BROKEN LIGHTS AND MENDED LIVES

Theology and Common Life
in the Early Church

By the same author

Theodore of Mopsuestia: Exegete and Theologian

The Captain of our Salvation: A Study in the
Patristic Exegesis of Hebrews

The Sermon on the Mount

Origen: An Exhortation to Martyrdom, Prayer,
and Selected Works

BROKEN LIGHTS AND MENDED LIVES

*Theology and Common Life
in the Early Church*

Rowan A. Greer

The Pennsylvania State University Press
University Park and London

Library of Congress Cataloging-in-Publication Data

Greer, Rowan A.
Broken lights and mended lives.

Includes bibliography and index.
1. Christian life—Early church, ca. 30–600.
2. Spirituality—History of doctrines—Early church,
ca. 30–600.   I. Title.
BR195.C5G74   1986   270.1   85-21823
ISBN 0-271-00422-3

Copyright © 1986 The Pennsylvania State University

Printed in the United States of America

Contents

Preface

Those who have kindly read this book in manuscript have pointed out to me something I already knew, that it is in several ways an odd sort of book. Let me take the opportunity here to address this issue, partly to supply a *caveat lector* and partly to explain the approach I have taken. The peculiarities of the book revolve around its structure and the fundamental attitudes which inform that structure. With respect to the first point, one of the readers put it quite succinctly by saying that the book has no argument but, instead, a theme. To put this judgment in my own words, I should say that the only thesis of the book is that theology in the early Church was always directly or indirectly concerned with the common life of Christians. From one point of view theologians attempted to put into words the corporate experience of the Church. The Christian story, continuously repeated in the reading of Scripture and in the liturgy, found its focus for the Fathers of the Church in the victorious Christ, the new humanity. And even more the technical aspects of early Christian theology were designed to explain this Christ and his significance. From another perspective the Fathers sought to use their ideology to explain and to shape the everyday life of Christians. To study the dialogue between theology and common life is to realize very quickly that no broad thesis is possible save to argue that there was a persistent concern with the dialogue. And that is the theme I shall endeavor to explore from a variety of angles.

The peculiarity of the structure of the book implies a peculiarity in one of my basic assumptions, that theology is an important dimension of early Christianity and must be considered carefully and sympathetically in assessing it as a social phenomenon. In dealing with the patristic period scholars have for the most part tended to do one of two things: Either they have concentrated upon patristic theology with little reference to its social setting, or they have tended to discount theology and to limit their attention to the Church as a social and institutional phenomenon in late antiquity. I am far from wishing to deny the value of both these approaches and should hope to understand my own approach as complementary rather than contradictory of what others have done. Indeed, in some sense writers like Peter Brown and Robert Wilken have prepared the way for me. Their work takes its point of departure from the Church as a social phenomenon, but seeks to show how theological ideas are involved in complicated ways in the life of the Church. Without making any claims about my success, I am suggesting that the terms can be reversed and that we can begin with theology and ask how it is related to Christianity as a social phenomenon.

In the preface to his *The Cult of the Saints* Peter Brown points out that he has examined the question from the point of view of the "highly articulate," "a distinctive and influential clerical elite" (pp. xiv, xv). He suggests that more can be done by attempting to understand the cult of the saints from other points of view. The inference I should draw from his remarks is that no one approach is correct, but that there are many valid ways of gaining an understanding of the early Church. And I should argue that a theological approach is one such way and needs to be taken seriously. Of course, the different avenues that lead to early Christianity give us differing visions of what it was like. But they supply different views of the same thing. We cannot oppose, say, popular to official Christianity; instead, we must seek to use the two angles stereoptically to gain a deeper imagination of the early Church. There are, to be sure, risks and limits to the approach I have chosen. A focus upon theology means that we are more likely to be dealing with what the Church Fathers believed ought to be than with what was really the case. And I shall be more interested in theological views of everyday life than with the social, economic, and political structures themselves. Then, too, I shall focus upon theological aims rather than their success or failure in practice. These limitations, however, need not be considered arguments against a theological approach, provided we understand theology to be one among other factors involved and provided we try always to keep other approaches in mind.

One final peculiarity of the approach I have followed is that I treat the Fathers of the Church sympathetically. This means, I think, two rather different things. First, it suggests no more than that I have attempted so far as possible to enter into the world of early Christianity and to imagine it on its own terms. If history is the imaginative reconstruction of the past, as Collingwood said, then sympathy is crucial for the historical imagination. Of course, this sympathy is difficult to acquire—not merely because many of the conventions of the Church in late antiquity are uncongenial to us, but also because we cannot entirely free our minds of contemporary concerns and cannot always know when our sympathy is more for our own prejudices than for what was true long ago in a very different world. Nonetheless, the willingness to seek an understanding of the ancient world on its own terms is crucial to the historian's task.

The second sense in which I am sympathetic to the early Church is that I find myself a convinced Christian, at least as convinced as an Anglican can be. This may seem an abandonment of objectivity and a repudiation of the conventions of modern scholarship. But I should argue that the appearance is misleading. The ghost of the Enlightenment continues to seduce us into believing that there can be such a thing as pure objectivity. While I should agree that we must aim for a disinterested and impartial assessment of the historical, I become increasingly convinced that we deceive ourselves if we think we can ever remove our prejudices altogether. Indeed, the pretense of objectivity can sometimes be as prejudicial as approaches that assume what may seem to some a subjective point of view. Disinterested observers are never quite so disinterested as they appear to be or even as they would like to suppose. It seems to me far more sensible to recognize one's prejudices and assumptions for what they are and to hope that even though this may not always enable one to discount those prejudices, it will enable the reader to do so. Consequently, I have made no secret of the fact that my sympathy for the early Church springs in part from the fact that I share its commitment to the Christian Gospel.

To these preliminary observations I should like to add some words of thanks. No one works alone, and I have made an attempt to indicate my debt to other students of the early Church in the footnotes and the bibliography. I also owe much to my first teacher, Dr. Norman Pittenger, who succeeded in interesting me in the patristic period. There have been other teachers along the way, but equally important to me are those who have encouraged my work. The Religion and the Arts Program at Yale Divinity School has put me in touch with my colleagues John Cook and Peter Hawkins, and chapters six and seven of this book are in part the product of that association. Cynthia Shattuck of the Cowley Press and Robert Wilken were helpful readers of the manuscript. And I owe more than I can say to the moral support of Judah and Grace Goldin and of

Stanley, Anne, and Adam Hauerwas. Last but not least I am indebted to Mr. Philip Winsor of the Pennsylvania State University Press. Like his namesake on the road from Jerusalem to Gaza, he appeared in my office from nowhere and has since then combined so careful a treatment of the manuscript with so kind a consideration of its author that one can almost believe in the coincidence of justice and mercy.

Abbreviations Used
in Citing Primary Texts

ACM	*The Acts of the Christian Martyrs*, Eng. tr. & ed. Herbert Musurillo (Oxford: At the Clarendon Press, 1972)
ACW	Ancient Christian Writers
	16 Irenaeus, *Proof of the Apostolic Preaching*, Eng. tr. & ed. Joseph P. Smith (Westminster, Md.: Newman Press, 1952)
	27 Methodius of Olympus, *The Symposium: A Treatise on Chastity*, Eng. tr. & ed. Herbert Musurillo (Westminster, Md.: Newman Press, 1958)
	31 John Chrysostom, *Baptismal Instructions*, Eng. tr. & ed. Paul W. Harkins (Westminster, Md.: Newman Press, 1963)
	34 Palladius, *The Lausiac History*, Eng. tr. & ed. Robert T. Meyer (Westminster, Md.: Newman Press, 1965)
AH	Irenaeus, *Against Heresies* (see *ANF* 1)
ANF	*The Ante-Nicene Fathers*. American reprint of Edinburgh edition by A. Roberts & J. Donaldson, revised by A. C. Coxe (Buffalo, 1884–86)
Ant.	Gregory of Nyssa, *Antirrheticus adversus Apolinarium* (see Jaeger 3.1)
Apol.	Tertullian, *Apology* (see *ANF* 3)
1 Apol.	Justin Martyr, *First Apology* (see *ANF* 1)

2 Apol.	Justin Martyr, *Second Apology* (see *ANF* 1)
ARI	Gregory of Nyssa, *Address on Religious Instruction* (see LCC 3)
Bidez	L'Empereur Julien, *Oeuvres complètes*, French tr. & ed. J. Bidez (Paris: Société d'édition "Les Belles Lettres," 1960)
Casson	*Selected Satires of Lucian*, Eng. tr. & ed. Lionel Casson (Chicago: Aldine, 1962)
CC	Origen, *Contra Celsum* (see Chadwick)
CCC	Gregory of Nyssa, *Commentary on Song of Songs* (see Jaeger 6)
CG	Augustine, *City of God* (see PC)
Chadwick	Origen, *Contra Celsum*, Eng. tr. & ed. Henry Chadwick (Cambridge: At the University Press, 1953)
Clarke	*The Ascetic Works of Saint Basil*, Eng. tr. & ed. W. K. L. Clarke (London: S.P.C.K., 1925)
Con.	John Cassian, *Conferences* (see *NPNF²* 11)
Conf.	Augustine, *Confessions* (see PC)
CWS	The Classics of Western Spirituality
	Athanasius, *The Life of Antony and the Letter to Marcellinus*, Eng. tr. & ed. Robert C. Gregg (New York, Ramsey, & Toronto: Paulist Press, 1980)
	Gregory of Nyssa, *The Life of Moses*, Eng. tr. & ed. Abraham J. Malherbe (New York, Ramsey, & Toronto: Paulist Press, 1978)
	Origen, *An Exhortation to Martyrdom, Prayer, and Selected Works*, Eng. tr. & ed. Rowan A. Greer (New York, Ramsey, & Toronto: Paulist Press, 1979)
De gub.	Salvian, *De gubernatione Dei* (see Sanford)
De hom. op.	Gregory of Nyssa, *De hominis opificio* (see *On the Making of Man*, *NPNF²ᵢ* 5)
De inc.	Athanasius, *De incarnatione* (see *On the Incarnation*, LCC 3)
Dem.	Irenaeus, *Demonstration* (see *Proof of the Apostolic Preaching*, ACW 16)
De perf.	Gregory of Nyssa, *De perfectione* (see Jaeger 8.1)
De princ.	Origen, *De principiis* (see *ANF* 4)
Div. inst.	Lactantius, *Divine Institutes* (see *ANF* 7)
DL	Cassiodorus, *Divine Letters* (see Jones)
DT	Augustine, *De trinitate* (see *NPNF¹* 3)
EM	Origen, *Exhortation to Martyrdom* (see CWS)
Ench.	Augustine, *Enchiridion* (see *NPNF¹* 3)

Enn.	Plotinus, *Enneads* (see MacK.)
Ep.	Epistle
Euch.	Paulinus of Pella, *Eucharisticus* (see LCL Ausonius)
Ex.	Clement of Alexandria, *Exhortation to the Heathen* (see *ANF* 2)
HE	Eusebius of Caesarea, *Ecclesiastical History* (see LCL)
Hom.	Homily
Inst.	John Cassian, *The Institutes* (see *NPNF*² 11)
Instr.	Clement of Alexandria, *The Instructor* (see *ANF* 2)
Jaeger	*Gregorii Nysseni Opera*, ed. Werner Jaeger (Leiden: E. J. Brill, 1921—)
Jones	Cassiodorus Senator, *An Introduction to Divine and Human Readings*, Eng. tr. & ed. Leslie Webber Jones (New York: Columbia University Press, 1946)
LA	Athanasius, *Life of Antony* (see CWS)
LC	Eusebius of Caesarea, *Life of Constantine* (see *NPNF*² 1)
LCC	Library of Christian Classics

3 *Christology of the Later Fathers*, Eng. tr. & ed. E. R. Hardy (Philadelphia: Westminster Press, 1954)

6 *Augustine: Earlier Writings*, Eng. tr. & ed. John H. S. Burleigh (Philadelphia: Westminster Press, 1953)

12 *Western Asceticism*, Eng. tr. & ed. Owen Chadwick (Philadelphia: Westminster Press, 1958)

LCL   Loeb Classical Library

Ammianus Marcellinus, *History*, Eng. tr. & ed. John C. Rolfe, 3 vols. Cambridge, Mass.: Harvard University Press, first printed 1935–40, revised and reprinted 1948–52)

Apostolic Fathers, Eng. tr. & ed. Kirsopp Lake, 2 vols. (Cambridge, Mass.: Harvard University Press, 1912–13)

Ausonius, *Works*, with the *Eucharisticus* of Paulinus of Pella, Eng. tr. & ed. Hugh G. Evelyn White, 2 vols. (Cambridge, Mass.: Harvard University Press, 1921)

Saint Basil, *The Letters*, Eng. tr. & ed. Roy J. Deferrari, 4 vols. (Cambridge, Mass.: Harvard University Press, 1926–34)

LM	Gregory of Nyssa, *Life of Moses* (see CWS)
LPIR	*The Last Poets of Imperial Rome* (see PC)

LR	Basil of Caesarea, *The Longer Rules* (see Clarke)
MacK.	Plotinus, *The Enneads*, Eng. tr. & ed., Stephen MacKenna, 2nd ed. rev. by B. S. Page (New York: Pantheon Books, 1957)
NPNF¹	*A Select Library of Nicene and Post-Nicene Fathers of the Christian Church*, Eng. tr. & ed. Philip Schaff and Henry Wace (Buffalo & New York, 1886–1900), first series
NPNF²	Ibid., second series
OFW	Augustine, *On Free Will* (see LCC 6)
OSR	Gregory of Nyssa, *On the Soul and the Resurrection* (see *NPNF²* 5)
OTR	Augustine, *Of True Religion* (see LCC 6)
PC	Penguin Classics
	Augustine, *Confessions*, Eng. tr. & ed. R. S. Pine-Coffin (Harmondsworth: Penguin Books, 1961)
	Augustine, *The City of God*, Eng. tr. Henry Bettenson, intr. & ed. David Knowles (Harmondsworth: Penguin Books, 1972)
	The Last Poets of Imperial Rome, Eng. tr. & ed. Harold Isbell (Harmondsworth: Penguin Books, 1971)
Ref.	Hippolytus, *The Refutation of All Heresies* (see *ANF* 5)
Sanford	Salvian of Marseilles, *On the Government of God*, Eng. tr. & ed. E. M. Sanford (New York & London: Columbia University Press & Oxford University Press, 1930)
SC 21	Éthérie, *Journal de Voyage*, French tr. & ed. H. Pétré, Sources chrétiennes 21 (Paris: Les éditions du cerf, 1948)
Sol.	Augustine, *Soliloquies* (see LCC 6)
Strom.	Clement of Alexandria, *The Stromata* (see *ANF* 2)

Introduction

Years ago I encountered a literate madman in the Worcester State Hospital, who pointed out that the peculiarity of Kafka was that, whereas in reading most books we try to become the people in the book, Kafka's characters have a way of becoming us. This is a vivid way of explaining the effect that studying the Fathers of the Church has had upon me. What has increasingly impressed itself upon me is that a constant dialogue was maintained between theology and the life of the Church.[1] Even those who elaborated a technical theology were also preachers in the Church, and their aim was to articulate and to shape the experience of ordinary Christians. In general terms, this dialogue seems to me one that has been lost in the Church and that very much needs to be restored. In the academy the separate disciplines of history, biblical studies, theology, and liturgy have tended to make theology not only a school discipline but one discipline among others. In the parish church what I have found is a broad loss of theological awareness and a tendency to focus upon the moral demands of Christianity rather than upon the promises of the Gospel. What seems to me to have been a unity in the early Church has become fragmented in our own time. The reading and study of Scripture, the liturgy, preaching, and the arts have tended to go separate ways. Theology and life have been divided from one another.

I should not want to argue that we should in our time simply revive what happened in the patristic Church. That would be neither possible nor desirable. Nor do I wish in the main body of what follows to use patristic opinions as a way of solving modern problems. Instead, my aim is to describe important aspects of what was thought and done as a way of arguing for the liveliness of the dialogue between theology and life. In Tennyson's phrase the theological views of early Christians were understood as "broken lights" that reflected dimly the ineffable glory of God. And these broken lights sought to articulate the Church's experience of God's presence in its life. The movement from experience to theology was balanced by a movement in the opposite direction. The broken lights in various ways mended human lives, and theology functioned to order and shape Christian experience. Part one will explore what it means to say that theology for the Fathers of the Church was the articulation of Christian experience, while part two will turn toward various aspects of the Christian's life in order to examine the shaping effect of theology and the mending of human lives. And it is my hope that these studies will spur some to reflect upon the perennial issues raised as they appear in our own world. Let me begin by spelling out in more detail what I mean by the two movements I have mentioned.

THEOLOGY: THE CHURCH'S ARTICULATION
OF ITS EXPERIENCE OF GOD

The experience of God is certain and steadfast for the believer, but it is ineffable for the simple reason that God himself transcends human knowledge. Gregory Nazianzen in his *Second Theological Oration* uses a tag from the *Timaeus* and puts it this way (*Oration* 4; LCC 3, p. 138): "It is difficult to conceive God, but to define him in words is an impossibility, as one of the Greek teachers of divinity taught. . . . But in my opinion it is impossible to express him, and yet more impossible to conceive him." A distinction is to be made between God's nature (what he is) and God's active operation (how he is). Were God not present in the created order and in human nature itself, the possibility of discourse about God would be eliminated altogether. As it is, to speak of the ineffable God is a possibility, though one hedged about with qualifications. There is no need to try to systematize this understanding by discussing the themes in patristic theology that come later to be rationalized as *viae negativae*, *viae eminentiae*, and other forms of analogical language about God. The important point is that the reasoning involved reflects an a priori conviction that God exists and makes himself known and that the Church can neither refrain from speaking of this knowledge nor exhaust its significance. The lover finds the beloved in one sense unknowable, but in another sense known. And so in halting terms the lover must find words for his experience, however much he understands that the words do not begin to exhaust or even to express his experience. Similarly the Church's theology attempts to describe an unknown God who nonetheless makes himself known.

It must be added that for people like Origen, Athanasius, and the Cappadocians, as well as for such different figures as Theodore and John Chrysostom, the conviction just outlined implies a further conclusion. In his homilies on Song of Songs, Gregory of Nyssa reflects upon the meaning of the question the daughters of Jerusalem address to the bride: "What is your beloved more than another beloved?" (Song 5:9). The bride is, of course, the Church; and the difficulty in her answering is that in his uncreated aspect Christ, the Beloved, can neither be understood nor explained (*CCC* 13; Jaeger 6, p. 381):

> Since, therefore, His uncreated, pre-existent, and eternal aspect remains totally incomprehensible and ineffable to every nature, but His appearance through the flesh to a certain degree comes to our knowledge, for this reason the teacher pays attention to these considerations and composes her account concerning those things that can be received by her hearers. What I mean is the great mystery of our religion through which God was manifested in the flesh. [cf. 1 Tim. 3:16ff.]

A certain pride of place is given the Incarnation, which brings into focus the revelation of God in Creation and which establishes for all humanity the possibility of receiving the gift of the Spirit. From one point of view, a highly christocentric approach is adopted. Yet for the Cappadocians and for all thought after the adoption of the trinitarian dogma in 381, to experience the Incarnate Lord is also to experience the Father and the Spirit. In other words, the Incarnate Lord, worshipped by the Church, is the experience of God that requires theological articulation.

THE CHURCH'S EXPERIENCE

It will be evident from what has already been said that to speak of "the Church's experience" is to use the word experience in a slightly eccentric way. We must eliminate the individualistic and strictly emotional connotations the word, I suspect, has for us. And in defining what is meant by the Church's experience it is possible to begin with the sort of view Irenaeus elaborates as early as 180 C.E. in his treatise *Against the Heresies*. In his opinion the apostolic faith is the Church's response to Christ and in this way preserves the Church's experience of Christ. This faith is available to Christians in two forms, the Scriptures of the Old and New Testaments and the Rule of Faith. The Rule, for Irenaeus, is a trinitarian credal affirmation that can be expressed in slightly differing words but that later develops into the fixed forms of creeds like the Apostles' Creed and the Nicene Creed.[2] A metaphor helps clarify what Irenaeus means. It is as though a rich man were to put his money in a bank. Similarly, the apostles deposited in the Church their faith; and they did so by bequeathing to the Church the Scriptures and the Rule of Faith (*AH* 3.4.1). Moreover, they saw to it that this apostolic deposit would be guarded carefully. They appointed bishops to succeed them, and lists of bishops in succession to the apostles guarantee that what is guarded in the Church is the true coinage of faith and not counterfeit.

Christians, then, can draw upon the apostolic experience and make it their own. If they are unable to read or to understand the Scriptures, they have the Rule of Faith. Thus, ". . . those barbarians who believe in Christ do assent, having salvation written in their hearts by the Spirit, without paper and ink . . . carefully preserving the ancient tradition" (*AH* 3.4.2; *ANF* 1, p. 417). While they can be distinguished from one another, Scripture and the Rule are identical in proclaiming the same faith. It makes no difference whether one's dollar consists of ten dimes or of four quarters. Irenaeus specifies the relation between Scripture and the Rule by using the metaphor of a mosaic made of precious stones (*AH* 1.8.1) The many passages of Scripture have been ordered to make a magnificent portrait of a king. That is, Scripture is meant to portray God. The difficulty is that the stones of the mosaic can be wrongly arranged. This is what the heretics do. They put the passages of Scripture in a wrong relationship to one another and so construct the picture of a fox or a dog, a false god. It is the Rule of Faith that explains how Scripture must be arranged. The metaphor becomes vivid when we remember that in the Roman Empire mosaic floors were often shipped disassembled, and a key or plan (*hypothesis*) was provided in order to explain how the sections were to be laid. Similarly the Rule of Faith is the "plan" that ensures a correct reading of Scripture. What became in the sixteenth-century Reformation an either/or question (Scripture *or* tradition) is for Irenaeus a both/and question (Scripture *and* the Rule).[3]

The key word to use in describing Irenaeus' point of view is "witness." Scripture and the Rule are apostolic in the sense that they preserve the original experience of the Church and testify to Christ. They do not possess authority in and of themselves, even though they may be thought to be inspired by God's Spirit. Final authority rests in Christ, while Scripture and the Rule function to give access to that authority. In this way the Church's experience is, first of all, its appropriation of the past.

Just as the lore of a family represents a fundamental and important part of a child's experience growing up, so the Church is rooted in its past as that past is linked to the coming and work of the Saviour. Theology, then, is largely the attempt to put into words this past and common experience of the Church. And, in great measure, theology is the interpretation of Scripture. In this sense, patristic theology is biblical, even though the Fathers by no means think themselves confined by biblical categories. Of course, Irenaeus' view is an ideal one. He does not take account of differing interpretations, differing rules of faith, and disagreements among bishops. For the moment, however, let me argue that the first way we can define the Church's experience of God is by saying that it is the apostolic witness to the Incarnate Lord. It must be pointed out, as well, that this includes the Old Testament witness not only to Christ but also to the Creator God and to the activity of the Spirit prior to and in the Incarnation.

The next step that must be taken is to guard against a possible misunderstanding of Irenaeus' view of the apostolic witness. That witness is not conceived as an objet d'art to be preserved in a museum. On the contrary, it is bound up with the preaching of the Church, which is equatable with our faith (*AH* 3.24.1; *ANF* 1, p. 458):

> . . . which, having been received from the Church, we do preserve and which always, by the Spirit of God, renewing its youth, as if it were some precious deposit in an excellent vessel, causes the vessel itself containing it to renew its youth also. For this gift of God has been entrusted to the Church, as breath was to the first created man, for this purpose, that all the members receiving it may be vivified: and the [means of] communion with Christ has been distributed throughout it, that is, the Holy Spirit, the earnest of incorruption, the means of confirming our faith, and the ladder of ascent to God.

The apostolic witness is a living one which, though not equated with the Spirit, is by the Spirit enabled increasingly to vivify the Church and to guide it toward its heavenly destiny. Moreover, Irenaeus understands the renewal of the witness to be the way in which the universal summing up (*anakephalaiôsis*) that was initiated in Christ is brought to consummation. Granted that in the passage from which I have just quoted Irenaeus goes on to speak of those who "deservedly wallow in all error" and are not united in Christ, the logic of his view is that the Church, preserving its witness and guided by the Spirit, ever renews the work of unification.

The perpetual renewal of the Church is not, therefore, an end in itself, but only a means of conveying God's saving power to the world.

One point to be made with respect to this second aspect of Irenaeus' understanding of the Church's experience is that it allows for a development of that experience, as well as of its articulation. To return to the analogy of the lover and the beloved, it is the case not only that the lover will be obliged perpetually to express his love in words but also that his apprehension of that love and of the beloved will continue to change and to grow. It is not that a new revelation or a new Christ is given the Church, any more than in a long marriage a new husband is substituted for an old. But as in the marriage, so in the Church's experience of Christ, new apprehensions of the beloved are always appearing. The revelation of God in Christ is a constant, but the experience of that revelation and the witness to it are constantly "made young." It would be wrong to think of this process in a progressivist way, save in an ultimate sense. Instead, the process can be thought to reflect the response of the Church to changed circumstances. Like the bride in Nyssa's interpretation of the Song of Songs, the Church always "composes her account concerning those things that can be received by her hearers." The renewal of the Church's experience is correlative with the Church's function to bear her witness to the world. The Incarnate Lord, the activity of the Spirit, and the situation of the Church in the world combine to form a dynamic that can be regarded as analogous to the dynamic of a long and genuine marriage.

A second point to make concerns the locus of the Church's developing experience. We must remind ourselves that we are still speaking in corporate terms, and at a general level, it is possible to speak of the corporate life of the Church as this locus. More specifically, however, that corporate life is expressed in the sacraments of Baptism and the Eucharist. By Baptism the corporate character of the Church is established, and in the Eucharist it is expressed and renewed. The concept is a difficult one for us to grasp because we persist in thinking of ourselves as centers of consciousness and of communities of people as alliances of individuals understood in this sense. The logic of writers such as Gregory of Nyssa runs in the opposite direction. Individuals are defined not from within but by means of their relationship to Christ and Christ to one another. The divine power which is in process of recreating the world is evident in the sacraments of the Church. In the Eucharist both in reality and in symbol the new Creation is manifested.[4] The human experience of the Church's worship, then, is not merely an appropriation of the past. It is, as well, a present experience that must become part of the theological articulation of the Church's faith. The preacher's task, for example, is to put into words what the Church is experiencing, its present appropriation of the Saviour. In sum, the theologian must try to describe a vision that helps explain what the Church is doing.

Finally, it will be clear that the sacramental shaping of the Church's experience does not imply that the Church's worship is the locus of theological articulation in such a way as to introduce a division between worship and life. On the contrary, the Fathers are convinced that worship informs life and life informs worship. Consequently, the Christian moral life represents a part of the present experience of Christ that needs to be put into words. The daily experience of Christians is drawn into the theological vision. The differing stories of Christians are integrated into the story of Christ. Present and past are bound together in a corporate experience, and the theologian's task is to create a visionary account of it.

THE FUNCTIONS OF THEOLOGY AS THE ARTICULATION OF THE CHURCH'S EXPERIENCE

In the first instance theology functions to put into words the twin aspects of the Church's experience I have just described. With respect to the "witness" side of the coin it would not be far from the mark to say that this function is tantamount to the exegesis of Scripture. But, of course, since the argument from Scripture and the argument from tradition are regarded as identical by the Fathers, there are certain assumptions made about exegesis that seem somewhat foreign to us. Since the creeds are thought to represent the "scope" of Scripture, interpretation is always concerned both with the biblical text and with the credal key to its general meaning. Thus, exegesis represents the interpretation of the apostolic witness. Moreover, a distinction is made by all between the narrative meaning (*historia*) of Scripture and the spiritual meaning (*theoria*). This distinction reflects the conviction that prime authority rests in the revelation itself and not in the letter of Scripture. By moving from the *historia* to the *theoria* the Fathers believe they are gaining closer access to the meaning of the Incarnation with all its implications. I should add at this point that I am assuming from this point of view no radical difference between typological and allegorical exegesis. Both the Antiochene and the Alexandrian schools of interpretation make the distinction to which I have referred, and neither is prepared to adopt a strictly literal reading of the text. The essential difference between the two schools has to do with axiomatic theological presuppositions. The Antiochenes insist upon the narrative meaning's function "for contemporary use" and believe that the *theoria* represents an "indication" of future realities.[5] The Alexandrians employ a spatial metaphor and regard the narrative meaning as an earthly pointer to heavenly realities. These

two perspectives do begin to imply fairly radical differences in interpretation, but their starting points are not quite so far apart as much of the
secondary literature has made it seem.

Since theology is the interpretation of the apostolic witness and seeks
to penetrate to the object of that witness, the door is opened for theology
to become the interpretation of the renewed and developed aspect of the
Church's experience. The unity of the "witness" and the "renewed" aspects of the Church's experience is assumed. Consequently, one can identify the interpretation of Scripture with, for example, the interpretation
of the Christian life within the Church. Origen's homilies on the Old
Testament make this equation, as do in a different way Theodore's
Catechetical Homilies. Concerns of a specific kind that create problems
for Christian life also act as a shaping principle guiding the interpretation of both aspects of the Church's experience. Theological debates, the
exigencies of trying to lead the Christian life in a city such as Antioch or
Constantinople, and the perils and challenges of the monastic life are
examples of practical issues that determine the interpreter's questions of
the Church's experience. It may be somewhat over simple, but I should
think some analogy may be found in what our Supreme Court does.
Specific questions are addressed to the court, and its decisions are meant
to be an interpretation of the Constitution and of the precedents which
have arisen from it.

What I am suggesting is that theology functions to bind together past
and present experience, just as the Supreme Court in its decisions attempts to integrate the Constitution with contemporary problems by
interpreting its spirit. One way of understanding this is to compare the
role of theology in the patristic Church with the sort of *interpretatio
Graeca* found in Plutarch's *On Isis and Osiris* or Iamblichus' *On the
Mysteries.* Particularly in the case of Iamblichus the function of his neo-
Platonic *interpretatio Graeca* is to bind into a single system a traditional
body of cultic practice and a group of sacred texts, notably Homer and
Hesiod.[6] What Plutarch and Iamblichus sought to do was to supply a
broad theoretical structure that would order and bind together the sacred texts that were the legacy of the past with the cult practices of the
present. In a similar way early Christian theologians sought a way of
integrating the meaning of Scripture, understood by the Rule of Faith,
with the present liturgical experience of the Church, including the lives
brought into that experience. The pagans failed for a number of reasons,
not least of which was the diverse character of the elements to be integrated. They had no clear canon of Scripture, despite the function of
Homer and Hesiod as sacred texts. And the cult practices with which
they had to reckon were as diverse in origin as they were in expression.

Christians were able to deal with more focused materials, and we can argue that their enterprise had greater success for this reason.

A few examples from the writings of Clement of Alexandria (fl. 200) will illustrate what I mean by saying that theology functions to order experience and to bind past experience with present. Clement begins his *Exhortation to the Heathen* by arguing that the experience of Christ reorders pagan experience by freeing it from bondage to custom and idolatry and by informing it with the presence and power of God's Word. He gives what amounts to an allegorical interpretation of Eunomos the Locrian and the Pythic grasshopper in order to make his central point clear and vivid. As the story goes, Eunomos was competing in a lyre contest at Delphi when one of his strings broke. A grasshopper flew to his lyre and supplied the missing note. The Greeks regarded this as a tribute to Eunomos' excellence as a musician. Not so, says Clement. Instead, the grasshopper represents the divine song which transforms and completes the human song of Eunomos. This divine song is "the new, the Levitical song" and is equated with "the celestial Word, the true athlete crowned in the theatre of the whole universe (*Ex.* 1; *ANF* 2, p. 171)." It is this song, the Word of God, that "composed the universe into melodious order, and tuned the discord of the elements to harmonious arrangement, so that the whole world might become harmony." And it is this song that "has come to loose, and that speedily, the bitter bondage of tyrannizing demons; and leading us back to the mild and loving yoke of piety, recalls to heaven those that had been cast prostrate to the earth. It alone has tamed men, the most intractable of animals (p. 172)." The new song is identified with God's agent in Creation and Redemption, and Clement appeals to both to the scriptural witness to the Redeemer and to Christian experience of Redemption as a vision of new freedom and a transformation of the moral life. And he exhorts the heathen to turn away from their old songs and turn to the Word, who desires to "open the eyes of the blind, and unstop the ears of the deaf, and to lead the lame or the erring to righteousness, to exhibit God to the foolish, to put a stop to corruption, to conquer death, to reconcile disobedient children to their father (*Ex.* 1; *ANF* 2, p. 172; cf. *Ex.* 4, 12)."

Another example of how Clement links the Church's witness to Christ with present experience of salvation as the transformation of the old life and its conventions may be found in his identification of Christ with "the Sun of righteousness" (Mal. 4:2). This Sun, "who drives His chariot over all, pervades equally all humanity . . . and distills on them the dew of truth. He hath changed sunset into sunrise, and through the cross brought death to life; and having wrenched man from destruction, He hath raised him to the skies, transplanting mortality into immortality, and translating earth to heaven" (*Ex.* 11; *ANF* 2, p. 203). This passage reflects Clement's Christian Platonist theology. The Word of God, like the Platonic World Soul, is a cosmic principle in which our souls can participate and so receive truth and life. The Incarnate Word makes what was possible fully actual by enabling us to know God and to have the assurance of the resurrection. This theology, however much it employs philosophical conventions, nonetheless roots those conventions in the biblical witness to Christ. We may think, for example, of John's Gospel and its equation of Christ with "light" and with the Word of God that "enlightens every man coming into the world" (e.g., John 1:1–9). At the same time, Clement's theology points toward the present experience of his audience. As pagans they were familiar with the worship of the sun, and they are told that this worship must be transformed into worship of Christ, the true Sun. Clement alludes to what must be a baptismal hymn—"Hail, O Light." And we are put in touch with the ritual realities of early Christian Baptism, which took place after a vigil lasting all night and was celebrated at dawn. The new light of the Christian life was symbolized by the way Baptism was administered. Clement's theology integrates pagan and Christian experience and biblical and philosophical themes with his larger vision of Christ as the Saviour. And, in his view, this larger vision is true to the apostolic witness to Christ.

One further point can be made regarding Clement's enterprise: His theological vision correlates with what Christians saw as well as with what they heard in Scripture and in the words of the liturgy. Christ was often represented in ancient Christian art as an Apollo figure, and a remarkable mosaic depicting Christ as the Sun God, driving his four-horse chariot across the sky, has been preserved in the Vatican. Another image Clement uses of Christ is that of the Shepherd who teaches his sheep (e.g. *Ex.* 11; *Instr.* 1.9; cf. Ecclus. 18:13–14). Again we find the fusion of biblical and philosophical themes with Christian experience in the present. The Shepherd is the Good Shepherd of Scripture and the Truth of which Plato speaks. And his teaching of the sheep immediately conjures up the catechetical practices of the early Church. And, of course, early Christian art constantly depicts Christ as the Shepherd, often teaching his sheep. In all these ways, then, we find theology exercising an integrative function by elaborating a vision of the Saviour that tries to be true to past and to present.[7]

The theological vision, however, is not to be equated with sight. As I pointed out earlier, God cannot finally be known; and so theology is an ever-developing attempt to apprehend God in Christ without ever claiming to comprehend Him. Origen, in the generation following Clement, puts it this way (*De princ.* 4.3.14; CWS, pp. 202f.):

"How unsearchable are the judgments of God and how inscrutable His ways" (Rom. 11:33). For he [St. Paul] did not say it was difficult to search out the judgments of God, but that it was altogether impossible. Nor did he say that it was difficult to investigate His ways, but that they could not be investigated. For no matter how far a person advances in his investigation and makes progress by a keener zeal, even if the grace of God is within him and enlightens his mind, he cannot arrive at the perfect end of the truth he seeks. No mind that is created has the ability to understand completely by any manner of means, but as it finds some small part of the answers that are sought, it sees other questions to be asked. And if it arrives at those answers, it will again see beyond them to many more questions that they imply must be asked.

It is this attitude that explains why patristic theology is not systematic. The assumption is made that the theologian's vision puts him on the road to truth, but his destination lies beyond the confines of this life. The visions are "broken lights," but they are all we have. And they are sufficient to point us in the right direction as we move toward the time when we shall know even as we are now known by God.

The "broken lights" character of theology explains why it has a second and negative function: Positively, theology is meant to integrate the Church's past and present experience in order to light the way toward the future; negatively, theology functions to exclude false directions, a role best seen in the dogmatic development of the conciliar period. I am arguing for a distinction between doctrine and dogma. Doctrine expresses Christian convictions in positive terms, but dogma aims at excluding error and at doing so as economically as possible. The two issues that concerned the Church in the fourth and fifth centuries were the trinitarian and the christological questions. The dogma of the Trinity was worked out at the councils of Nicaea (325) and Constantinople (381). And the dogma, though couched in the formula "one *ousia* and three *hypostaseis*," was primarily meant to exclude the errors of Arius and Sabellius. The Chalcedonian Definition of Christ's person (451) ratified the acts of the council of Ephesus (431) and excluded the views of Apollinaris, Nestorius, and Eutyches. But the dogmas in excluding error by no means required any one doctrine. A number of doctrines are thought to be valid positive interpretations of the dogmas. Thus, theology functions positively to articulate Christian experience and negatively to rule out false articulations of Christian experience.

THEOLOGY AND THE SHAPING OF CHRISTIAN EXPERIENCE

The other movement that characterizes the theology of the early Church is that from theology to Christian experience. At the outset, it seems to me that this movement is an easier one to grasp. What I mean is this: I can understand that my convictions as a Christian are somehow the product of my experience, but it is extremely difficult to explain how this has happened. Clearly my experience in struggling for meaning in my life and in coping with suffering, sin, and evil, as well as my associations with other people, have all contributed to my basic perspective in explaining my world. But the process has been so complex that I cannot finally explain it. As well, we could raise the question why more or less identical sets of experience produce radically different responses. It is much easier to see how my convictions order and inform my experience. Imperfect though they may be, they supply the mainspring for what I think about my life and my behavior. In principle, the Christian vision is meant to be translated into virtue; the faith that apprehends God's gratuitous forgiveness in Christ must be translated into a radical obedience to him.

The early Christians were convinced that this sort of translation of theology into life ought to and often did take place. The point is crucial to Justin Martyr, who addressed his apologies to the Roman emperors in the middle of the second century. While Justin takes the opportunity to consider the larger question of the truth of Christianity and its relation to philosophical truth, his specific purpose is to ask the emperors that Christians be given a fair hearing and not be punished simply for being Christians. In order to make his request credible he is obliged to prove that, at least in principle, the stock charges levelled against Christians are untrue. If it were in fact the case that Christians are atheists and immoral people, and as so subversive of Roman society, then it would be right that they be punished simply as Christians. But, Justin argues, none of this is true. He admits that Christians deny the pagan deities, but insists that they worship the true God. It is hard to see how this admission enables Christians to escape the charge of atheism from any point of view but their own. And yet Justin's arguments against pagan religion are in large measure borrowed from the Stoics and would have been familiar to the emperors. He seems to be saying that our supposed atheism is really no different from yours, and we cannot be held atheists on that account.

Justin's refutation of the charge that the Christians were immoral is more convincing. At one level, he bases his argument on the teaching of Christ, which Christians are expected to follow. They are commanded to be chaste, to repent, to care for the poor, to love all and avoid retaliation, to speak the truth without oaths, and to obey and pray for the civil authorities (*1 Apol.* 15–17). Those who claim to be Christians but do not obey these rules are no more Christians than philosophers can claim that name if they fail to practice what they preach. Moreover, Justin can point to concrete illustrations of Christian virtue. Christians do not expose their children (*1 Apol.* 27), a point we find made repeatedly in early Christian literature and one that must have a basis in fact. Faith in Christ enables people to change their lives in radical ways for the better (*1 Apol.* 14; *ANF* 1, p. 167):

> . . . we who formerly delighted in fornication . . . now embrace chastity alone; we who formerly used magical arts dedicate ourselves to the good and unbegotten God; we who valued above all things the acquisition of wealth and possessions, now bring what we have into a common stock, and communicate to every one in need; we who hated and destroyed one another, and on account of their different manners would not live with men of a different tribe, now, since the coming of Christ, live familiarly with them, and pray for our enemies. . . .

Justin cites the specific examples of a man in Alexandria who sought official permission from the governor to make himself a eunuch for Christ's sake (*1 Apol.* 29) and of a dissolute woman whom Christianity converted to chastity and who brought trouble upon herself by trying to reform her husband (*2 Apol.* 2). The mending of human lives, then, is Justin's proof that Christians are not immoral.

It is Christian convictions that explain the reformation of morals. From one point of view, it is belief in the Last Judgment that supplies the motive and sanction for good life. God will mete out eternal rewards and punishments (*1 Apol.* 20), and even now no one can "escape the notice of God" (*1 Apol.* 12). Thus, the rules for the Christian life, which agree with but go beyond what constitutes good citizenship, are enforced by sanctions far more effective than the law administered by the emperors and their civil servants. From another point of view, Christians voluntarily choose to pursue the good, hoping for the reward promised them according to their merits (*1 Apol.* 43). And there is at least the hint that freedom in this sense is also the gift of God. Christians receive Baptism "in order that we may not remain the children of necessity and of ignorance, but may become the children of choice and knowledge, and may obtain in the water the remission of sins formerly committed" (*1 Apol.* 61; *ANF* 1, p. 166). The mended lives, then, are not merely the product of obedience to a new set of laws but are fashioned by the illumination of Baptism. To know the good is to do the good, and the Christians' knowledge of the Truth in Christ frees them and enables them to do that Truth in their lives.[8]

There are at least two problems with the way Justin puts it. First, as is the case with any ethic of intent, it is hard to see necessary connections between a Christian intention and Christian behavior. The same vision has the possibility of producing a number of different sorts of lives. And so it becomes necessary to bring into the picture certain rules which specify the limits on translating intention into practice. In a similar way, the Stoics, for whom outward actions were a matter of indifference, were obliged to adopt a calculus of preferred actions. The second problem is not theoretical but practical. To what degree is Justin correct in seeing the Christians as holier than other people? The question probably admits no clear answer for the simple reason that in religious terms the criterion for sanctity is God's judgment and not the moral effect of Christianity on the surrounding society. These two problems will keep arising as we look at the Christian life in the early Church. Lives are mended in differing ways, and the impact of Christianity on the world of late antiquity is extremely difficult to assess. My chief concern, however, is with the aim of theology to order life and not necessarily with its success in doing so.

Another place to look for an understanding of how Christian convictions shaped human lives is Origen's treatise *Against Celsus*. Celsus, a Platonist philosopher, had written a treatise against the Christians called *The True Word*. There is reason to believe that Justin Martyr is the specific Christian Celsus seeks to refute, and in any case Celsus' book appeared about 180.[9] Origen wrote his response almost seventy years later; and what he does is simply to offer a running commentary on Celsus' book, responding point by point. At one level, the issues are theoretical. Where can we find Truth? How can Christ be divine and yet suffer? Is the Christian hope an unworthy one? But at another level, Celsus uses ad hominem arguments. The Christians are immoral yokels. Origen's response to the second part of this accusation is to insist that there are Christians who equal the wisdom of pagan philosophers, and that the existence of simple people in the Church is not at all an argument against Christianity. On the contrary, the glory of Christianity is its ability to convey truth not merely to an elite but to simple people (*CC* 3.52ff.). It is this second point that enables Origen to refute the first part of Celsus' accusation.

The Christians, in conveying their message to all, excel the philosophers not only by persuading simple people but also by reforming their lives (*CC* 3.56; Chadwick, p. 166):

. . . we deliver women from licentiousness and from perversion caused by their associates, and from all mania for theatres and dancing, and from superstition; while we make boys self-controlled when they come to the age of puberty and burn with desires for sexual pleasure. . . .

Origen's platform is somewhat puritanical even by the standards of his own day, but his point differs in no way from Justin's. One proof of the Gospel lies in its power to reform lives. Origen goes on to argue that Christians are quite right to summon the immoral to repentance, and he even admits that in one sense sinners are preferred. The sinner "who realizes his own sin" and repents is better than the person who in conceit fails to see his sin and his need of God, who "alone is able to complete our deficiencies" (*CC* 3.64; Chadwick, p. 171).

Christian ascetics and martyrs provide Origen with proof of his view (*CC* 3.68; Chadwick, pp. 173–74):

But when we consider that the doctrines which Celsus calls *vulgar* have been filled with power as though they were spells, and when we see that the words turn multitudes all at once from being licentious to living the most tranquil life, and from being unrighteous to nobility of character, and from being cowards or effeminate to such bravery that they even despise death for the sake of the piety which they believe to be right, are we not justified in admiring the power in the message?

Christian lives, then, in Origen's view are the best apology for the truth of the Gospel. The devotion of ascetics and martyrs shows what Christian belief can do. Throughout the world "numberless throngs of people . . . have left their ancestral laws and those they supposed gods, and . . . have dedicated themselves to the observance of Moses' law and to the discipleship and worship of Christ" (*De princ.* 4.1.1; CWS, p. 172). And they have done this despite persecution and the possibility of martyrdom.

The same sort of argument we have found in Justin and Origen persists in early Christianity. And the appeal gradually becomes one made not merely to the character of the Christian life but also to the multitudes of those converted to it. The Truth is vindicated by its power of persuasion. Athanasius wrote his treatise *On the Incarnation* very shortly after the Emperor Constantine had conquered by the sign of the cross at the Milvian Bridge (312 C.E.). Constantine's gift of imperial patronage to the Church almost certainly explains Athanasius' triumphant appeal to the daily influx of pagans into the Church (*De inc.* 30; cf. 27–28). What had been for Origen a confident hope becomes for Athanasius a reality in the process of completion. The whole world was about to become Christian. The "triumph" of the Church was, however, ambiguous. Many became Christians not out of conviction but in order to benefit by imperial patronage. And it is doubtless true that it became harder to see the mended lives of Christians. Both the development of strict catechetical practices and the rapid rise of monasticism are in large part protests against a Church gone public and atttempts to preserve the moral rigor of the earlier Church. It is against this historical development and in the light of the watershed of Constantine's recognition of the Church that we must examine the ways the Christian life expressed itself.

CONCLUSION

The preceding reflections have been designed to convey something of the perspective I shall adopt in what follows. I really have two concerns. The first is to examine the theologies of the early Church as "broken lights." What I mean is that the Fathers believe that they have encountered God's presence in their own Christian experience—in the Church's Scriptures and tradition, in their worship, and in their attempts to live as Christians. They firmly believe that what they have experienced transcends this world; and so in articulating their experience of God in Christ, they are pointing beyond that experience to its ultimate grounding in God. They would, I think, have agreed with Tennyson (*In Memoriam*, lines 17–20):

> Our little systems have their day;
>   They have their day and cease to be:
>   They are but broken lights of thee,
> And thou, O Lord, art more than they.

A correlation is assumed a priori between Christian experience and its object. The inadequacy of the experience is explained by the inexhaustability of its final object. In this way the empirical character of early Christian thought must be radically distinguished from much of what we take for granted today. It is not that truth can be concocted out of our experience. On the contrary, we experience a truth that transcends our experience and that is alone to be understood as "real." The Fathers of the Church are for the most part Christian Platonists. And what I wish to examine is the "broken lights" character of their thought.

    Part one will begin with an account of Irenaeus' theological vision (ca. 180) and will conclude by describing the versions of the Christian vision found in the works of Gregory of Nyssa and Augustine. In one sense we shall discover three very different interpretations of the Christian message. At the same time, we shall find some common themes and problems. All three writers are concerned with the Christian story and with Christ's victory as the climax of that story. Moreover, their preoccupation is with articulating the story in such a way as to show how Christ's victory becomes the Christian's. And the victory over death, sin, and Satan is one that in differing ways the three writers locate within the common life of the Church. Their views also raise two fundamental problems. First, is the common life of the Church to be regarded as a present participation in Christian destiny, or is it rather to be understood as an anticipation of that destiny? The question is not so much one that requires a sharp decision one way or the other as one that implies the issue of where our emphasis should lie. Second, how must we envisage the common life of the Church not only in relation to the Christian destiny but also in relation to human life as a whole. Gregory of Nyssa is a universalist and makes no final distinction between the Christian and human destiny. At the opposite extreme, Augustine sharply distinguishes the fate of the elect from that of humanity as a whole. Irenaeus appears to take something of a middle view. The logic of his thought implies that the course of human history must be understood as one in which Christ's headship comes to be acknowledged by all. And yet he recognizes that those who take Satan's part will suffer condemnation with him.

My second concern is with the function of the theological broken lights in the Christian life. In other words, what does the theological development have to do with Christian behavior? The problem, of course, is a perennial one. But more often than not accounts of patristic theology focus rather narrowly on controversy, and the complexities of the development make it hard to see that there were practical as well as theoretical issues at stake. My basic assumption is that, at least in principle, theology acts as an articulation of the religious convictions that supply the motives for Christian life. The broken lights are meant to mend lives; vision ought to be translated into virtue. And the theological issues I have just noted become crucial in trying to make that translation. How may the Christian destiny, the vision of Christ's victory, be related to the Christian life? To what degree does that life participate in the destiny, and to what degree does it merely anticipate it? Moreover, is the translation one meant to include all people and capable of doing so? These issues could be addressed in a number of ways. For example, we might examine what were supposed Christian virtues with a view to discovering their relation to theological themes. But what seems remarkable to me about the Christian vision of Christ's victory is the consensus of the

Fathers that this victory is mediated to us through the common life of the Church. For this reason I have chosen to examine the Christian life in its relation to various structures of human community. Chapters four through six will examine the family, hospitality, and citizenship in order to see how being a Christian affected understandings of the ordinary human associations in which people found themselves. Chapter seven will discuss monasticism primarily as a Christian attempt to actualize the ideal Christian community. And chapter eight will examine Christian attitudes to the collapse of Western imperial society. In these ways central aspects of the social dimension of early Christianity can be examined in order to consider how human lives were mended by religious convictions put into practice. The question for the reader, as well as for myself, will be how far the general point of view I have tried to set forth at the outset makes sense of the evidence to be examined.

I

Broken Lights

1

The Victory that
Sums Up God's Purposes

In the Vatican in Rome there is a late-third-century sarcophagus. The sculptor has carved on it many episodes from the Bible, but the focal scenes portray the story of Jonah. The prophet is thrown overboard from a small boat towards the jaws of a sea serpent that looks more like the Loch Ness monster than a whale. A second scene shows Jonah disgorged by the monster head first, and a final one has Jonah lying at ease under his gourd bower. The scenes are stereotypes in early Christian art and are found not only on sarcophagi but also as frescoes in catacombs.[1] There is nothing original about them. Everywhere we find the same conventions operating, conventions adapted from pagan art to Christian purposes. Whenever Jonah was carved or painted, it was the same way—head first into the monster, head first out of the monster, and an almost sensuous luxuriating beneath the gourd bower. It was, of course, not a question of art for art's sake. Instead, a statement was being made for the Christian. In the martyr's tomb and on the dead Christian's sarcophagus we find Jonah as a claim and an answer. Victory is the word that puts it most clearly. The point is not Jonah's reluctance or the remarkable repentance of the Ninevites. It is Jonah's deliverance and the refreshment given him by his victory. The sign of Jonah points to the Resurrection of Christ, and by that hope to the triumph of life over death for the martyr and, indeed, for all Christians.[2]

If we were to seek for one way of describing the experience of early Christians, it would be to point to a representation of victory like the

Jonah story. Christ's victory by his death and Resurrection is found in Jonah's deliverance from the whale, Daniel's deliverance from the lions' den, the three young men's deliverance from the burning fiery furnace, and above all in the deliverance of Israel from bondage in Egypt. What did the victory mean to the early Christian? In one sense, it was a way out. The social, political, and economic evils that made up a large part of life in late antiquity would all be left behind as the Christian passed through death to life. And the new age is pictured as the obverse of this life. A banquet would replace the hunger and poverty of the present. Peace and rest would replace toil. But in another sense, the victory was a way in. For many early Christians the Church provided for the first time a place to belong, a community of hope in what must often have seemed a hopeless world.[3] And for all Christians the victory was a moral one. The life of virtue enabled them to see that what really counted was what could not pass away.

Both the sense of victory and this understanding of it breathe through one of the most fascinating documents preserved for us from the ancient Church. Cyprian, the bishop of Carthage in North Africa in the middle of the third century wrote a letter to his friend Donatus in which he tried to put on paper what his conversion to Christianity meant to him. He apparently writes the letter from his country estate outside Carthage in the autumn. It is the time of the vintage festival, "and the pleasant aspect of the gardens harmonizes with the gentle breezes of a mild autumn in soothing and cheering the senses (Ep. 1; *ANF* 5, p. 277)." Cyprian is clearly well-to-do, and his conversion to Christ probably cut him off from a promising career in the imperial civil service or from some other place of prominence in provincial Roman society. But he has no regrets. Indeed, he comes close to describing himself as a Jonah delivered from "lying in darkness and gloomy night, wavering hither and thither, tossed about on the foam of this boastful age" and placed in the peace of a "bower" where the "neighbouring thickets ensure us solitude, and the vagrant trailings of the vine branches creeping in pendent mazes among the reeds that support them have made for us a porch of vines and a leafy shelter" (ibid.).

Cyprian's conversion has delivered him from a world of sin and misery. He asks Donatus to imagine himself on "one of the loftiest peaks of some inaccessible mountain" in order to survey the world (Ep. 1; *ANF* 5, p. 277). The catalogue that follows gives a realistic description of the conditions of life in the middle of the third century. Travel is blocked by robbers and pirates. Civil war involves the whole world in "the bloody horror of camps." Murder committed on a grand scale becomes a virtue. The lust for blood and vice infects the cities by gladiatorial games and theatrical performances. The immorality and depravity hidden from view is worse than what meets the eye. The rich live in constant anxiety lest they be plundered by robbers or, more quietly, by "malicious lawsuits." "The power of those whom power makes terrible to others, is first of all, terrible to themselves" (Ep. 1; *ANF* 5, p. 279). Cyprian is, indeed, living in a world that had plunged into a civil and social chaos impossible to exaggerate. The anarchy of the third century is obscure to us. Often coin hordes supply the only evidence of what was taking place. The Roman Empire had lost control. Civil wars and barbarian invasions were compounded by famine and plague. Only toward the end of the century with Aurelian, Diocletian, and Constantine was order restored. It is from this world that Cyprian, Jonah-like, has found in Christ an anchorage in "the harbor of salvation" (Ep. 1; *ANF* 5, p. 279).

Cyprian's deliverance, however, is one that gives him a new vision and a new freedom in this life. His baptism washed away "the stain of former years," and he found himself enlightened and empowered to do "what before had seemed difficult" (Ep. 1; *ANF* 5, p. 276). The gift he received was the freedom of virtue, what he calls "liberty of action" (ibid.):

> How great is this empire of the mind, and what a power it has, not alone that itself is withdrawn from the mischievous associations of the world, as one who is purged and pure can suffer no stain of a hostile irruption, but that it becomes still greater and stronger in its might, so that it can rule over all the imperious host of the attacking adversary with its sway.

The mind that is enlightened by Christ is no longer captive to outward circumstances, but instead has victory over them and power to live in hope and freedom.

The experience that Cyprian describes is central to early Christianity. From the time of the New Testament writers on it was the victory of the cross and the new life given by the risen Lord that stood at the center of the Christian claim. Miracles and particularly the exorcism of demons in Christ's name were concrete signs of the triumph, and we must remember that regular and ritual exorcism was part of the preparation for baptism throughout the patristic period.[4] Christian lives and the deaths of Christian martyrs also witnessed to Christ's victory. And it was the aim of Christian theology to put that witness into words that would encourage Christians to remain steadfast in their faith and would persuade the world to commit itself to the Saviour. Indeed, it is not going too far to say that the whole of the patristic theological development is preoccupied with answering the question, Who is the Saviour? In this sense, the articulation of Christian experience is an explanation of the risen Lord that seeks to understand his relation to God and his purposes for Israel and the Gentiles and his relation to us as human beings. The New Testament itself must be regarded as a series of desperately human attempts to explain Christ. These attempts lead in differing directions and employ a wide variety of categories. Is Christ the Messiah? a prophet like Moses? the son of Man? the Wisdom of God? The only rule that works for the New Testament is that Christ is whatever you are hoping for, but he always fulfills those hopes in an unexpected way. Christian writers after the New Testament were obliged to find ways of explaining their own experience of Christ in the light of the initial responses preserved in the New Testament. Let me turn to Irenaeus as an example of one who tries to put into words the sort of experience described by Cyprian and who seeks to do so in a way true to Scripture.

IRENAEUS AND HIS SAVIOUR

We know very little of Irenaeus' life save that he was the bishop of Lyons from about the year 177. He does tell us that as a child he was familiar with the household of Polycarp, the bishop of Smyrna in Asia Minor who was martyred at the age of eighty-six in 156:[5]

> I remember the events of those days more clearly than those which happened recently, for what we learn as children grows up with the soul and is united to it, so that I can speak even of the place in which the blessed Polycarp sat and disputed, how he came in and went out, the character of his life, the appearance of his body, the discourses which he made to the people, how he reported his intercourse with John and with the others who had seen the Lord. . . .

Irenaeus' was in a sense an apostolic childhood. Through Polycarp he was brought up in the shadow of eyewitnesses to Christ and his Resurrection. He must have received a good but modest education, if we can judge by his writings. In 177 the Churches in Lyons and Vienne suffered a great persecution. The bishop, Pothinus, was martyred; and the Christians in Gaul wrote a detailed account of the persecution to the Churches of Asia and Phrygia.[6] Irenaeus was selected to succeed Pothinus. And as the leader of a martyr Church, he was also obliged to do battle against Christian heretics. He did so in part by writing a treatise in five books called "The Detection and Overthrow of the Knowledge Falsely So

Called." The work, commonly known as *Against Heresies*, and a small book called *The Demonstration of the Apostolic Faith* give us a good insight into Irenaeus' understanding of Christianity. And his view is clearly common property. We can reconstruct from Irenaeus' writings the earliest theological synthesis in the history of the Church.[7]

Like Cyprian a little more than half a century later, Irenaeus concentrates upon Christ as the Saviour. In speaking of the long-suffering of God, he says (*AH* 3.20.1; *ANF* 1, pp. 449f.):

> . . . so also, from the beginning, did God permit man to be swallowed up by the great whale, who was the author of transgression, not that he should perish altogether when so engulphed; but arranging and preparing the plan of salvation, which was accomplished by the Lord, through the sign of Jonah. . . .

The entire human race, imprisoned as it were in the belly of Satan, has been delivered by Christ. What Irenaeus has in mind is death, for it is Satan who has brought death upon us (*AH* 5.23). But death infects human life in many different ways. The fact that we shall ultimately rot and decay betrays itself in the calamities to which we are subject and in the corruption of vice. Moreover, the path to incorruption leads through suffering and death. The martyrs, who "strive to follow the footprints of the Lord's passion," supply the paradigm case. Their death enables them to "attain to glory," and the reality of their new life depends upon the reality of their willingness to suffer for Christ. Similarly, the victory of Christ would be specious had "the Word of God the Father . . . made man" not in reality suffered (*AH* 3.18.5–6; *ANF* 1, p. 447). The Christian message is one of salvation and involves a number of claims that Irenaeus is obliged to sort out. Christ is the Word of God made man; and his story, climaxing in his death and Resurrection, is the culmination of God's arrangements for salvation.

To put the matter this way raises a good many complicated problems. First, the relations of Christ to God and of Christ's human aspect to his character as the divine Saviour immediately involve the trinitarian and christological issues that preoccupy the early Church. If the Saviour is somehow God and if Christians are to remain true to their Jewish heritage as monotheists, then some form of trinitarian monotheism must be developed. And if this development can insist upon the full divinity of Christ, however that might be understood, then it is hard to see how Christ can equally be human. Irenaeus is aware of these problems even though he cannot be said to have solved them satisfactorily.[8] But a second set of difficulties is more important to him. If Christ is the

Saviour, how is his work to be related to what God did at Creation and in the Old Testament? The reason Irenaeus must worry with these problems has to do with his opponents, the Gnostics. For Christian Gnostics salvation involves several denials. The Saviour rejects the material creation, the Creator God, and the Old Testament. In these ways Gnostic salvation is discontinuous with our world. Irenaeus must respond by insisting that salvation is not merely from the world but for it.

For Irenaeus the debate with Gnosticism is in no sense abstract. A Valentinian Gnostic teacher named Marcus is active in Lyons and has seduced, both figuratively and literally, many women from the Church. He engages in magical practices, and encourages foolish women to prophesy (AH 1.13). Irenaeus attacks the teaching that lies behind these practices. Marcus, as the other Gnostics, undermines the unity of God by speaking of a large number of divine "aeons" in a divine "pleroma" and by arguing that the Creator God (Demiurge) of the Old Testament is inferior to the divine pleroma. His work is also inferior, and the entire material creation is equated with evil. "Knowledge" enables the Gnostics to see the world and themselves in their true light for the first time. The Gnostics are really spiritual beings who have fallen from the divine pleroma and become imprisoned in bodies. Once they realize this, they have the power to destroy the entire physical creation, disengage their "inner man" from the body, and find salvation by identifying themselves with the divine pleroma. Irenaeus' problem is clear: He must define salvation in such a way that it is continuous with the physical creation and the Saviour so that he may be continuous with the God of Creation and the Old Testament.

In a crucial passage (AH 3.16.6) Irenaeus summarizes the view he wishes to oppose to the Gnostics' understanding of salvation. He sets the story of Christ's death, Resurrection, and return in glory "to raise up all flesh, and for the manifestation of salvation, and to apply the rule of just judgment to all who were made by Him" within a larger context. The dead and risen Lord is identified with God's "only-begotten Word, who is always present with the human race." Irenaeus goes on to say (AH 3.16.6; ANF 1, pp. 442f.):

> There is, therefore, as I have pointed out, one God the Father, and one Christ Jesus, who came by means of the whole dispensational arrangements [connected with Him], and gathered together all things in Himself. But in every respect, too, He is man, the formation of God; and thus He took up man into Himself, the invisible becoming visible, the incomprehensible being made comprehensible, the impassible becoming capable of suffering, and the Word

being made man, thus summing up all things in Himself: so that as in supercelestial, spiritual, and invisible things, the Word of God is supreme, so also in things visible and corporeal He might possess the supremacy, and, taking to Himself the pre-eminence, as well as constituting Himself Head of the Church, He might draw all things to Himself at the proper time.

Irenaeus, of course, is talking about the Saviour, the Head of the Church who is the object of Christian worship. The story of this Saviour is of God's Word united to humanity in Christ Jesus, crucified and raised from the dead, and destined to return at the end of the world.

It is this story, together with its implications, that defines what Irenaeus means by the Incarnation. His word for it is "the Economy," and by Economy he means the dispensations God uses to govern his household, the universe. Thus, "Incarnation" does not refer in a limited way to Christ's nativity or to a technical account of his person as divine and human. Instead, the term refers to the entire story from Christ's birth of Mary to his return in glory. Moreover, *the* Economy is the last and consummating dispensation of the Word of God. It brings to focus the previous economies of the Word, "who is always present to the human race." Irenaeus' word for the consummating function of the Incarnation is borrowed from Ephesians 1:10 (*anakephalaiôsasthai*). It occurs three times in the passage I have cited above and is translated "gathered together," "took up," and "summing up."[9] And to speak of Christ as the Head of the Church is also to refer to his work of "summing up." All these points require elaboration, and I shall attempt to explain them more fully in what follows. The story of Christ Jesus is placed within the larger story of the Word's activity, beginning with the Creation of the world. Consequently, the Saviour who is the Head of the Church is thought to have played a role in the whole of human history and, particularly, in the history of Israel. The argument will proceed by exploring the Saviour's relation to Adam and to the entire course of human history understood as a growth from innocent childhood to experienced maturity. Then I shall be able to return to the question of what Irenaeus means by "summing up," "heading up" (*anakephalaiôsis, recapitulatio*).

THE SAVIOUR AND ADAM

Irenaeus follows St. Paul in describing the Saviour as the new Adam, but he elaborates the typological comparisons we find in Romans 5 and 1 Corinthians 15 and adapts them to his own purposes. The argument in Romans 5:12ff. depends upon the fact that both in Adam and in Christ a

single act has universal consequences. Adam sins and is punished by
death, and the pattern he introduces into human life is one in which the
entire race participates. This participation, though explained by Adam's
disobedience, is nonetheless free and responsible. All humans die *because*
they all sin (Rom. 5:12). A commonsense distinction between the explanation for the human predicament and the issue of moral responsibility
makes sense of the argument, which otherwise lends itself to complicated
and frustrating reflections about God's sovereignty and human freedom.[10]
In a similar way, Christ's act of obedience explains a possibility open to
all. The pattern of his death and Resurrection represents God's loving
purpose for all humanity. St. Paul's aim in using this typology of contrast
between Adam and Christ is not to construct an elaborate theological
account of Redemption. Rather, it is to make a fairly simply point about
the dead and risen Lord. A comparison, obviously, will be used to explain
something less clear by what is accepted and known. St. Paul is not
explaining Adam. Instead, he must explain Christ and how Christ's act in
the past can have relevance to the Romans in the present. So, he says,
remember that you believe Adam's act to have had universal consequences for humanity. Similarly, believe that Christ's act is effective for
you. In the same way, in 1 Corinthians St. Paul uses the old Creation in
Adam as a way of explaining the new Creation in Christ.

Needless to say, St. Paul's argument supplies a point of departure for
further reflection, and Irenaeus accepts the implicit invitation. He reworks the argument in the interest of a central point he wishes to make
against the Gnostics. Redemption must not be construed as the abolition
of the old Creation. Rather, it needs to be seen as its transformation. The
Adam pattern is undone not by being rejected but by being turned into
the Christ pattern. Irenaeus, depending on Romans 5:12ff., puts the
point this way (*AH* 3.18.7; *ANF* 1, p. 448):

> For as by the disobedience of the one man who was originally
> moulded from virgin soil, the many were made sinners, and for-
> feited life; so was it necessary that, by the obedience of one man,
> who was originally born from a virgin, many should be justified
> and receive salvation.

What happened in Adam is reversed in Christ and reversed *for* Adam
(*AH* 3.23). Christ "fought and conquered; for He was man contending
for the fathers, and through obedience doing away with disobedience
completely. . ." (*AH* 3.18.6; *ANF* 1, pp. 447f.). Irenaeus' logic depends
upon noticing that the two patterns overlap. Death in the Adam pattern
is the penalty for sin and the end of the road for human beings, but in

the Christ pattern death becomes the gateway to life and incorruption in the new age of the resurrection.

Irenaeus delights in elaborating the details of the typology. In the passage cited above he argues that just as Adam was made from virgin soil, so Christ was born of the Virgin (see also *AH* 3.21.10). And just as Adam died on the sixth day, the very day he was created, so Christ died to bring life on the sixth day (*AH* 5.23.2). Luke traces seventy-two generations from Adam to Christ, and so Christ brings life to the seventy-two nations of the world (*AH* 3.22.3). Moreover, the typology can be extended to include Eve and Mary. As Eve was disobedient and led astray by the voice of the devil, a fallen angel, so Mary was obedient to the angel's command (*AH* 3.22.4; 5.19). Virginal obedience undoes virginal disobedience (*AH* 5.19.1; *ANF* 1, p. 547):

> For in the same way the sin of the first created man receives amendment by the correction of the First-begotten, and the coming of the serpent is conquered by the harmlessness of the dove, those bonds being unloosed by which we had been fast bound to death.

As well, the tree by which Adam and Eve fell corresponds to the tree of the cross by which Christ brings life (*AH* 5.16.3, 17.3). And the "seed" of Eve, Christ, bruises the head of the serpent (Gen. 3:15) when he defeats Satan in the wilderness temptation, thereby fulfilling the promise made to Eve (*AH* 5.21.1–2). Irenaeus drives the typology toward his conclusion that the new Adam is the victor over Satan, who holds humanity captive to sin and death. Christ binds "the strong man" and plunders his goods (*AH* 3.18.6, 23.1; 5.21.3). And in freeing the captives, Christ redeems not only the children of Adam and Eve but the original captives themselves (*AH* 3.23.2).

The central figure of Irenaeus' reflections upon the Adam typology is, of course, the Saviour. And Irenaeus makes one point explicit that is merely implicit in Romans 5:12ff. The Saviour must be man, for "unless man had overcome the enemy of man, the enemy would not have been legitimately vanquished" (*AH* 3.18.7; *ANF* 1, p. 448). And so Irenaeus insists upon the reality of Christ's human experience, suffering, death, and Resurrection (*AH* 3.22.1). At the same time, "unless it had been God who had freely given salvation, we could never have possessed it securely. And unless man had been joined to God, he could never have become a partaker of incorruptibility (*AH* 3.18.7; *ANF* 1, p. 448). In other words, the new Adam, while fully human, is not a mere man, but "the Son of God made Son of man." The first Adam was "of an animal nature . . . that he might be saved by the spiritual one" (*AH* 3.22.3; *ANF* 1, p. 455: 1 Cor. 15:45ff.). Irenaeus does not explain how this can be, and it remains for the later theological development to try to make sense of his conclusion. Nevertheless, his view does draw a legitimate inference from the Pauline texts. The new Adam of 1 Corinthians 15 is "the man from heaven," and Romans 5:15 implies that the act of Christ is not a merely human act like Adam's but the working of "the grace of God and the free gift in the grace of that one man, Jesus Christ." Elsewhere in his writings St. Paul explicitly treats Christ as the divine Redeemer, who though "in the form of God" took "the form of a servant" by emptying himself (Phil. 2).

Defining Christ as the Word of God made man implies that the new Adam transcends the old and suggests that Irenaeus does not mean to treat the typology as though Christ simply reversed what happened with Adam. Of course, at one level what was done by Adam was undone by Christ; and the typology depends upon a number of comparisons and contrasts of the two. Nonetheless, while Irenaeus seeks to preserve the analogy (*AH* 3.21.10), he places it within a broader framework. His treatment of the Scriptural judgment that Adam was made in the image and likeness of God indicates the larger context in which the typology appears. He can say that in Christ we have recovered what was lost in Adam, namely to be in God's likeness and image (*AH* 3.18.1). But passages in Book 5 explain what he means by saying this. Adam was made "in the likeness of God" by the Son and the Holy Spirit as "the hands of the Father" (*AH* 5.6.1; *ANF* 1, p. 531). But this likeness, which Adam lost in the fall, was not complemented by the image of God (*AH* 5.16.2; *ANF* 1, p. 544):

> For in times long past, it was *said* that man was created after the image of God, but it was not [actually] *shown*; for the Word was as yet invisible, after whose image man was created. Wherefore also he did easily lose the similitude.

In the Incarnation the Word made flesh "showed forth the image truly" and "re-established the similitude after a sure manner, by assimilating man to the invisible Father through means of the visible Word." In other words, Christ's reversal of the Fall is merely preliminary to the granting of God's image as the fulfillment of God's intent at Creation.[11]

Irenaeus, then, thinks of Redemption primarily as the completion of Creation. This enables him to refute Gnostic views that would see Redemption as requiring the destruction of the material creation. And it allows him to think of the movement of the human race from Adam to

Christ on the analogy of the growth of an individual from infancy to maturity. Adam's sin was "child-like" and the moment he saw what he had done, he repented and clothed himself with irritating fig leaves to punish his body. God, compassionately recognizing the childishness of Adam's sin, exchanged the fig leaves for coats of skin (*AH* 3.23.5). This assessment of the Fall minimizes its importance without denying that Adam brought punishment on himself and his posterity. But the Fall becomes a stage in the growth of humanity to maturity; and, however unfortunate and unnecessary, it seems as inevitable as an adolescent's rebellion. God created humanity infantile because created things are inferior to the Creator and must grow to their perfection (*AH* 4.38). This is what Irenaeus means when he says that the Incarnate Word "summed up [*recapitulavit*] in himself the long line of human beings, furnishing us with salvation in epitome, that we might recover what we had lost in Adam, that is, existence according to the image and likeness of God" (*AH* 3.18.1). The emphasis is not upon the recovery, but upon the summing up which takes us beyond recovery to the fulfillment of God's original intention at Creation.

FROM INFANCY TO MATURITY

Irenaeus' insistence upon the continuity of Adam and Christ and of Creation and Redemption means that he can understand the whole of human history as a process of growth that finds its term in the new humanity of the Incarnate Word. This process is identical with the story embodied in Scripture and the Rule of Faith. In his *Demonstration of the Apostolic Preaching* Irenaeus puts it this way (*Dem.* 6; ACW 16, p. 51):

> And this is the drawing-up of our faith, the foundation of the building, and the consolidation of a way of life. God the Father, uncreated, beyond grasp, invisible, one God the maker of all; this is the first and foremost article of our faith. But the second article is the Word of God, the Son of God, Christ Jesus our Lord, who was shown forth by the prophets according to the design of their prophecy and according to the manner in which the Father disposed; and through Him were made all things whatsoever. He also, *in the end of times* (Dan. 11:13), for the recapitulation of all things, is become a man among men, visible and tangible, in order to abolish death and bring to light life, and bring about the communion of God and man. And the third article is the Holy Spirit, through whom the prophets prophesied and the patriarchs were taught about God and the just were led in the path of

justice, and who *in the end of times* has been poured forth in a new manner upon humanity over all the earth renewing man to God.

Creation, the Old Testament, and the Incarnation mark the major episodes of the story, and the Word plays a role in all of them. We must look at the story in more detail in order to understand the continuous work of God's Word and the focal dispensation of the Incarnation.

If there is a single theme that Irenaeus stresses, it is the conviction that there is but one God and that he is the Creator. Obviously, the conviction is directly opposed to the complicated speculations about the origin of the world that preoccupy the Gnostics. As well, Irenaeus insists that the same Creator God is the God of both the Old and the New Testament (*AH* 4.32). Moreover, he approves of Plato's opinion that God's goodness is his motive in creating the world (*AH* 3.25.5). And he cites as scriptural proof the first mandate of *The Shepherd of Hermas:* "First of all believe that God is one, 'who made all things and perfected them, and made all things to be out of that which was not,' and contains all things, and is himself alone uncontained" (LCL 2, p. 71; *AH* 4.20.2). This mandate is constructed from traditional Jewish elements. That God is one derives from the *Shema* (Deut. 6:4), the "creed" of Israel. The mother of the seven Maccabaean martyrs (2 Macc. 7:28) speaks of God who made everything "out of what did not exist." And the notion of the uncontained God who contains all things is used by Philo and the rabbis to explain what it means to call God "the Place." Irenaeus' monotheism has deep roots in ancient Judaism.

The last phrase of the mandate from *Hermas* occurs with great frequency in Irenaeus' work and is the basis for much of his argument in Book 2, where he is concerned to refute the Gnostic doctrine of God. To say that God is uncontained means affirming his transcendence. And his transcendence requires his unity and his incomprehensibility. The Creator differs radically in nature from his creation, and for this reason he cannot be comprehended. He is the unknown God. On the other hand, in saying that God contains all things, Irenaeus is speaking of God's providential ordering of all things. God's activity informs the whole creation. While He cannot be comprehended in his greatness, he can be apprehended in his love (*AH* 4.20.1). And so, the Gnostics are wrong on two counts. By arguing that "the spiritual" are saved because of their natural identity with God, as sparks of the divine, they deny God's transcendent nature. By denying that knowledge of God was available before the revelation of "gnosis" in the Saviour, they fail to acknowledge the continuous working of God's providence, the love by which he always makes himself known.

Within this understanding of the creator Irenaeus includes the Word of God and his Spirit. God made all things through his Word (*AH* 3.11.1). God always has present with him his two hands, the Word or Son and Wisdom or the Spirit, "by whom and in whom, fully and spontaneously, He made all things" (*AH* 3.20.1). The use of the plural in Genesis 1:26 ("Let *us* make") indicates the trinitarian character of Creation. Psalm 33:6 ("By the *word* of the Lord the heavens were made, and all their host by the *Spirit* of His mouth") makes the point still more explicit.[12] More-over, a mystical interpretation of the first verse of Genesis establishes the conclusion that God created the heavens and the earth "by his Son" (*Dem.* 43). The first word of the Bible (*bereshith*), usually translated "in the beginning," is a very peculiar expression in Hebrew that could as easily mean "by his first fruits" or "by his beginning." Christ, then, as God's first fruits, is the Beginning by means of which "God created the heavens and the earth." Precedents for this interpretation may be found in Proverbs 8:22 and Ecclesiasticus 24:5, and it lies behind verses in the New Testament such as John 1:1ff., Colossians 1:15, and Revelation 3:14. Christ, as God's Beginning, is the agent of God in Creation and revela-tion. An obvious problem begins to emerge. How can Irenaeus insist upon the absolute unity of God and yet recognize the distinct existence and activity of his Son and Spirit? Irenaeus sees the problem, and that is why he can sometimes speak of the persons of the Trinity as no more than aspects of the same God. The Son and Spirit are God's hands. The Son is God's "reason" and the Spirit his "spirit," on the analogy of an individual human being. Thus, we are still speaking of God as a single "person." At the same time, Irenaeus is unwilling to give up speaking of Father, Son, and Spirit as three. He is caught between, on the one hand, insisting on God's unity to refute the Gnostics and retain his commit-ment to the monotheistic heritage of Judaism, and, on the other hand, being true to a Christian recognition of the distinct character of the Son and the Spirit. He knows what he wants to say, but he can find no persuasive way of saying it. Nor does the Church find a solution till two centuries later at the Council of Constantinople in 381.

The Word is not only the Father's agent in creation but is also the means of revealing the Father to the creation. In *Against Heresies* 4.6 Irenaeus discusses the meaning of Matthew 11:27 (". . . no one knows the Father except the Son and any one to whom the Son chooses to reveal him"). Since the verse uses the present tense, it cannot mean that the Son's revelatory work in the Incarnation is to be contrasted with a previ-ous time when no one *knew* the Father. On the contrary, Matthew refers to the Son's continuous manifestation of the Father. The Lord reveals God the Creator "by means of the creation itself," and "by the law and the prophets did the Lord preach both Himself and the Father alike." Finally, the revelation finds its full focus in the Incarnation. The same trinitarian problem that emerges in Irenaeus' doctrine of creation betrays itself in his doctrine of revelation. Once again his battle with the Gnostics obliges him to deny any division between Father and Word. The Father is the invisible aspect of God; the Word, the visible aspect (*AH* 4.6.6). On the other hand, the tradition that Irenaeus follows and that we find in Justin Martyr's writings found the Word of God present in the Old Testament as a distinct figure. Wherever God was said to appear or to descend, the Word came on stage. It was the Word who spoke to Moses from the burning bush and who descended to see the Tower of Babel. These logophanies were presented as dress rehearsals for the Incarnation, and they implied the Word's separate identity.

Irenaeus does not solve the difficulty, but his attempt to paper over it shows that he sees it. He attempts to redefine what Justin had thought of as actual appearance of the Word and treats the phenomenon as a kind of prophetic dispensation of God. For example, Irenaeus says that before the Fall the Word of God was constantly walking in the Garden of Eden (Gen. 3:8). But lest we take this too literally, he adds: "He would walk round and talk with the man, prefiguring what was to come to pass in the future, how He would become man's fellow, and talk with him, and come among mankind, teaching him justice" (*Dem.* 12; ACW 16, p. 55). The walking has become a prophetic talking, and Irenaeus comes close to suggesting that "Word" is simply a way of speaking of God's prophetic activity. Just as the Word, "the visible of the Father," is present in the created order, so "the Son of God is implanted everywhere throughout his writings" (*AH* 4.10.1). In this sense, the Old Testament is "the words of Christ" (*AH* 4.2.3). Christ is the treasure hid in the field (Mt. 13:44); "but the treasure hid in the Scriptures is Christ, since He was pointed out by means of types and parables" (*AH* 4.26.1; *ANF* 1, p. 496). In other words, everything in the Old Testament finds its true reference in Christ.

Two points must be added. First, Irenaeus is using "prophecy" to mean more than verbal predictions of Christ. The Old Testament narratives contain types and parables of Christ, and these must also be regarded as "prophetic." When Moses lifts up the brazen serpent in the wilderness, he is foreshadowing Christ's exaltation on the cross. And this type is as prophetic as Isaiah's prediction of the virgin birth. Second, the references of the Old Testament to Christ can be seen only retrospectively and from the perspective of faith in Christ: ". . . every prophecy, before its fulfilment, is to men [full of] enigmas and ambiguities. But when the time has arrived, and the prediction has come to pass, then the prophecies have a clear and certain exposition" (*AH* 4.26.1; *ANF* 1, p. 496). The treasure hid in the field is "brought to light by the cross of Christ." Thus, the Incarnation functions to clarify the previous revelatory work of the Word, declaring God's "dispensations with regard to man." For Irenaeus "prophecy" is drawn into the broader notion of God's providential dispensations.

THE OLD TESTAMENT AS GOD'S DISPENSATION

The significance of Irenaeus' treatment of the Old Testament as a record of God's dispensations leading to the Incarnation emerges only when we compare it with earlier Christian understandings. Of course, most Christians regarded the Old Testament as something that pointed beyond itself to its fulfillment in Christ and the Church. The prophecies and promises of Scripture are fulfilled in him and his work, and the narratives of the Old Testament are a mystical and typological foreshadowing of the New. And Irenaeus shares this understanding. The difficulty, however, is that such a view gave little room for attaching value to the Old Testament in its own right. This problem was compounded by the fact that most Christians rejected the Jewish practices that appeared to be required by the Old Testament. The observance of circumcision, the Sabbath, the food laws, and the Temple service was thought abolished by Christ. And Christians used the Old Testament to prove that this was so. As well, the destruction of the temple in 70 C.E. and the prohibition of Jews from Jerusalem after the Hadrianic revolt of 132 C.E. were both used as empirical proof that God willed the abolition of Jewish practices. All this meant that it was difficult to reject Judaism without rejecting the Old Testament. Indeed, Marcion and the Gnostics took the logical step of doing just that and, as well, denying the one Creator God of the Old Testament.

As a result, the problem for Irenaeus was to find a way of retaining the traditional interpretation of the Old Testament and yet preventing it from being given a Marcionite or gnostic conclusion. Let me begin by saying something about the way in which Irenaeus preserves the traditional understanding by arguing that the Old Testament is prophetic both of Christ and of the rejection of Judaism. The prophets, including for Irenaeus Moses and David, predicted what came to pass in Christ. The stock verses are cited. Isaiah 7:14 predicts the Virgin birth, while Isaiah 9 and 11 supply a detailed description of the prophesied child (*AH* 3.9.3, 16.3, 17.3, 19.2–3, 21; 4.33.11). Isaiah 61 ("The Spirit of the Lord is upon me") is quoted by Christ in Luke 4:18 as a text fulfilled in his person and ministry. Isaiah 53 (the suffering servant) and Psalm 22 (the forsaken righteous one) are fulfilled in Christ's passion (*AH* 3.12.8, 19.2, 20.8, 23.2, 33.1, 12; 5.31.2). Psalm 110:1 (the exalted Lord), Daniel 7 and 2 (the Son of Man and the Stone), and Zechariah 12:10 (the pierced one) predict the Resurrection, exaltation, and second coming of Christ (*AH* 2.28.7; 3.6.1, 10.5, 16.3, 19.2, 20.11; 5.33.1, 11). Predictions are found for the whole story of Christ's birth, life, death, Resurrection, and return in glory. Examples could be multiplied, and the predictions are made to extend beyond Christ's life and fate to their effect. The Old Testament is also fulfilled by the inclusion of the Gentiles in the people of God and the rejection of the Jews. Moreover, the prophetic character of Scripture may be found not only in what "they proclaimed by word" but also in what "they indicated typically by means of [outward] action" (*AH* 3.20.8; *ANF* 1, p. 490). Thus, the paschal lamb is a type of Christ, the true Passover (*AH* 4.10); and when Moses lifts up his arms in the battle with Amalek or the brazen serpent in the wilderness, he is acting out a type of Christ (*AH* 4.24.1).

Equally traditional is Irenaeus' use of the Old Testament to prove that Jewish practices have been abolished. These practices, can, of course, be given a spiritual interpretation that finds its fulfillment in Christian beliefs. The spiritual circumcision is Christian Baptism, and the true Sabbath rest will be found in heaven (*AH* 4.16.1–2). The Temple sacrifices point towards the pure offering of Christian worship (*AH* 4.17–18). But in themselves these practices are not only no longer of value, they were actually given to the people of Israel "on account of their hardness of heart" (*AH* 4.15.2). Irenaeus, following earlier tradition as we find it in Barnabas and Justin, thinks of the sin of the Golden Calf (*AH* 4.15.1; *ANF* 1, p. 479):

> But when they turned themselves to make a calf, and had gone back in their minds to Egypt, desiring to be slaves instead of freemen, they were placed for the future in a state of servitude suited to their wish. . . .

In other words, the Law in its literal meaning is really a divine punishment for the rebellion of Israel. "The laws of bondage . . . were one by one promulgated to the people by Moses, suited for their instruction or for their punishment" (*AH* 4.16.5; *ANF* 1, p. 482). Taken merely as punishment, the Law would have no purpose for the Jews save to reject them, and the anti-Jewish argument runs the risk of being driven in a Marcionite direction.

Irenaeus avoids this danger by associating instruction with punishment. The traditional arguments can be retained, but the punishment for the people of Israel is now thought to be remedial and, consequently, has a purpose beyond that of mere retribution. So it is that the Jews "had therefore a law, a course of discipline, and a prophecy of future things" (*AH* 4.15.1; *ANF* 1, p. 479). In Greek the word for "punishment" (*paideusis*) also means "education." Irenaeus' emphasis is upon the second meaning. The punishment of the hard-hearted people is meant for their instruction. The law of bondage was meant to train slaves to serve God (*AH* 4.13.2). In this way God "prepared a people beforehand, teaching the headstrong to follow God," and "in a variety of ways He adjusted the human race to an agreement with salvation" (*AH* 4.14.2; *ANF* 1, p. 479). The whole of the Temple service was designed to draw the people away from idolatry, "calling them to the things of primary importance by means of those which were secondary; that is, to things that are real, by means of those that are typical; and by things temporal, to eternal; and by the carnal to the spiritual; and by the earthly to the heavenly" (*AH* 4.14.3; *ANF* 1, p. 479). God is thought of as the wise teacher, who gradually educates his people so that they can grow from infancy to maturity. The covenants with Adam, Noah, and Moses are designed for this purpose (*AH* 3.11.8, 12.11). And the law of bondage given by Moses corresponds with Adam's fall. Just as Adam must pass through an adolescent rebellion on his way to maturity, so the people must live for a while as slaves. But once Christ comes and brings "the new covenant of liberty" he abolishes the laws of bondage and increases and widens "those laws which are natural, and noble, and common to all" (*AH* 4.16.5). Irenaeus has drawn the traditional anti-Jewish polemic into the framework of his metaphor of growth. The Old Testament represents a stage in human development and testifies not only to the completion of that development in Christ, but also to the dispensations by which God guides it towards the final and focal dispensation of the Incarnation.

THE INCARNATION AND "SUMMING UP"

The Incarnation represents for Irenaeus the culminating Economy of God. The work of the Word in Creation and in the Old Testament finds its completion when the Word is made flesh. Irenaeus can think of this in terms of Ephesians 1:9–10: "For he has made known to us in all wisdom and insight the mystery of his will, according to his purpose which he set forth in Christ as a plan for the fulness of time, to unite all things in him, things in heaven and things on earth." The Greek word translated "to unite" (*anakephalaiôsasthai*) means to head up or sum up, but its Latin rendering (*recapitulare*) implies the additional notion of "once again." Thus, Irenaeus' doctrine has usually been called "recapitulation," and has often been understood to mean that the paradise lost in Adam is restored in Christ. As examining Irenaeus' use of the Adam typology has shown, this is not what Irenaeus means to suggest. Instead, the summing up is one accomplished for the first time in Christ; and the Incarnation represents the attainment of human maturity in the New Man as opposed to the childlike character of the old Adam.[13] The very fact that Irenaeus can speak of summing up when he explains why God did not create Adam perfect to begin with argues for the correctness of the interpretation I am suggesting (*AH* 4.38.1). The theme of summing up is one Irenaeus finds not only in Scripture (Eph. 1:10) but also in the writings of Justin Martyr (*AH* 4.6.2). And it is one that he introduces into his statement of the Rule of Faith (*Dem.* 6, cited above p. 31).

The passage from Irenaeus' work that makes the best point of departure for his understanding of summing up is the one I have cited above, page 26 (*AH* 3.16.6). The Incarnation is placed within the dispensational scheme (*per universam dispositionem*), and is said to "sum up" humanity and all things in Christ. At one level, the cosmological understanding we find in the theology of Ephesians (and Colossians) is echoed by Irenaeus. The supremacy of God's Word in "super-celestial, spiritual, and invisible things" is extended to "things visible and corporeal." In other words, the Incarnation, as Ephesians 1:10 says, unites heaven and earth. But this union has primary reference to humanity and to Christ's constitution as the Head of his body the Church. Thus, the binding of heaven and earth is understood to effect the "communion of God and man" (*Dem.* 31; ACW 16, p. 67). That communion must be understood in the light of Irenaeus' doctrine of salvation, to which I shall turn in a moment. In trying to understand what Irenaeus means by this dimension of his doctrine, we might think—anachronistically—of the metaphor of the keystone in a medieval cathedral. The keystone is what holds the fabric together by balancing the architectural stresses of the building. So Christ, who is the Son of God made Son of Man, holds together the whole of God's house, the entire universe. In this way he does not reproduce what had been the case for Adam, but fulfills for the first time the promise of Adam's creation. The summing up is referred by Irenaeus both to the Incarnation (*AH* 3.16.6) and to Christ's second coming at the end of the age (*AH* 1.10.1). It seems clear that we should understand that what is in principle true in Christ is made true in fact at the end of the age. Or, to put it another way, human destiny, which is presently fulfilled in the Incarnate Lord, will be consummated in the age to come.

This last point begins to shift attention to a second, and for Irenaeus more important, dimension of summing up. The spatial metaphor yields to a temporal one. To return to *Against Heresies* 3.16.6, the summing up takes place so that Christ "might draw all things to Himself at the proper time." The summing up is a drawing together and has a double reference to the previous dispensations of the Word and to the work of Christ's body the Church in completing his work. For this reason Irenaeus more often than not associates the summing up with the Adam typology (*AH* 3.18.1, 7, 21.9–10, 22; 5.1.2, 21.1; *Dem.* 30–34). But Christ not only brings the image promised to Adam, while renewing the lost likeness, he also gathers together and so sums up every stage of human life (*AH* 3.18.7) and all nations (*AH* 3.22.3). In this way, summing up is integrated with Irenaeus' vision of the course of human history as a growth from infancy to maturity and with his conviction that God, like a wise teacher, has done everything to train humanity for perfection in Christ. If Irenaeus begins his theology by meditating upon the Saviour who brings him the kind of deliverance that saved Jonah from the whale, he ends by thinking of that Saviour and his story as part of a larger story that begins with Creation and ends with Redemption and a new age. Indeed, Creation and Redemption are really nothing more than two different ways of speaking of the same story or process; "Creation" focuses upon its beginning and "Redemption" on its ending. By considering Irenaeus' doctrine of Redemption we can complete an account of his attempt to articulate Christian experience.

THE VISION OF GOD AS THE LIFE OF HUMANITY

Irenaeus' point of departure in defining Redemption is the Christian belief in the resurrection of the dead, including the sort of apocalyptic scenario we find in the book of Revelation. Virtually the whole of Book 5 of the *Against Heresies* is a treatise on the resurrection. A variety of arguments proves that all flesh will be raised at the end of this age. God's power in creating humanity shows he has power to raise the dead (*AH* 5.3). It is as absurd to deny that flesh can partake of life as it is to say that a "sponge could not possibly partake of water, or a torch of fire" (*AH* 5.3; *ANF* 1, p. 530). The long lives of the ancients in Genesis and the preservation of Enoch, Elijah, the three young men in the burning fiery furnace, and Jonah indicate the possibility of the resurrection (*AH* 5.5). Christ's own Resurrection assures us of ours (*AH* 5.7), as do his miracles in raising the dead (*AH* 5.13). The Incarnation itself shows that God wills the redemption of our flesh (*AH* 5.14). Isaiah (26:19 and 66:13) and Ezekiel (37) predict the resurrection. These arguments and others are aimed against the Gnostic denial of the resurrection. Irenaeus goes on to make it clear that the general resurrection is not to be equated with the

End. Instead, it is the "the commencement of incorruption" and the beginning of the millennium which precedes the End (AH 5.32).[14]

However committed Irenaeus is to this typical early Christian view of the last things, he understands it in his own way. His usual way of speaking of the resurrection is to talk of incorruption. And while he nowhere uses the technical terms we should expect, he does appear dependent on the stock Stoic notion of a human being as a psychosomatic entity, a mind controlling and vivifying a body. In a commonsense way the idea depends upon noting that the mind and the body affect one another. We can all think of experiences in which a mental vigor enlivens our bodies—the athlete who runs faster than he thought possible, the mother who performs a remarkable feat to save her child. Writing all this large gives a way of thinking of a body so informed by mind as to overcome death itself. So it is that for Irenaeus the incorruption of the resurrection has a double meaning. It involves the perfection of the capacities of the soul or mind, what we should call the personality. And it involves rendering our bodies incapable of deteriorating into death. Irenaeus takes a physical view of incorruption, but his concern is with the redemption of human beings as psychosomatic unities. The resurrection overcomes our tendency to change, as well as our tendency to rot and die.

Irenaeus also integrates his understanding of our final destiny of incorruption with his basic metaphor of growth. Thus, in the present it is possible for us to grow towards incorruption (AH 5.8.1; ANF 1, p. 533): "But we do now receive a certain portion of His Spirit, tending towards perfection, and preparing us for incorruption, being little by little accustomed to receive and bear God." Even though the term of the process is located beyond the limits of this age, the process itself begins with Baptism. As we have seen, God chose not to create humanity perfect from the beginning. Rather, creation is followed by growth, strengthening, abounding, and recovering (AH 4.38.3). For the Christian the baptized life is the context for this development towards perfection. Just as wheat must be moistened to make bread and the earth watered for plants to grow, so "our bodies have received unity among themselves by means of that layer which leads to incorruption; but our souls, by means of the Spirit" (AH 3.17.2; ANF 1, p. 445). The growth is a corporate one by which gradually a new humanity is fashioned.

At one level the process finds a moral meaning and is a growth in obedience and virtue. By decreeing Adam's death, God placed a limit on sin "so that man, ceasing at length to live to sin, and dying to it, might begin to live to God (AH 3.23.6; ANF 1, p. 457). While God has no need of human obedience, "He grants to those who follow and serve Him life and incorruption and eternal glory" (AH 4.14.1; ANF 1, p. 478). It may be that Stoic conventions are operating in Irenaeus' thinking at this point. The control of body by mind is for the Stoics equatable with virtue. Vice is to be understood as the mind's being overwhelmed by the body and its passions. The loss of the mind's control is revealed in lust or anger, and reasserting its control transforms lust to love and anger to courage. Thus, there is a moral meaning that can be given to corruption and incorruption. And for Irenaeus the moral sense of incorruption is a harbinger of the perfect control of mind over body that he equates with the resurrection.

In addition to the moral meaning he gives the beginnings of growth toward the final incorruption, Irenaeus is concerned with a spiritual meaning. Baptism not only unites us with one another, it also brings us into fellowship with God, preparing us for "the adoption of sons" (*AH* 3.19.1). Of course, this fellowship has a moral dimension because it is reconciliation. But it also represents a developing vision of God. No one can see God in his greatness and glory, "for the Father is incomprehensible; but in regard to His love, and kindness, and as to His infinite power, even this He grants to those who love Him, that is, to see God" (*AH* 4.20.5; *ANF* 1, p. 489). In this way Irenaeus harmonizes the contradiction in Scripture between passages which insist God cannot be seen and passages which speak of seeing God. The kind of vision of which Irenaeus speaks is one that grows in clarity. What the prophets saw prophetically in the Spirit, we see "adoptively through the Son." The paternal vision is reserved for heaven (*AH* 4.20.5). The perfection of the vision of God in the age to come will bring us "within the light" and enable us to "partake of its brilliancy." And God's splendor vivifies the redeemed. To see God is to receive life. In other words, the perfected vision marks the term of the soul's growth and immediately involves rendering the body incorruptible. It is in this sense that "the vision of God is the life of humanity" (*AH* 4.20.7).

CONCLUSION

Irenaeus' theology is really a story about himself and his Saviour. Christ's birth, life, death, and Resurrection not only show Irenaeus the path he must follow, they also grasp and shape him for his destiny. Christ's victory reveals the end of the story not merely for him but also for Irenaeus and for all Christians. By being caught up into Christ's story Irenaeus gains hope and freedom for the present. Moreover, to be caught up in Christ's story is to find oneself in a drama that goes beyond the Incarnation to involve the whole of God's purpose in Creation and in the calling of Israel. The Saviour supplies the perspective from which we can see for the first time the true meaning of Creation and of the Old

Testament. The death and Resurrection of Christ discloses the new birth with which the created order has been in labor and which the period of the Old Testament anticipates. Irenaeus employs this basic vision positively to create a theological structure that integrates the diverse points of view of Scripture with the Church's developing Rule of Faith. His most important contribution is to retain the earlier Christian arguments against the Jews by transforming them so as to avoid a Marcionite conclusion. The punishment of the hard-hearted becomes an education, and the Old Testament a training and preparation for the New. Negatively, Irenaeus' theology functions to refute the Gnostics. Since Creation, the history of Israel, and the Incarnation are aspects of a single divine plan unfolded in time, the chief points of the Gnostics find their refutation. The one Creator God dispenses both testaments and reveals himself fully and focally in Christ.

Irenaeus' theology is no private exposition of his own faith. Instead, it puts into words the apostolic faith and is the articulation of the Church's experience. That this is so finds confirmation in what we know of early Christian worship. Melito of Sardis, a contemporary of Irenaeus, and Hippolytus, who wrote little more than a quarter of a century later, enable us to have some idea of what the Christian passover was like.[15] The feast celebrated Christ's death and Resurrection together and was the occasion when catechumens were baptized. The paschal feast was preceded by prayer, fasting, and exorcism and, on the Saturday evening, by a vigil which lasted all night. A ceremony conducted in the dim light of oil lamps must have made a profound impression on people who had been fasting for several days and who were used to going to bed and getting up with the sun in a world without electricity. At dawn the baptisms took place and were followed by the paschal Eucharist. Everything revolved around the story of Christ's death and Resurrection and the believers' participation in that story. His victory became theirs. But the readings from Scripture and the prayers exploded the story so that it could be seen everywhere. In particular, to die and rise with Christ was to participate in the new Creation and the new Exodus. Hippolytus tells us that the newly baptized were given a cup of milk and honey together with the bread and wine to remind them that they had ritually entered the true promised land, redeemed from the Egypt of their old lives by the cross.

What I am suggesting is that Irenaeus' theology, in its positive as opposed to its polemical function, attempts to put into words the liturgical experience of the paschal mystery. That experience united the sacramental acts of Baptism and the Eucharist with readings from Scripture and, we may presume, with iconographical interpretations of the Christian message. Both the experience and Irenaeus' explanation of it revolve around Christ's victory. And Irenaeus insists upon defining that victory as the completion and the climax of God's economies in Creation and in the Old Testament. To be sure, when the Christian appropriated the victory, he found it both a promise enabling the life of virtue and a demand requiring it. But the promise and the demand of the victory bound the believer to the Christian community and were mediated to him in that setting. These themes remain constants throughout the patristic period, and we shall find them in the thought of Gregory of Nyssa and of Augustine. Both these later figures, however, are less concerned with the relation of Christ's victory to what preceded it and more preoccupied with what follows it. For Nyssa, as we shall see, the emphasis lies upon the way we can even now participate in Christ's victory. For Augustine a sharper distinction is made between the Christian life and Christian destiny. For him the Christian is at best a pilgrim and a convalescent awaiting the perfect goal of healing in the age to come. Despite the fundamental continuity with Irenaeus' basic view, we shall find in Nyssa and Augustine two very different versions of the story of victory told by Irenaeus.

2

The Leaven and the Lamb

The basilica of San Vitale in Ravenna was completed by the middle of the sixth century. Its most striking feature is a mosaic in the dome of the apse depicting Christ as the majestic risen Lord. Wearing the purple imperial robe, a beardless and serene Christ is seated upon a blue circle representing the universe. With his right hand he bestows the crown of martyrdom upon St. Vitalis, and in his left he holds the scroll sealed with seven seals. To his left stands Bishop Ecclesius with a model of the basilica in his hand. Both the martyr and the bishop are attended by an angel. From beneath Christ's feet flow the four rivers of paradise, watering a greensward filled with spring flowers. The New Adam is depicted in the new paradise of an eternal spring, and the renewal of the earth is placed within the universe now made subject to the risen Lord.[1] The mosaic should not surprise us. It expresses the faith in the exalted and victorious Saviour that we have seen to be the predominant vision of Christ in the early Church. Yet I suggest that it bears closest relationship to what Gregory of Nyssa says about his Lord.

Without suggesting that there is any conscious dependence of the Ravenna mosaic on the writings of Nyssa, I should argue that it follows a tradition that Nyssa as much as anyone else shaped. In one of his sermons he gives us what can be regarded as a verbal meditation on the mosaic (*In diem luminum*; Jaeger 9, p. 241):

> You, O Sovereign Lord, are truly the pure and everflowing wellspring of goodness. You justly turned away from us—and in your

love for mankind had mercy on us. You hated—and you reconciled. You cursed—and you have blessed. You drove us from paradise—and you have summoned us back. You stripped us of the
shameful covering of the fig leaves and have clothed us with a
precious robe. You have opened the prison and released the condemned. You have sprinkled us with pure water and cleansed us
from our stains. No longer is Adam ashamed when you summon
him, nor rebuked by his conscience does he hide cowering in the
thicket of Paradise. No longer does the fiery sword circle paradise
and make its entrance unapproachable to those who draw near.
All is turned to joy for us who were the heirs of sin. And paradise
is trodden under foot of men—even heaven itself. The whole
creation in the world and above the world, which once warred
with itself, is bound together in the harmony of love. And we men
join our voices with the angels, singing with them God's praises.

The Saviour is the New Man, but our attention is shifted away from the
old paradise to the new one of heaven itself. The promise of Creation is
fulfilled in the total "harmony of love."

In what follows I want to argue that Nyssa tells the same story that
Irenaeus does, even though he shifts the emphasis somewhat and sharp-
ens the details. The cosmic Christ remains the hero; and the story that
begins with Creation culminates in the Incarnation and ends with the
destruction of this world order and the establishment of the new age.
Irenaeus' attention, however, is focused upon the relationship of the
central part of the story to what preceded it; the Incarnate Lord is
brought into continuity with Creation and the dispensation of the Old
Testament. Nyssa's interest, on the other hand, lies in what follows the
Incarnation. It is not merely that his concern is to show how Christ's
victory becomes ours rather than to relate that victory to God's previous
economies; it is that he is convinced that the present availability of our
future destiny supplies the mainspring of the Christian life. As well, for
Nyssa the hero of the story attains clearer definition. The trinitarian
dogma and the christological issues of the Apollinarian controversy are
very much in the forefront of Nyssa's mind. And these theological
themes not only define Christ but have a marked effect on Nyssa's version of the Christian story taken as a whole. In broad terms these differences within similarity are the product of two very different situations.
Irenaeus was obliged to defend the Christian story against those who
sought to deny its relation to the created order and to Israel. Nyssa, one
of the architects of fourth-century orthodoxy, sought to make the story
the basis for a vision of the monastic life.

Gregory of Nyssa's life work coincides with these two enterprises. He was born about 330, a younger brother of Basil the Great. Unlike Basil he was unable to attend any of the great schools of his time. But he did become a teacher of rhetoric and married. We cannot be certain of the chronology, but gradually Nyssa came to devote himself exclusively to the Church. As a young man he followed his mother's wishes by attending the feast in honor of the Forty Martyrs of Sebaste and ended by dreaming that the martyrs beat him with rods for his failure to take Christ seriously. This experience was not decisive, but his sister Macrina's persuasions were.[2] He left his secular life and joined his brother in his monastic retreat in Pontus. When Basil became bishop of Caesarea in Cappadocia in 370, he appointed Gregory bishop of Nyssa. And so the younger brother shared in Basil's work to revive the Nicene faith. He was present at Constantinople in 381 as the newly elected archbishop of Sebaste. For more than a decade afterwards he was active both as a preacher at the imperial court and as a writer of treatises designed to put the monastic life into words as an ideal for all Christians.

Nyssa's thought is prismatic rather than systematic. What I mean is that he clearly has a relatively coherent view of the Christian story and its theological meaning. And this view is articulated by a profound knowledge of Scripture as well as a sophisticated understanding of the philosophical themes that were part of the lingua franca of Christian Platonism, the dominant theology of the period. But in his writings he tends to treat a single theme in all its many aspects in such a way that it reflects the other central themes in his thought. As we shall see, to think of the image of God mirrors for us Nyssa's understanding of the Trinity, of the "epectasy" of contemplating God, of the triple character of the Christian life as moral, intellectual, and spiritual, and of a vision of the transfigured physical universe. As a result, I must warn that the order in which I shall describe Nyssa's thought is artificial and interpretive. I shall begin by examining his vision of human destiny, together with the "way" that leads to its fulfillment, go on to speak of his understanding of Christ, and conclude by treating his approach to the Christian life.

THE IMAGE OF GOD—A VISION OF HUMAN DESTINY

In 379 Basil the Great died. He failed to see the final achievement of his work at the council of Constantinople in 381, but one hopes that like Moses he saw the promised land from afar. His younger brother wrote a treatise as a gift in memory of Basil shortly after his death. Nyssa refers in his preface to Basil's sermons on the six days of Creation, which death had prevented him from completing. And so the "gift" is intended "to

add to the great writer's speculations that which is lacking in them . . .
so that the glory of the teacher may not seem to be failing among his
disciples" (*De hom. op.*, pref.; *NPNF*[2] 5, p. 387). What was lacking in
Basil's sermons was treatment of the sixth day on which humanity was
created. Nyssa's treatise *On the Making of Man*, then, completes Basil's
work; but it does so at the level of the "speculations" that inform the
sermons. In other words Nyssa concentrates on the theological underpin-
nings of Basil's view without translating the theology into homiletical
form. In effect, what he does is to give an allegorical interpretation of
Genesis 1:26–31, the last part of the sixth day of Creation. The first
fifteen chapters supply a vision of humanity as God intended it to be,
and the central theme is our creation in the image of God.

Nyssa begins by setting the stage. The created order is constantly
changing either by the mutations that characterize things on earth or by
the movements we find in the heavens. But these changes are ordered by
God in perfect harmony. The world is the perfection of beauty and order,
and God prepares it for humanity the way a good host prepares his feast.
That humanity is created last proves its excellence. And this is why it is
only before this creation that God deliberates by saying, "Let us make
humanity in our image, after our likeness" (chs. 1–3). The great guest,
then, that God brings to the feast of Creation is an image of his own
sovereign freedom (*De hom. op.* 4; *NPNF*[2] 5; pp. 390ff.):

> . . . the best Artificer made our nature as it were a formation fit
> for the exercise of royalty, preparing it at once by superior advan-
> tages of soul, and by the very form of the body, to be such as to
> be adapted for royalty: for the soul immediately shows its royal
> and exalted character, far removed as it is from the lowliness of
> private station, in that it owns no lord, and is self-governed,
> swayed autocratically by its own will; for to whom else does this
> belong than to a king? And further, besides those facts, the fact
> that it is the image of that Nature which rules over all means
> nothing else than this, that our nature was created to be royal
> from the first.

Like a prism this passage reflects major themes in Nyssa's doctrine of
the image. The biblical emphasis upon humanity's role as God's vicegerent, exercising dominion over the rest of creation, informs three themes
with philosophical connotations. The soul itself mirrors God. It functions
to govern the body. Finally, humanity is meant to rule over the Creation.
The first of the three philosophical themes reproduces what by Nyssa's

time is the accepted and traditional understanding of "the image." The human soul, for the early Athanasius as well as for Origen, Irenaeus, and Justin, is created akin to the Word of God, identified as the World Soul. Nyssa reworks this antique Christian theology by treating humanity as the image of the entire Godhead, since otherwise the consubstantiality of the three divine persons would be undermined. But the old associations of the image theology are retained, and the human soul thought consti- tuted capable of grasping Truth, since like is known by like.[3] Nyssa elaborates his basic understanding by showing that the human soul reflects in the created order the basic attributes of God. Just as the divine archetype is one, incorporeal, and ineffable, so the human soul possesses the same character (De hom. op. 6, 11). The soul is a single faculty that orders and uses the multiplicity of sense perceptions, and its unity re- quires it to be incorporeal. The invisible soul or mind also defies our comprehension and so reflects the incomprehensibility of God. Moreover, just as God is the perfection of moral virtues, of "mind and word," and of "love," so the image reflects the moral, intellectual, and spiritual aspects of God (De hom. op. 5). We have been created with capacities that take form in the Christian life.

The one difference between the archetype and the image, between the Trinity and humanity, is that involved in distinguishing between the Creator and creation. The created order is always involved in the inter- vals (diastemata) of time and space, while God transcends them. He is "adiastematic." God is pure, unchanging Being; and we are always changing, always becoming—even, as we shall see, in heaven. Part of what this involves is that the incorporeal soul is embodied. Nyssa em- ploys the Stoic understanding of the mind-body relation in a revised form to make his point. Unlike the Stoics he insists upon the incorporeal- ity of the mind or soul, but like them he regards the proper governance of the body and its passions by the mind as equatable with the life of virtue. He relates this aspect of the image to the Platonizing theme of the soul's likeness to God as follows (De hom. op. 12.9; NPNF[2] 5, p. 399):

> . . . the mind, as being in the image of the most beautiful, itself also remains in beauty and goodness so long as it partakes as far as is possible in its likeness to the archtype. . . . And as we said that the mind was adorned by the likeness of the archetypal beauty, being formed as though it were a mirror to receive the figure of that which it expresses, we consider that the nature which is governed by it is attached to the mind in the same relation, and that it too is adorned by the beauty that the mind gives, being, so to say, a mirror of the mirror; and that by it is

swayed and sustained the material element of that existence in which the nature is contemplated.

When the natural likeness of the mind to God is properly actualized, the mind is empowered to govern the body. Knowing the good becomes doing the good, and Nyssa's emphasis on human beings as psychosomatic unities carries with it this moral meaning. As well, the perfection of the mind's governance of the body involves the physical perfection of the transfigured life of the resurrection.

Nyssa's doctrine of the image includes a third philosophical theme that may derive from Posidonius, one of Cicero's teachers.[4] The fundamental idea is that humanity functions to order and harmonize the world. Nyssa's version of the idea depends upon two distinctions—of the intellectual or spiritual and the corporeal, and of the uncreated and the created (*De hom. op.* 8). The first, of course, is Plato's distinction between the intelligible order, which is incorporeal and alone "real," and the world of sense appearances. Since humanity is to be defined in terms of embodied souls, it is related to both orders. The soul ties humanity to the angelic creation; the body, to beasts, plants, and even sticks and stones. In this way humanity is meant to bind together and harmonize the whole of the created order, and the image of God governs creation as well as the human body. The second distinction is biblical and takes Nyssa beyond the Posidonian view that humanity is a microcosm ordering the world (*De hom. op.* 16.1). Humanity not only harmonizes creation, but divinizes it. Uncreated and created are bound together as well as spiritual and corporeal. The idea requires two further themes for it to make sense. First, we must think of humanity in corporate terms; and, second, we must find in Christ, the Incarnate Lord, the principle that ties humanity to God.

The first of these themes is explicit in *On the Making of Man.* "In saying that 'God created man' the text indicates, by the indefinite character of the term, all mankind" (*De hom. op.* 16.16; *NPNF*[2] 5, p. 406). It would be possible to understand this statement as though Nyssa were speaking of a Platonic form or universal in which individual humans participate. But it is clear this is not what he means. "All mankind" is "the entire plenitude of humanity . . . included by the God of all, by His power of foreknowledge, as it were in one body" (*De hom. op.* 16.17; *NPNF*[2] 5, p. 406). In other words, we are to think of all human beings who ever have been or will be born as constituting a single body. The point may be clarified by appealing to the argument of *To Ablabius*, where Nyssa uses the analogy of a corporate humanity to explain the Trinity. "Human nature" in the strict sense applies to a single common nature, and "to speak of 'many men' is a customary misuse of language" (LCC 3, p. 257). In some way individuals on the human level correspond to the persons or *hypostaseis* of the Godhead. And, once we see that Nyssa has rejected philosophical models in his trinitarian theology, we can begin to understand what he means.[5] He is giving a theomorphic definition of humanity. Just as the Trinity is a single ineffable nature with individuation, so humanity is a single ineffable nature with individuation. We are "relations" of a single nature. An individual is to be defined not as a center of consciousness but by his relatedness to other individuals. In a fallen world we as individuals are more often than not divided from others, but ideally we remain different from them but fully united.[6] The destiny of the soul is neither to be disembodied nor to lose its individuality by being merged with the World Soul.

The second of the themes I have noted is required to complete Nyssa's vision, but it is only implicit in *On the Making of Man*. The treatise concludes with the following words (*De hom. op.* 30.33–34; *NPNF*[2] 5, p. 427):

> Thus Paul, advising those who were able to hear him to lay hold on perfection, indicates also the mode in which they may attain that object, telling them that they must "put off the old man," and put on the man "which is created after the image of Him that created him" (Col. 3:9–10). Now may we all return to that divine grace in which God at the first created man, when He said, "Let us make man in our image and likeness"; to Whom be glory and might for ever and ever. Amen.

The allusion indicated by the Pauline text is to the Incarnate Lord. In Christ we find true humanity, and in him human nature acquires its capacity to harmonize and to divinize the whole of creation. And, presumably, we find our destiny in becoming relations to one another of the corporate human nature of Christ. Nyssa's vision revolves around the theme of the image of God, and it is the vision of a perfectly ordered harmony of all reality and of a transfigured world.

THE "WAY" TO THE VISION

In chapter 16 of *On the Making of Man* Nyssa recognizes that his vision has no apparent relationship to the world of his own experience. He is unwilling to relinquish his vision, but cannot deny the world in which he lives (*De hom. op.* 16.4; *NPNF*[2] 5, p. 404): "Neither does the Word of God lie when it says that man was made in the image of God, nor is the pitiable suffering of man's nature like to the blessedness of the impassible Life." Scripture supplies "some guidance in the question." Nyssa believes that a careful reading of Genesis 1:26–27 reveals that God's intention is not identical with what he does. God intends to make humanity in his image ("Let us make man in our image"), but in fact he creates humanity in the image but with the distinction of male and female. The male-female creation, then, differs from God's intent; and it also differs from the fulfillment of God's intent in Christ, "for 'in Christ Jesus,' as the apostle says, 'there is neither male nor female' (Gal. 3:28)" (*De hom. op.* 16.7; *NPNF*² 5, p. 405). Thus, Nyssa's vision is equated both with God's intention and with the eschatological fulfillment of that intention. It remains to explain what "is now manifested in wretchedness."

Nyssa's argument is extremely difficult to follow, but some sense of it can be made by defining his basic perspective and by seeing that he gives two rather different explanations of why God created humanity with the male-female distinction.[7] The basic perspective insists that time and space are irrelevant to God but necessary for us. The distinction between intention and fulfillment is meaningless to God, since "to God's power nothing is either past or future, but even that which we expect is comprehended, equally with what is at present existing, by the all-sustaining energy" (*De hom. op.* 16.18; *NPNF*² 5, p. 406). On the other hand, "the created nature cannot exist without change; for its very passage from non-existence to existence is a certain motion and change of the non-existent transmuted by the divine purpose into being" (*De hom. op.* 16.12; *NPNF*² 5, p. 405) Thus, human beings are situated between the divine purpose and its fulfillment after the end of this world order. Nyssa's vision is a hope. But since God's purpose is eternal, the hope is assured; and the course of human history is moving towards its realization. In a sense, Nyssa is speaking of a continuous Creation. What we normally call Creation is not so much an event as the initiation of a process. And "Creation" and "Redemption" merely refer to different aspects of the same process. Like Irenaeus, Nyssa regards Redemption as the completion of Creation.

With this understanding in mind Nyssa turns to his first explanation of human misery and the absence of his vision of human destiny. Scripture, we remember, says that God created humanity as his image together with the male-female distinction. In other words, he created embodied souls. It is the body that enables us to be related to the beasts and the sensible order of creation (*De hom. op.* 16.9). Nyssa does not carry the argument forward, but it is possible to see how he might have or should have done so by consulting his *Address on Religious Instruction.* There he speaks of the Resurrection of Christ as the reunion of body and soul (*ARI* 16; *LCC* 3, p. 294): "In the same way he conjoined the intelligible and sensible nature on a larger scale, the principle of the resurrection extend-

ing to its logical limits." What I think Nyssa means is that in the risen
Lord humanity finally attains its destined function of harmonizing and
divinizing the creation.[8] Thus, the body is required for the image of God
to fulfill its appointed role. God, then, creates humanity with the body so
that the human race may develop and become the king of creation.

I am obliged to admit, however, that a second explanation of our
misery and of the male-female creation occupies center stage in *On the
Making of Man*. Nyssa's argument is a strange one to us. He assumes
that the plenitude of human beings requires the begetting of children.
Humanity ought to have reproduced angelically in order to make up this
fullness of the corporate human nature. But God foresaw that Adam and
Eve would fall from their angelic state in paradise and would no longer
be capable of angelic procreation. Consequently, he prepared a remedy
for the Fall by creating Adam and Eve with bodies so that they would be
able to reproduce like the beasts (*De hom. op.* 16–18). Nyssa understands
the Fall as the loss of the mind's governance of the body. Human passions like anger, lust, and cowardice are "a likeness to the brute nature"
(*De hom. op.* 18.3; *NPNF*[2] 5, p. 408). When the mind is dominated by
them, virtues are transformed into vices. And "the misery that encom-
passes us often causes the Divine gift to be forgotten, and spreads the
passions of the flesh, like some ugly mask, over the beauty of the image"
(*De hom. op.* 18.6; *NPNF*[2] 5, p. 408). One problem is how to integrate
this idea with the first explanation. We should have to argue that the
body functions in two ways, to overcome the effects of the Fall and to
enable the image to perform its cosmic function. And we should have to
say that overcoming the Fall is the means to completing God's creative
intention. But the deeper problem with the view is that the body, though
a remedy in one sense for the Fall, is also its occasion. Like Narcissus the
mind is seduced by its own image in the body. Or like the dog in Aesop's
fable, the soul drops the real bone in its mouth to pursue the reflection
of the bone in the stream (*ARI* 21; LCC 3, p. 298). It begins to look as
though God created humanity fallen.

It is clear, however, that Nyssa does not want to pursue this logic. In the
Address on Religious Instruction he takes seriously the distinction between
Creation and the Fall, and he gives a more straightforward and less allegorical interpretation of the story in Genesis 1–3. He begins by admitting
that the first humans possessed all blessings. The "most excellent and
precious" of these was "the gift of liberty and free will" (*ARI* 5; LCC 3, p.
277). But human freedom is mutable; it can turn towards evil as well as
good. This is why some of the angels fell and became devils. Envy explains
why Satan turned from God, and it was his envy of Adam that explains
Satan's tempting of Eve in paradise. He "mingled evil with man's free

will" and made it easier for Adam and Eve to sin by disobeying God (*ARI* 6; LCC 3, pp. 280f.). Nyssa follows the biblical narrative, but interprets it by employing some of his central themes. Both the fall of Satan and of the first human beings are explained by their misuse of a mutable freedom. God is not to blame for giving them a gift they failed to honor. Nevertheless, the choices of good and evil are not to be placed on the same level. "We must not think of virtue as opposed to vice in the way of two existing phenomena" (*ARI* 6; LCC 3, p. 279). Just as blindness is not a thing but merely a privation of sight, so vice and evil have no ontological status, but are merely privations of the good. This neo-Platonic theme is qualified when Nyssa speaks not of blindness but of closing one's eye to the sun (*ARI* 6; LCC 3, p. 280). There is something rebellious and active about the choice of evil, however much it must be regarded as a privation.

Freedom and evil, understood in this way, help explain Adam's fall. But a further theme drives towards an assessment of that fall not totally unlike Irenaeus'. Two points need to be taken together. First, human beings in virtue of their creation are perpetually becoming, and this "continual change" is either towards good or towards evil (*ARI* 8; LCC 3, p. 286). Second, if evil is the privation of good, then it is bounded and limited by good (*ARI* 21; LCC 3, p. 298). What this means is that our movement towards good can never find an end any more than we can cease counting to infinity. But our movement towards evil is limited. If we imagine the shadow cast by an eclipse as a truncated cone, we can move into the shadow, but no matter how we move, if we keep on going, we shall inevitably re-emerge into the light (*OSR; NPNF*² 5, p. 443). This assessment of freedom as choice needs to be balanced by appealing to Nyssa's doctrine of providence. From another point of view, our movement into evil brings punishment upon us. And God's providential punishment is remedial; it functions to educate us so that we shall begin once more to choose the good. These themes will occupy our attention when we speak of Nyssa's view of the Christian life at the end of this chapter. But for the moment it is enough to point out that they underline the temporary character of Satan's fall as well as Adam's. Both, guided by God's providence, will inevitably move through evil to good. Even Satan will be saved because Christ's punishment of him and victory over him is God's way of healing "the very author of evil himself" (*ARI* 26; LCC 3, p. 304). Nyssa's philosophically oriented ideas explain why he believes that everyone will be saved, and they preserve the way the Christian story is understood by Irenaeus. The creation of humanity initiates God's purpose; and the Fall, however unfortunate and disastrous in its immediate consequences, is an inevitable episode on the way to perfection and the completion of God's purpose. That way, of course, includes the history of Israel. But Nyssa, unlike Irenaeus, is not primarily concerned with the steps along the way before Christ. Instead, his preoccupation is with the crucial step of the Incarnation and the effect of that step on the Christian life.

Nyssa's Christology in Dialogue with Apollinaris

Nyssa, of course, wrote before the outbreak of the Nestorian controversy; we therefore cannot expect to find the impact of the christological dogma on his thought the way we find that of the trinitarian dogma. Nevertheless, he was an opponent of Apollinaris; and I shall suggest that he sees deeply into the problem of relating what he would call Christ's uncreated aspect with his created aspect. Indeed, long before Chalcedon, he sees that we cannot penetrate the mystery. The technical issues emerge most clearly in Nyssa's *Antirrheticus Against Apollinaris*. As is the case with most ancient polemics, the argument does not progress in what we should consider an ordered fashion. Nyssa takes what Apollinaris says and refutes it point by point. And yet it is easy enough to see that Nyssa attacks Apollinaris in two different ways. First, Apollinaris' inadequate account of Christ's human nature undermines the possibility of our salvation: What Christ has not assumed he has not redeemed. Here the issue is Apollinaris' omission of a human soul in Christ. Second, the highly unitive character of Apollinaris' Christology leaves the Word open to being affected by his body and thereby rendered mutable and reduced from his divine status. Both the soteriological and the theological attacks against Apollinaris are effective, but they do produce considerable confusion with respect to Nyssa's own views, as we shall see in a moment.

Apollinaris defines the new humanity as the Man from heaven, that is, the Word joined to a human body.[9] The scriptural warrant for the view is found in 1 Corinthians 15:45–49. Nyssa uses the passage to attack Apollinaris from the soteriological perspective (*Ant.*; Jaeger 3.1, pp. 145f.). When St. Paul says "as is the man of heaven, so are those who are of heaven" (verse 48), he presupposes the total identity of Christ with human beings. Hebrews 4:15 affirms this understanding by stating that Christ shares every aspect of our condition save for sin. Since the human mind is not by nature sinful, Christ must share our mind as well as our body. The Incarnate Lord must possess a human soul if he is to bring us Redemption. Using a metaphor drawn from Matthew 18:12ff., Nyssa puts the matter this way (*Ant.*; Jaeger 3.1, pp. 151f.):

> For who does not know the divine mystery, that the captain of our salvation [the Word] went after the lost sheep. And we hu-

mans are that sheep, who have wandered away by sin from the spiritual hundred. And He takes the whole sheep on His shoulders. For the wandering of the sheep was not in part, but since the whole sheep strayed, the whole sheep is also led back. The hide is not carried, and the inside of the sheep left behind, as Apollinaris wants to say. But the sheep is put on the shoulders of the Shepherd, that is on the divinity of the Lord, having been made one with it by the assuming.

In the Incarnation the Word appropriates the whole of human nature; and Apollinaris, by failing to recognize this, gives an inadequate account of Redemption.

Nyssa takes with utter seriousness the total identity of the Word with humanity and insists at this level on a highly unitive account of Christ's person: "Compare what happens in the case of the ocean. If someone puts a drop of vinegar in the sea, the drop also becomes sea by being assimilated to the quality of the sea" (*Ant.;* Jaeger 3.1, p. 201). Similarly, the humanity of Christ is transformed by its relation to "the sea of immortality." All the attributes of "the flesh" were changed along with it "to the divine and pure nature." It would be difficult to find a more extreme view of the unity of Christ and the divinization of his humanity.

Nyssa's other line of attack upon Apollinaris proceeds from a theological point of view. Apollinaris' unitive Christology carries with it the danger of making the Word of God subject to passion and change (*Ant.;* Jaeger 3.1, p. 136). Christ's birth, the swaddling clothes, the growth of his body, sleep, toil, the sufferings of his passion, the nails, the spear, the grave—none of these can possibly be referred to the eternal and unchanging Word of God (*Ant.;* Jaeger 3.1, p. 167). Here Nyssa takes seriously the force of the Arian argument from the human operations and sufferings of Christ.[10] If we attribute them to the Word by nature, then they affect that nature, and we can only conclude that the Word is less than God. As a result, we must make a sharp theological distinction between the Word and "the Man mingled with God" (*Ant.;* Jaeger 3.1, p. 146). Just as a unitive Christology is implied by attacking Apollinaris from a soteriological perspective, so a divisive Christology is implied by attacking him from a theological perspective.

It is not as though Nyssa fails to see the dilemma that is created. He rightly sees the necessity of rejecting Apollinaris' views for both soteriological and theological reasons. But he also sees that what makes sense at the level of refutation does not add up to a viable positive view. In speaking of Christ it is necessary to insist both on the full union of God and humanity and on their distinction. To put it, anachronistically, in the language of the Chalcedonian Definition, the two natures must be undivided and unconfused. It is Nyssa's recognition of this that suggests he sees the issues that will later trouble the Church in the Nestorian controversy. And he understands that a point comes at which the mystery of the Incarnation can only be protected but not explained. For that reason he does not hesitate to speak of the union of natures, alternatively, as a "mingling" and as a "fellowship." The "mingling" means they are united; the "fellowship" insists on their distinction.

This interpretation of Nyssa's reaction to Apollinaris and to the Christological issues raised in his day is confirmed by a long passage in the *Antirrheticus* (*Ant.*; Jaeger 3.1, pp. 183f.):

> . . . he [Apollinaris] prefers this charge against us, saying that those are wrong who assert that the union of flesh and the assumption of man are the same thing. Even if what I am saying seems to be fairly simple-minded, I shall not disguise the truth that neither of these phrases which I am accustomed to use is meant as an accurate definition . . . "union" is understood in many senses. . . . What, then, is the union of flesh? . . . And the assumption of man—how does it happen? . . . Just as much as in the case of the first expression, the answers are unknown to us. For as long as someone expounds the word of the mystery without seasoning it with the divine salt of the Scriptures, the insipid salt of the pagan wisdom, abandoned by the faithful, is still present.

The mystery, then, is sufficiently revealed in Scripture; and we must resist the temptation to turn it into some kind of philosophical doctrine. The true error of Apollinaris is to suppose that human categories can adequately define Christ.

The same point of view informs the central argument of Nyssa's *Address on Religious Instruction*. Having spoken of God, the Creation, and the Fall, he turns in chapter nine to the Incarnation (*ARI* 9; LCC 3, p. 286):

> One who has followed the course of our argument up to this point will probably agree with it, since we do not appear to have said anything unbefitting a right conception of God. He will not, however, take a similar view of what follows. . . .

What he means is that the Incarnation requires two contradictory conclusions. The Word of God remains unchanged and impassible in it; and yet the Word truly lives a human life, suffers, and dies. The faith obliges us to insist upon both propositions. The objections are obvious and could easily be removed if we could "actually see what we only hope for. But our hopes await the ages to come, so that there may then be revealed what at present our faith alone apprehends" (*ARI* 17; LCC 3, pp. 294f.). Nonetheless, Nyssa does make a stab at reconciling the two propositions. The central objection, as he sees it, is that the Christian belief makes the Word passible and subject to change. How, then, shall we say that the Word remains impassible even in the Incarnation?

Two ways of answering the question occur to Nyssa. If by "passion" we mean vice, then so long as the Word remains sinless in the Incarnation, he can be said to remain impassible (*ARI* 9, 15; LCC 3, pp. 287, 291). But this answer is inadequate, since "passion" can also mean the weaknesses and natural changes to which human beings are liable. A second answer would redefine these "weaknesses" as "modes of activity" (*ARI* 16; LCC 3, p. 292). Nyssa sails perilously close to Apollinaris' opinion that the human operations of Christ are really divine activities. And he senses the inadequacy of this answer, as well. The objection is raised once more, and this time he answers the objection not by explaining it away but by dismissing it and ruling it out of court. "Sick people do not prescribe to doctors their manner of treatment" (*ARI* 17; LCC 3, p. 294). And so, he gives up trying to explain the union of natures in Christ's person. Instead, he turns to an argument that sees in the Incarnation the perfect expression of God's goodness, wisdom, justice, and power (*ARI* 20ff.; LCC 3, pp. 296ff.). We cannot explain the Incarnation, but we can see in it the character of God himself.

Implicit in what I have said so far is the chief peculiarity of Nyssa's account of Christ. He can sometimes speak of Christ's humanity in generic or corporate terms. It is the lost sheep placed on the divine Shepherd's shoulders. It is the patient healed by the divine Physician. On the other hand, he can speak of Christ's humanity in individual and concrete terms. The humanity is "the Man He [the Word] assumed" (*ARI* 16; LCC 3, p. 294). It is tempting to interpret this peculiarity by arguing that Nyssa hesitates between an Alexandrian and an Antiochene Christology. Like Athanasius and Cyril he can think of the humanity as the entire nature, and this way of putting it correlates with the unitive aspect of his Christology. Like Theodore and Nestorius he can define the humanity as a concrete individual man, and this would correlate with his insistence on distinguishing the natures. Arguing this way may not be entirely beside the point, but it does not take us far enough. It seems anachronistic to employ the terms of the later controversy to explain Nyssa's thought. And even if Nyssa deliberately retains contradictory ideas because he recognizes the insolubility of the mystery, this does not quite

explain why he would treat the humanity as well as the union of humanity and divinity in two different ways.

I want to suggest that we can find a fuller explanation of the peculiarity of Nyssa's Christology by relating what he says to the basic structure
of his thought. The distinction he makes between the vision that defines
human destiny and the "way" that leads to that destiny correlates with
the two ways he treats Christ's humanity. Let me begin with a passage
from his *Commentary on Song of Songs*. In Song of Songs 5:9 the virgin
daughters of Jerusalem ask the bride: "What is your beloved more than
another beloved?" Nyssa understands the question to mean how shall she
describe Christ to them. He points out that "in the case of Christ one
aspect is created and another is uncreated." In the first aspect Christ is
"totally incomprehensible and ineffable to every nature." As a result, the
bride gives her answer by speaking of what is comprehensible to the
virgins in the mystery of the Incarnation. He describes this mystery in
the language of 1 Timothy 3:10ff. and Philippians 2, and goes on to say
(*CCC* 13; Jaeger 6, pp. 380ff.):

> And since He once for all drew to Himself the perishable nature
> of flesh through the first fruits which He assumed through the
> incorruptible Virgin birth, He always hallows the common lump
> of the nature together with the first fruits. He nourishes His own
> body the Church through those who are united with Him by the
> fellowship of the mystery.

Christ thereby gives harmony to his body and "brings to the perfection of
beauty" all the members in their own order. Song of Songs 5:10ff. is then
interpreted as a description of the Incarnation and its saving effect.

The passage can be examined from two points of view. As a moving
and beautiful description of the salvation brought by Christ, it makes
perfect sense. God the Word makes himself known through the "first
fruits." And by faith we become members of the Body of Christ. Salvation involves both the activity of God and our response. Its aim is the
perfection of the Body of Christ, and we can assume that this means the
completion of the New Creation in which individuals find their identity
in the corporate image of God. On the other hand, the "first fruits" of
our nature looks like an allusion to the Man, a concrete individual distinct from the "common lump" of humanity. The implied metaphor of
the leaven leavening the whole lump (1 Cor. 5:6ff., Gal. 5:9) points in the
same direction. And what is involved is a "way" or process leading
towards a future destiny.

The association of the Man, Christ's humanity regarded as a concrete individual, with the leaven, which initiates a process, betrays itself whenever Nyssa discusses or uses New Testament passages that speak of Christ as the first fruits, the first-born, or the beginning (cf. 1 Cor. 15:20, Rom. 8:29, Col. 1:15, 18, Hebr. 1:6). Characteristic of Nyssa's account of Christ is his interpretation of Song of Songs 5:16: "This is my beloved and this is my neighbor, O daughters of Jerusalem" (*CCC* 14; Jaeger 6, pp. 426ff.). In this section of Song of Songs the bride is thought to be explaining the Beloved by speaking of the Incarnation. Luke's parable of the Good Samaritan, which explains the meaning of "neighbor," is regarded as an explanation of "the economy of God's love for humanity." The man fallen among thieves is the human race, which has "descended," lost its incorruptible "clothes," received the "wounds" of sin, and suffered the "advance of death over half our nature." The Law, symbolised by the priests and the Levites, in no way aided the human condition. Nyssa goes on (*CCC* 14; Jaeger 6, pp. 427f.):

> This could only be done by the One who put on the whole of human nature by the first fruits of the lump, in which was a share (*meros*) of every nation, Jew, Samaritan, Greek, and absolutely all men. He, together with His body, that is the beast, stopped at the place of man's ill treatment and healed his wounds, and made him rest on His own beast, and made His own love of man a lodging for him in which all who toil and are burdened may find rest.

Presumably we must identify "body" with "first fruits" and must understand "body" to refer to the whole human nature.[11] On this reading the allegorical meaning of the parable identifies the good Samaritan with the Word of God and his beast with the Man, the first fruits that leavens the whole lump of human nature.

From the perspective of the process the leaven may be distinguished from the lump of dough it leavens, but once the process has been completed the distinction is no longer necessary. In this life we are joined to the leaven, to the individual humanity of Christ. And this union envisages the completion of the process (*De perf.*; Jaeger 8.1, p. 206):

> So we too as the lump through similar paths shall be joined to the Father of incorruptibility through imitation so far as possible of the Mediator's impassibility and immutability. So we shall become the Only Begotten God's crown of precious stones, becoming glory and honor by our life.

In other words, once the leavening process has been completed, we become aspects of a single corporate human nature the way jewels are aspects of a single crown. Christ in his humanity is the image of God.[12] He realizes the vision of *On the Making of Man*, and our destiny is to become relations of the corporate humanity of Christ. Thus, when he is thinking of the "way," Nyssa refers to Christ's humanity in concrete, individual terms; but when he is speaking of the destination and the completion of the process, he uses corporate terms. The "leaven" is meant to become the "lamb" the Good Shepherd puts on his shoulders, and Nyssa's Christology is explained by the basic themes in his thought rather than by technical Christological issues.

THE CHRISTIAN LIFE AND DESTINY

It will be obvious that Nyssa's understanding of the Christian life must be related to the larger pattern of his thought. That pattern involves a double process or story. God's Creation of the universe and of humanity initiates a drama that is completed beyond this world order in the restoration of all things. The story drives towards this fullfillment. As well, however, within the larger process the Incarnate Word introduces the leavening that makes that fulfillment possible. At the risk of inviting the reader to block the metaphor, we could say that Creation is the assembling of the ingredients, the Incarnation the introduction of the leaven, and the age to come the baked bread. The Christian life, then, is in broad terms our incorporation into this pattern. And, in Nyssa's view, once we have been made part of the story we already begin to participate in our destiny even though the goal of the Christian life is placed beyond the limits of this world order.

Incorporation into the process that can be called either Creation or Redemption depends upon the two dynamics of God's providence and human freedom. Nyssa virtually reproduces Origen's understanding of the two.[13] He begins by defining providence as a general and universal operation of God, the effects of which are to be explained by how providence is used by human freedom. Rightly received, providence benefits us; wrongly received, it punishes us. It is as though we misused someone's love, when we bring God's punishment upon ourselves; we cannot blame God when, like Pharaoh, we cause him to harden our hearts. When Scripture speaks of God hardening Pharaoh's heart, it really means that Pharaoh has hardened his own heart and caused providence to have a punitive effect. To blame God is "as if someone who has not seen the sun blames it for causing him to fall into the ditch" (*LM* 76; CWS, p. 71). Nyssa employs a legendary reading of the story in Exodus to make the point clear.[14] Following a Jewish tradition, he believes that the Hebrews lived in the same cities as the Egyptians and yet escaped the plagues sent by God, while the Egyptians did not. This means that (*LM* 80; CWS, p. 72):

> It was not some constraining power from above that caused the one to be found in darkness and the other in light, but we men have in ourselves, in our own nature and by our own choice, the causes of light or of darkness, since we place ourselves in whichever sphere we wish to be.

It is not that we create providence, since the divine operation is greater than our choices and is the context in which we make our choices. But what we choose does determine the effect of providence upon us. By choosing wrongly we make our "own plagues" (*LM* 86; CWS, p. 74). In this way our freedom explains the origin of evil. Providence, however, functions in another way. When we misuse God's love and bring punishment upon ourselves, God not only fits the punishment to our sin in a retributive fashion, he also uses the punishment as a remedy and educates us by our own mistakes. In this way sooner or later, even if it means purgatorial punishments after this life, God will persuade all of us to choose him and the good (*ARI* 35; LCC 3, p. 317).

Like Origen, Nyssa emphasizes our freedom. Providence refers either to the normal working of the universe, by which the consequences of our actions have a kind of inevitability, or to a mysterious but non-coercive divine power to guide our freedom towards the good. And so we are free, not to do anything we will, but to act as moral agents. Nyssa disavows any fatalism and insists upon our moral responsibility. One theme found in Origen's thought attains more prominence in Nyssa's. Implied in the view just outlined is the idea that the effects of providence are consequent upon our choices. And so God can be said to respond to us when we begin to do the good (*LM* 44; CWS, p. 64):

> For truly the assistance which God gives to our nature is provided to those who correctly live the life of virtue. This assistance was already there at our birth, but it is manifested and made known whenever we apply ourselves to diligent training in the higher life and strip ourselves for the more vigorous contests.

The theme of God's "assistance" by which he cooperates with our moral endeavors is one that gains prominence in Christian understandings of the monastic life. John Chrysostom and John Cassian, for example, use the theme, and it lies at the heart of Pelagius' elitist and ascetical ideal. It could imply that we can save ourselves and that God's grace is simply a way of talking about his rewarding our efforts. Nyssa, of course, does not mean to go that far. Divine assistance is available to us "at our birth," and in this way comes before as well as after our steps towards virtue. Our capacity to choose the good is, as well, a gift of God; and, as we shall see, that capacity is quickened in us by God the way the beloved quickens love in the heart of the lover.[15]

Nyssa's understanding of providence and freedom also informs his account of the sacraments of Baptism and the Eucharist: ". . . what happens in the sacrament of Baptism depends upon the disposition of the heart of him who approaches it" (ARI 39; LCC 3, p. 322). What he means is that the grace in Baptism, though it is fully real and operative, has its intended effect only if it is rightly received. If someone crosses the Red Sea in the waters of Baptism and discovers the host of Pharaoh, the passions, still pursuing him, then he has not used Baptism rightly (LM 127; CWS, .p. 84). The sacraments mediate to us the saving power of Christ's death and Resurrection. That pattern seeks to grasp us so that the leaven of the new life can begin its work in us. But we must choose to ally ourselves with that new pattern and accept the leaven. And we need to add that there is an attraction in the pattern that elicits our response without violating our freedom. Thus, in worship and in the reading of Scripture the beauty of God's purpose and love draws us towards him. The Beautiful "is essentially capable of attracting in a certain way every being that looks towards it" (OSR; NPNF[2] 5, p. 449).

In this way Nyssa's understanding of the interaction of providence and freedom in the Christian life must be set within the framework of what is really a neo-Platonic theory of love.[16] Interpretations of Plato's *Symposium* and *Phaedrus* echo in Nyssa's words. We have been created capable of loving, and love is at one level an appetite like hunger or thirst. The purification of this appetite takes us beyond the world of appearances to the Beautiful itself, in other words to God. And there we find that "enjoyment takes the place of desire," and fellowship with God empowers us to love in a creative way, imitating so far as possible the love that explains God's Creation of the world. Our power to love is not only given by God, it is also quickened by our natural attraction to him and its exercise constantly embraced by his overarching providence. However much Nyssa can be understood to have sown the seeds of Pelagianism, it is only by divorcing the theme of God's "assistance" from the full context of his thought that he can be regarded as a Pelagian before Pelagius.

The dynamic of love that defines the Christian life has three aspects. Following Origen Nyssa correlates these with the three books of Solomon. Proverbs stands for the moral life, the elimination of vice and the acquistion of virtue. The theme of Ecclesiastes that all is vanity suggests that an intellectual examination of the created order reveals that it is contingent upon God. And Song of Songs speaks of the love by which "my beloved is mine and I am his." From one point of view these three aspects are stages in the Christian journey. It is "the guidance of virtue" that "leads us to know that light which has reached down even to human nature" (*LM* 20; CWS, p. 59). Primarily what this means is that the more we grow in virtue the more we are able to have a "sure apprehension of real Being" (*LM* 23; CWS, p. 60). Moses' vision at the burning bush (Ex. 3) is such an apprehension, since (*LM* 24; CWS, p. 60):

> . . . he came to know that none of those things which are appre-hended by sense perception and contemplated by the understand-ing really subsists, but that the transcendent essence and cause of the universe, on which everything depends, alone subsists.

In other words, we move from the life of virtue to an intellectual under-standing that God exists and that the created world of becoming de-pends on him.

The final stage, represented by Song of Songs, is what Nyssa calls "epectasy." He borrows the term from Philippians 3:13 ("*straining for-ward* to what lies ahead") and uses it to explain allegorically Moses' entrance into the dark cloud (Ex. 20:21) and his vision of God's back (Ex. 33:18–23). The darkness shows that the vision of God lies beyond all human conceptions and is, paradoxically, the vision of the unknown and unseen (*LM* 162–69; CWS, pp. 94–97). And the passage from Exodus 33 teaches that the true vision of God is "never to be satisfied in the desire to see him" (*LM* 219–55; CWS, pp. 111–20). That Moses saw God's back implies that seeing God is really following him; and since God is infinite, we shall never cease in our pursuit of him. And yet that pursuit is a "stable" motion, an endless falling towards God. It is not that our desire for God is frustrated. On the contrary, God satisfies our desire and in doing so creates in us a greater appetite for him. And the cycle goes on endlessly and joyously. The goal of the Christian life is, then, a redeemed and purified becoming that perfects the dynamic of love between the Christian and God. In this final stage we are taken beyond what we could ordinarily attain to a properly mystical union with God.[17]

As I have implied, the goal of "epectasy" is available to us in this life. Thus, in one sense, no firm line is drawn between the Christian's life and his destiny. On the other hand, the goal is never finally attained in this life, where moments of pure contemplation are never to be regarded as ends in themselves. Instead, the mystical experience must function to empower the active life of virtue (*LM* 166; CWS, p. 96). If, from one point of view, it is moral virtue that enables us to move towards the "epectatic" contemplation of God, from another point of view that contemplation is meant to enable our moral life. For this reason what appear as stages in regard to our destiny are aspects of our life. It is important to note that Nyssa, like Origen, refuses to divide the active from the contemplative life. Both are necessary in this world, and it is the dialectic between them that characterizes the Christian life.

The Christian life as a free movement of love in its moral, intellectual, and spiritual aspects toward God is, of course, the way Nyssa describes our entrance into the leavening process that will finally establish our destiny. But it is also our becoming part of the Christian story. Nyssa can think of the Christian life as an imitation of Christ, and it is the Incarnate Lord that supplies the grace for this imitation. He is the rock on which Moses stands in order to see God's back. But the pattern we find in Christ is reflected in other biblical stories. Nyssa's *Life of Moses* takes this point of view and uses an allegorical interpretation of Moses' story as a way of explaining the Christian life. The story has the advantage of setting Moses' progress in the context of Israel's journey from Egypt to the promised land. One effect this has is to place the Christian life in the context of the Paschal mystery. The transformation of death to life effected in Christ's Resurrection reinterprets the Passover so that the Exodus becomes a deliverance from the Egypt of sin and death and a pilgrimage towards the life of the new Creation. Another implication of the way Nyssa tells the story concerns his understanding of the relation between the individual and the common nature. Moses progresses through the three stages of the Christian life, but his "epectasy" occurs in the middle of the story. This mystical experience enables him to be Israel's guide on its way to the promised land and to fulfill his role as the servant of God. Similarly, the individual's progress must always be located within that of the people as a whole.

The themes that we have considered may all be placed within the Christian's present experience, but they contribute to Nyssa's account of the Christian's destiny. In the present we find our freedom fulfilled by God's providence, which is available to us generally in life and particularly in the sacramental life of the Church. And we can make moral, intellectual, and spiritual progress as we learn to respond to God's love in Christ. We can even have momentary experiences of "epectasy" and of our relation to one another in Christ. But all these aspects of the Christian life come to full focus only in the age to come. There "epectasy" will be made permanent as we fall endlessly towards the infinite Good and need no longer live in the dialectic between contemplation and action. There we shall truly become relations of one another in the one human nature, the ineffable image of God that is Christ's corporate humanity. Finally, in addition to the perfection of these aspects of the Christian's life, we shall participate in a transfigured physical order. To the moral and spiritual dimensions of redemption in which we can already participate will be added the physical dimension that is not yet apparent. The resurrection will bring new life not just to human beings but to the entire material creation.

The themes by which Nyssa explains our destiny are broken lights and are, in some degree, the product of the trinitarian and christological debates of the fourth century. By broken lights I mean that the three major themes I have disengaged from Nyssa's thought are not fully integrated with one another, even though they clearly represent different aspects of the same Christian hope. The "epectasy" develops Origen's understanding of our destiny as the pure contemplation of God, and it is difficult altogether to purge the idea of individualistic and purely spiritual connotations. The particular way that Nyssa treats the corporate character of our destiny is his own contribution. And the emphasis on the physical dimension of Redemption follows Irenaeus' and Athanasius' emphasis on incorruption. Not only do the three themes drive apart from one another when looked at this way, they also betray the impact of developing fourth-century orthodoxy. It is Nyssa's insistence upon the biblical distinction between Creator and created that leads him to argue that even in Redemption we remain creatures that are continually becoming. His portrait of the corporate aspect of Redemption depends entirely on his views of the Trinity and of Christ's person. The image that is human nature is defined as a reflection of the Trinity, single and ineffable but with individuals as relations of the nature. And he equates this corporate human nature with Christ's, the lost sheep placed on the shoulders of the divine Shepherd. Finally, the physical redemption of the resurrection reflects Nyssa's insistence upon the importance and value of the physical creation.

These broken lights are, as well, rays that shine upon us from the future and from the consummation of the Christian story. In this respect Nyssa is in broad agreement with Irenaeus. The story begun with the creation of Adam is completed in the New Man and consummated in the new humanity of the age to come. The hero of the story unites the beginning with the end, and we are brought back to the central vision of the risen Lord as the new Adam. His victory is ours and even now we can participate in it. To put it this way raises one last question. How far does it make sense to speak of the Christian life as a present participation in a future destiny? It may be that Irenaeus is better understood to speak of the present as an *anticipation* of the future rather than a *participation* in it. In any case, the distinction becomes crucial for Augustine. He begins his career as a Christian teacher and thinker fully committed to a version of the Christian Platonism we have found in Nyssa. But he ends by emphasising the great abysses between our present condition and our first creation, on the one hand, and our future destiny, on the other. For Nyssa the broken lights are nonetheless lights and give us the presence of Christ. For Augustine their brokenness begins to take pride of place, and we become exiles and pilgrims longing to find the journey's end. In the next chapter I shall turn to Augustine's transformation of the Christian story and of Christian Platonism.

3

The Pilgrim and the Holy City

Emile Bréhier points out that a major problem in assessing Plotinus' thought is to decide whether his chief preoccupation is philosophical or religious.[1] Are we to emphasize his account of the hierarchy of Being, or is what he says about the One, Mind, and Soul a way of supplying a stage setting for the drama of the soul's return to God? The second alternative finds support in a passage like the following (*Enn.* 6.9.7; MacK. 2, p. 247):

> God—we read—is outside of none, present unperceived to all; we break away from Him, or rather from ourselves; what we turn from we cannot reach; astray ourselves, we cannot go in search of another; a child distraught will not recognise its father; to find ourselves is to know our source.

Augustine might himself have written these words. In his case, however much he raises philosophical questions, the religious concerns predominate. Moreover, these concerns revolve less about the problem of defining the Saviour than about exploring the way in which Christians can find their destiny. His anguished plea in the *Soliloquies*, written in 386 at Cassiciacum immediately after his conversion, is to know himself and God. As for Plotinus, the two forms of knowledge are equated with one another and involve an introspective pilgrimage into oneself. Augustine's deepest conviction is that God has made us for himself and "our hearts find no peace" until they rest in him (*Conf.* 1.1; PC, p. 21). These ideas find full consideration in *De Trinitate*, where the mature Augustine comes close to saying that to know himself as God's image is to know the Trinity so far as that may be possible for a human being.

From one perspective Augustine's focus upon salvation does not distinguish him in any radical fashion from Irenaeus and Gregory of Nyssa. As we have seen, both these writers understand Christianity as a religion of salvation, and both seek to examine how the Christian's story is integrated with Christ's. In the same way, Augustine understands Christ's story as the broad context in which the Christian life finds its meaning. The Incarnation, set within God's purpose in Creation and in the calling of Israel, supplies the possibility of salvation for those who find themselves united with Christ. At the same time, Augustine shifts the emphasis in this general perspective from Christ's story to the Christian's. If Irenaeus' central concern is to define Christ in relation to Creation and to the mission of Israel and Nyssa's is to explain the Saviour in the light of the controversies over the Trinity and Christ's person that marked his time, then Augustine's central concern is with the Christian life itself. What appears as no more than a shift of emphasis when we compare Augustine with his predecessors and contemporaries nonetheless begins to look like a radical new departure when we examine Augustine as the one who set the theological agenda for all of Western theology. Attention shifts from defining the Trinity and Christ's person as a way of explaining the hero of the Christian story to defining what salvation is and who will gain it. A set of anthropological issues begins to dominate—grace and freedom, faith, predestination, the elect and the reprobate.

A puzzle begins to emerge. Janus-like, Augustine is both continuous and discontinuous with the Christian Platonism of a writer like Nyssa. And yet putting it this way seems unsatisfactory to me. A passage in the *Confessions* points towards a better way of describing the puzzle and approaching Augustine's thought (*Conf.* 7.20; PC, p. 154):

> I believe that it was by your will that I came across those [Platonist] books before I studied the Scriptures, because you wished me always to remember the impression they had made on me, so that later on, when I had been chastened by your Holy Writ and my wounds had been touched by your healing hand, I should be able to see and understand the difference between presumption and confession, between those who see the goal that they must reach, but cannot see the road by which they are to reach it, and those who see the road to that blessed country which is meant to be no mere vision but our home.

In other words, Augustine finds Platonism no more than a stage along the way in his journey towards the knowledge of self that gives him the vision of God. Just as his conversion takes him a step beyond the ideas found in the Platonic books, so his development as a Christian soon leads him beyond the Christian Platonism to which he was converted. He differs from Nyssa not merely because his emphasis is upon salvation rather than the Saviour but still more because he has moved beyond the Christian Platonism he adopted at his conversion to a theological vision that partly transforms and partly rejects Platonic themes.

Central to this shift in Augustine's thinking is an altered religious sensibility. He no longer thinks so much of the ascent of the soul to God as of the road the Christian must travel to the Heavenly City. The Platonists "see the goal that they must reach, but cannot see the road by which they are to reach it." What for them is a "vision" is for Augustine "that blessed country . . . our home." The Christian is a pilgrim, and this perception leads Augustine to make a sharp distinction between the Christian life and the Christian destiny. The Christian pilgrim is far from home, in some degree cut off not only from his point of origin but also from his destination. And so what strikes the student of the mature Augustine most forcibly is the gap between the created Adam and his fallen posterity and the contrast the elect find between their pilgrimage and their destiny in the City of God. To shift the metaphor, Augustine can think of the Christian life as a process of healing, and it is crucial to his understanding of the metaphor that the healing is never completed till the Christian's destiny is achieved. This life is, at best, a long convalescence. Nor may we suppose that more than a few of Adam's posterity are in fact on the road to health.[2]

The point I am trying to make is that the key to understanding Augustine's thought may be found in his problematic attitudes towards Christian Platonism. More than in the case of most theologians it is necessary to see Augustine's ideas in relation to his life. In part his thought is unsystematic because like Nyssa he believes that the broken lights of God's truth cannot be fitted together completely until we attain our destiny. But in part the contradictions and difficulties that block the way to a coherent interpretation of his thought are to be explained by the fact that he is a pilgrim in his thinking as well as in his life. In 386 he was converted to the Christian Platonism of Ambrose, but he rapidly moved on to think of his faith in ascetical terms. And, finally, he renounced the elitist implications of the ascetical life and came to see himself as a bishop, presiding over the mixed life of the Catholic Church in North Africa, where "wheat" and "tares," the elect and the reprobate, lived together in one Church. His growth from Christian philosopher to ascetic to bishop represents a transformation of and a pressing beyond the kind of Christian Platonism we have seen in Nyssa's thought.

In discussing Augustine, then, I want to begin by describing his conversion to Christian Platonism and his reasons for moving beyond it to his mature predestinarian view. Then I shall turn to the account of the Christian story found in his later writings, primarily *The City of God*. And, finally, I shall examine his understanding of the Christian life by focusing upon *De Trinitate*. Obviously, there are other ways in which we can explain Augustine's thought. We could examine him in terms of his threefold battle against the Manichees, the Pelagians, and the Donatists. Or we could assess him in his relation to earlier Christian thought and to the Augustinian synthesis of the Western Middle Ages, as well as the recrudescence of an extreme Augustinianism at the Reformation. But these approaches would draw us away from Augustine himself. The most remarkable aspect of Augustine's writings is that he invites the reader into his own reflections upon the Christian story; following him as far as possible in his own development is a way of accepting that implicit invitation.

AUGUSTINE'S CONVERSION TO CHRISTIAN PLATONISM

A dozen years after it happened Augustine describes his conversion in Book 8.12 of the Confessions (PC, pp. 177ff.). He is with his friend Alypius in a garden in Milan. A "great storm" of tears leads him to withdraw from Alypius, when "all at once" he hears "the singsong voice of a child in a nearby house" chanting "Take it and read, take it and read." Remembering how Antony the Hermit found conversion by hearing the Gospel read in Church, Augustine returns to Alypius and opens his book of St. Paul's epistles at random, finding the words: "Not in revelling and drunkenness, not in lust and wantonness, not in quarrels and rivalries. Rather, arm yourselves with the Lord Jesus Christ; spend no more thought on nature and nature's appetites" (Rom. 13:13–14). So it was that God's grace effected his conversion by giving him the will to act upon what he longed for in his thoughts. His retirement from public life and his retreat to the country estate at Cassiciacum followed immediately, and at Easter of 387 he, his friend Alypius, and his son Adeodatus were baptized in Milan. Like St. Paul's experience on the road to Damascus, Augustine's has the character of a sudden intrusion of God into his life.

At the same time the divine intervention found long preparation in Augustine's quest for truth and in what he himself came to regard as a providential ordering of that quest. From this point of view the conversion consummated in the garden in Milan first began in Carthage, where the schoolboy Augustine "in the midst of a hissing cauldron of lust" (*Conf.* 3.1; PC, p. 55) read Cicero's *Hortensius*, an exhortation to the philosophical life: ". . . my heart began to throb with a bewildering passion for the wisdom of eternal truth" (*Conf.* 3.4; PC, pp. 58f). Abandoning the thought of a legal career and the possibility of preferment in the imperial civil service, Augustine embarked upon his profession as a teacher of rhetoric. It was at this time that his yearning for Truth led him to the Manichees, whose motto was "Truth and truth alone" (*Conf.* 3.6; PC, p. 60). A conversion to Cicero was rapidly followed by one to Manichaeism. Augustine's quest for Truth was clearly one for meaning, a way of explaining his own experience and, in particular, his deep sense of moral evil not least of all in himself. The dualism of the Manichees not only explained evil in terms of a cosmic principle of darkness but also assured Augustine that his true and good self was to be distinguished from the evil in which he found himself trapped. And as a religion of salvation Manichaeism promised Augustine deliverance from his own evil self.

Gradually Augustine found the Manichees' answers unsatisfactory and no longer capable of satisfying his questions about God, himself, and evil. In large measure Augustine's disillusion with the Manichees was intellectual. Part of the problem was the relation between science and religion, since the conclusions of the astronomers contradicted the Manichaen myth at various points. And when Faustus, a bishop and teacher highly esteemed by the Manichees, came to Carthage, he proved to be no more than an eloquent charlatan. Augustine found himself far better educated than Faustus (*Conf.* 5.3–7). Clearly Augustine's disillusionment did not lead to an immediate renunciation of his association with the Manichees. When he went to Rome in 383 to seek his fortune there, it was with the expectation of help from the Manichees. And this doubtless explains why the anti-Christian prefect of Rome, Symmachus, was persuaded to recommend Augustine for the chair of rhetoric in Milan in 384. If Manichaeism represented a stage on Augustine's journey towards truth, the Manichees themselves assisted that journey by sending him to Milan, where he met Ambrose and read the "Platonic books." On his arrival in Milan, however, Augustine found himself no longer persuaded by the Manichees or the astrologers and without any answers to the questions burning in his heart. He was further from the truth than ever. The two problems he could not solve were the character of God and the nature of evil (*Conf.* 7.1–8). With no answers to these questions, he could find no meaning for himself. The Platonic books, almost certainly Latin translations of Plotinus, filled the void. "These books served to remind me to return to my own self" (*Conf.* 7.10; PC, p. 146).

What Augustine read in the Platonic books cohered with what he heard Ambrose preach in the Christian Church, and this Christian Platonism gave him answers to his two fundamental questions. For the first time he realized that God was simultaneously totally transcendent and immanent in the whole creation (*Conf.* 7.10; PC, p. 147):

> Eternal Truth, true Love, beloved Eternity—all this, my God, you are. . . . Your light shone upon me in its brilliance, and I thrilled with love and dread alike. I realized that I was far from you. It was as though I were in a land where all is different from your own. . . . And, far off, I heard your voice saying *I am the God who IS* (Ex. 3:14). . . . I might more easily have doubted that I was alive than that the Truth had being. For we catch sight of the Truth, as he is known through his creation.

God, as pure Being, Truth, and Goodness, alone has reality; but the created order has life and receives knowledge of God by participating in him. Created things "are real in so far as they have their being from you, but unreal in the sense that they are not what you are" (*Conf.* 7.11; PC, p. 147). The distinction between God's transcendent nature and his immanent presence carries with it the idea that we can either participate in him or corrupt ourselves by depriving ourselves of God's presence. Evil, then, is not a substance, but our movement away from God and our failure to recognize and act upon God's abiding presence with us (*Conf.* 7.9–16).

Augustine's reading of the Platonic books prepared him for conversion but did not effect the change for which he longed. "In my weakness I recoiled and fell back into my old ways, carrying with me nothing but the memory of something that I loved and longed for, as though I had sensed the fragrance of the fare but was not yet able to eat it" (*Conf.* 7.17; PC, p. 152). In the *Confessions* between his account of the Platonic books and the description of his conversion in the garden, Augustine tells the stories of Marius Victorinus and Antony. Victorinus, the pagan Platonist become Christian who began by denying that walls make a Christian, ended by insisting on making public profession of his faith. And Antony acted upon his faith by embracing poverty and the ascetical life. Implicit in these stories Augustine finds that Christianity is no mere idea but requires in addition to the perception of truth the public expression of a life dedicated to truth and the commitment to do that truth fully in life. More important, Augustine notes the need of a Mediator. Only through Christ is it possible "to follow the high road to that land of peace, the way that is defended by the care of the heavenly Commander"

(*Conf.* 7.21; PC, p. 156). It is, of course the Mediator whose grace touches Augustine's will in the garden and enables him to become a Christian and, indeed, a Christian Platonist.

With the possible exception of the emphasis Augustine places upon grace, the view he takes of Christianity is essentially the same as that found in Nyssa's writings. The Platonic distinction between Being and Becoming is equated with the biblical distinction between Creator and created. And so the created order, as a derived reality, exists by its participation in the Creator. Human beings must affirm their participation in God by recognizing his presence in them and their world. They can, as well, deprive themselves of God's presence by moving away from him; and in this way their misuse of freedom introduces evil into the world, an evil that is deprivation of the good. This basic pattern might then be integrated with the Christian story of God's purpose in creating the world and his fulfillment of that purpose in the sending of the Incarnate Lord. But Augustine stops short of filling in the Christian Platonist pattern the way Nyssa does. From the very moment of his conversion to Christian Platonism Augustine betrays his unhappiness with central aspects of the view he inherits.

CHRISTIAN PLATONISM TRANSFORMED: TOWARDS THE PREDESTINARIAN SCHEMA

In reading Augustine's early works, those written, say, before he became bishop of Hippo in 395, I have the sense of someone frustrated by false summits. That is, just as in climbing a mountain we often think we are almost at the top when a few more steps show us the distance yet to climb, so Augustine increasingly finds what he had regarded as breakthroughs in his religious thinking and life to be no more than points of departure. The fundamental platform of Christian Platonism, which he begins by thinking of as a solution to his spiritual quest, soon becomes an ideal that stands in contrast to his own moral and spiritual state. The best example of what I mean occurs in Book I of the *Soliloquies*, a dialogue between Augustine and his Reason written in 386 at Cassiciacum during the retreat that intervened between his conversion and his baptism. Augustine is thinking through the Christian Platonism that gives articulation to his new found faith. "For many days I had been earnestly seeking to know myself and my chief good and what evil was to be shunned" (*Sol.* I.1; LCC 6, p. 23). The long prayer that follows this setting forth of the topic for discussion revolves around the dialectic between contemplation and action. To turn to God and participate in him as the Truth, the Good, and the Beautiful enables the Christian to be freed and to live the life of virtue. At the same time, God is he "whom no man finds unless he has been purified" (*Sol.* I.3; LCC 6, p. 24).[3]

Augustine's thinking revolves around the Platonist axiom "to know the good is to do the good." Knowledge of God is what enables virtue. But the axiom can be reversed, since virtue is required before a person can know God. Putting it this way leads Augustine to question the validity of the axiom, at least for himself. Reason promises him that he will see God with his mind "as the sun is seen with the eye" (*Sol.* I.12; LCC 6, p. 30). All that is required is the healing of the soul's eye, in other words the virtue that enables vision, the doing of the good that enables one to know the good. Augustine examines himself. His spiritual sight is no longer obviously hindered by passions for riches, honors, or marriage (*Sol.* I.17). But Reason cross-examines him (*Sol.* I.25; LCC 6, pp. 38f.):

> Do you remember how, yesterday, in complete assurance, we declared that we were free from disease, that we loved nothing but Wisdom; all else we sought and desired only for the sake of Wisdom? How sordid, how base, how execrable, how horrible the embrace of a woman seemed to you when we were discussing the desire for marriage! But as you lay awake last night and the same question arose, you found it very different with you than you had supposed.

Augustine realizes that a "spent pestilence is a very different thing from one that is merely quiescent" (*Sol.* I.19; LCC 6, p. 35). Dung does not stink until it is stirred up. And so Augustine comes close to despairing of the healed vision that will give him knowledge of God. He cannot know God without doing the good, and he cannot do the good without knowing God. The Platonic axiom instead of freeing him for the Christian life shows him that he is still the prisoner of a depraved will.

If doing the good seems problematic to Augustine, so from a slightly different perspective does knowing the good. In his treatise *Of True Religion,* written in 389, a year after his return to Carthage, he raises the question of how Plato would have responded to the Christian message. He and his disciples would have agreed that a healed mind can perceive and cleave to the truth and so gain eternal life. But they would have realized that "a great and divine man" was required "to persuade the peoples that such things were to be at least believed if they could not grasp them with the mind" (*OTR* iii. 3; LCC 6, p. 227). Christ, of course, fulfills this requirement. And Augustine is arguing for the primacy of faith over the knowledge available to reason alone. He is skeptical of the possibility of knowing the good without first accepting the authority of the Catholic faith: ". . . all those things which to begin with we simply believed, following authority only, we come to understand" (*OTR* viii.14; LCC 6, p. 233; cf. xxiv. 45, xxxviii.70). The insight that faith precedes and seeks understanding pervades Augustine's writings. The Christian begins by learning the Catholic faith, but must continue by making that faith his own.[4] In this way he gains a kind of knowledge that enables him to love the truths of the faith and to enter upon the task of understanding those truths (DT 13.20). "To know the good," then, can be translated into believing the Catholic faith.

One might suppose Augustine capable of redefining the second part of the axiom as well as the first. Just as he can think of a development in "knowing" from accepting the faith to believing to understanding, so we should expect him to argue that the Christian can make progress in doing the good. Indeed, it was in some such developmental way that Christian Platonists like Nyssa understood the axiom. The Christian life was for them a growth toward perfection, and as the Christian's knowledge grew, so did his virtue. Similarly, progress in virtue meant progress in knowledge; and the dialectic pressed the Christian forward toward his destiny. In *On Free Will*, completed in 391, the year he was ordained priest in Hippo, Augustine reflects upon the human capacity to will the good. He accepts the argument that "Nothing makes the mind a companion of cupidity, except its own will and free choice" (*OFW* I.xi.21). It follows that (*OFW* I.xiii.29; LCC 6, p. 129):

> whoever wishes to live rightly and honourably, if he prefers that before all fugitive and transient goods, attains his object with perfect ease. In order to attain it he has nothing to do but will it.

This conclusion is a straw man in the argument, since it is almost immediately followed by the perplexing question "Why, then, do not all obtain it [the happy life]?" Though in principle doing the good would appear easy, in practice it proves highly difficult. The explanation for this fact of human life is found in the fall of Adam and Eve. Ignorance and difficulty are "the penalty of man as condemned" (*OFW* III.xviii.52; LCC 6, p. 202). Presumably faith begins to supply a remedy for ignorance, while "divine aid" assists "any of Adam's race . . . willing to turn to God" (*OFW* III.xx.55; LCC 6, p. 203). Although we are no longer able to choose the good unassisted, nevertheless the soul remains capable of turning toward God; and with God's help we can be made free of our difficulty in doing the good.[5]

Augustine has not yet moved to the view that because of the Fall we all

stand condemned, incapable of the good because we are the prisoners of
our depraved wills. And he does believe that we can choose to seek and
to accept God's grace. Election is not yet for him a mysterious divine
operation that overrides human choices. "But since man cannot rise of
his own free will as he fell by his own will spontaneously, let us hold
with steadfast faith the right hand of God stretched out to us, even our
Lord Jesus Christ" (*OFW* II.xx.54; LCC 6, p. 203). A strong sense of his
own depravity, his ignorance and weakness, prevents him from a whole-
hearted commitment to the usual Christian Platonist understanding of
the moral life as implying a dialectical growth in knowing and willing
the good. We can see him moving towards his mature doctrine of original sin. He will eventually say that what we inherit from Adam is not
merely ignorance and difficulty but the incapacity to will the good. This
conviction lies at the heart of the later Augustine's theology, and it
obliges him to deny the Platonist axiom that he vainly had struggled to
understand and to redefine. Once he commits himself to the view that
the fall of Adam involves the condemnation of the entire human race,
his break with Christian Platonism is complete. His despair of healing
leads to his notion of the depraved will, and Scripture teaches him that
his depravity is the consequence of Adam's sin. The Christian hope, then,
is identified with God's election of the saints, whom his mercy delivers
from the "mass of perdition" for their destiny in the City of God. Augustine's mature, predestinarian understanding of the Christian story is
born from his difficulties with Christian Platonism and his eventual
denial of the axiomatic connection of knowledge and virtue.

The Christian Story and the Predestinarian Schema

I may summarize the argument thus far by saying that what proved for
Augustine initially a perspective that filled the void left by his renunciation of Manichaeism and paved the way for his conversion to Christ and
the Church became a difficulty that led him to elaborate his doctrine of
original sin, together with its predestinarian implications. The Christian
Platonist understanding of the relation of the human soul to God offered
Augustine the possibility of participating in God by freely choosing to
recognize his presence in the soul and by willing the good. And it explained evil as a turning away from God and a deprivation of being,
truth, goodness, and beauty. Nevertheless, though he retained belief in
this pattern as a way of explaining both the position of Adam in paradise
and the final state of the elect in the City of God, Augustine increasingly
found the pattern false as a description of what was currently available
to the Christian. As late as the *Confessions* (397–98) he maintained the

Platonist and even Plotinian belief .that an occasional participation in eternal Truth was possible for the Christian.[6] In Ostia he and his mother experienced this mystical participation, for while speaking of the eternal Wisdom, "longing for it and straining for it with all the strength of our hearts, for one fleeting instant we reached out and touched it" (*Conf.* 9.10; PC, p. 197). But increasingly Augustine saw the Christian life as an anticipation of rather than a participation in Truth. More a pilgrim than a visionary, the Christian even when delivered from the condemnation pronounced upon Adam and all his posterity was not yet freed from the disease and the curse brought by Adam on the whole human race. Like Irenaeus and Nyssa, Augustine locates the Christian between Adam's creation and fall and the final consummation of Christ's saving work in the new age. But while the story is the same, it is told in a new way, transformed by Augustine's radical interpretation of the Fall and its abiding effect even upon the elect.

Augustine begins the story with God's Creation of the universe. Like his Christian Platonist predecessors he argues that God created "out of pure disinterested goodness"; but his emphasis is upon "disinterested," "since he [God] had continued in no less felicity without them [his creatures] from all eternity without beginning" (*CG* 12.18; PC, p. 496). Without denying God's goodness, emphasis has shifted to his sovereignty; and Augustine's chief concern is to demonstrate the mystery that though God "willed to create the first man, as a new act of creation, at some particular time," he did so "without any alteration in his purpose and design" (*CG* 12.15; PC, p. 490). Whereas the tradition before him had at least implicitly recognized that Creation involves God in some form of self-limitation, Augustine is determined to avoid this implication so far as possible. For this reason he rejects any view that the world is co-eternal with God or is some sort of eternal process (*CG* 11.4). Instead, God's eternity and the created order's time-bound character are radically contrasted (*CG* 11.4–6, 12.10–21). God's being remains unaffected by the becoming of the creation, while he orders the creation not only in its nature as good but also in its fallen state.

The last point is necessary if Augustine is to maintain God's unqualified sovereignty over creation and, hence, his remaining unaffected by the order of becoming. He puts it this way (*CG* 11.17; PC, pp. 448f.):

> But God, who is supremely good in his creation of natures that are good, is also completely just in his employment of evil choices in his design, so that whereas such evil choices make a wrong use of good natures, God turns evil choices to good use.

Whether by nature or by utility God is the sovereign orderer of creation. In the second dimension God so orders good and evil that their opposition and antithesis makes up a total beauty (*CG* 11.18). This idea enables Augustine to insist that God always remains in control, but it introduces into his thought an approach to the problem of evil that carries him beyond Christian Platonism and accounts for the basic peculiarity of his view of the destiny of creation.[7] Evil is no longer merely a deprivation of good but is something that must be ordered into the total picture as contraries are ordered in speech. Once the Fall has taken place God deals with evil not so much by working to eliminate it as by ordering it into a total good. And there is a final end of evil just as there is a final end of good with the result that the new age becomes an ordering of good and evil. Evil is not eliminated, but merely tamed; and the damned, eternally tormented in the lake of fire, supply a counterpoint to the bliss of the saints in the City of God. The Christian story, then, is not one that tells how God gradually purges evil from his creation. Instead, it is one that shows how God's sovereignty constantly balances good and evil until the new age when the balance is made ultimate and stable.

It is within this basic understanding of God's sovereignty over creation, together with its implication that evil is not so much eliminated as tamed, that Augustine speaks of the creation and fall of angels and human beings. The angelic creation may be read allegorically into the first chapter of Genesis. For example, "Let there be light" may refer to God's creation of the angels, while the separation of light and darkness may refer to the fall of the evil angels (*CG* 11.9, 19–20, 32ff.). None of this is peculiar to Augustine, but his preoccupation with the question why the evil angels fell is. He has no difficulty defining the evil will that precipitated their fall. They chose pride, the love of self, instead of true existence by loving God; and they sought cleverness rather than knowledge and faction instead of love (*CG* 12.1).[8] In the long run Augustine recognizes that there is no explanation for the origin of this evil will; there is no efficient cause, only a deficiency because the evil angels failed to stand fast in the truth (*CG* 12.6–8). But in the short run Augustine worries with the problem why some of the angels fell and others did not. He has no doubt that the good angels now have not only bliss but the certitude of their perseverance in bliss (*CG* 11.13). But he raises the question of whether this was so to begin with. He states the dilemma without solving it. Either the angels were created unequal, the good ones with certitude of perseverance, or they were created equal, the good angels receiving certitude after the ruin of the evil ones (*CG* 11.13). Putting it another way, he can suggest that either the evil angels received less grace or the good ones received more (*CG* 12.9).

Augustine's consideration of these questions betrays his unwillingness to explain the fall of the angels simply in terms of their freedom to turn toward or away from God. For a Christian Platonist like Nyssa it is clear that the angels were created free and mutable and that, however mysterious at one level, the fall of some is to be explained by their misuse of freedom. Why is Augustine not satisfied with this explanation? In part the answer revolves around his high view of God's sovereignty. That is why God must have shortchanged some of the angels when he bestowed grace upon them. The dilemma is insoluble, for if we press the argument much further, then we shall make God responsible for the falling away of the evil angels. But, Augustine fears, if we place too much weight on their freedom to renounce God, we run the risk of qualifying God's sovereignty. A second consideration helps explain Augustine's questions. If the gift of freedom means that the angels have the capacity to choose God, to know him and serve him, why would they fail to use that capacity? The questions Augustine raises about the angels, then, correlate with two of his deepest convictions—that God is absolutely sovereign and that evil must be taken with utter seriousness as a rebellion within the created order that can be tamed but not eliminated.

These basic perspectives also color Augustine's account of the creation and fall of Adam and Eve. In order to show this let me begin by simply describing what Augustine says. At one level, he repeats the view that can be found in other of the Fathers, notably Athanasius (*De Inc.* 3). Adam was created capable both of immortality and of death (*CG* 12.22; PC, p. 502):

> But he [God] created man's nature as a kind of mean between angels and beasts, so that if he submitted to his Creator, as to his true sovereign Lord, and observed his instructions with dutiful obedience, he should pass over into the fellowship of the angels, attaining an immortality of endless felicity, without an intervening death; but if he used his free will in arrogance and disobedience, and thus offended God, his Lord, he should live like the beasts, under sentence of death, should be the slave of his desires, and destined after death for eternal punishment.

Adam ought to have chosen the first of these alternatives and so have completed the image of God by true existence, knowledge, and love (*CG* 11.24–29, 12.24). But instead Adam failed to act upon the possibility of not sinning and brought the second alternative upon himself. The implication is that Adam's imperfection must ultimately yield to the perfection of the redeemed in the new age, where the saints will attain the impossibility of sinning. In God's purpose the movement of human history is from imperfection to perfection, from Adam's unstable bliss to the persevering bliss of the City of God. And so Redemption will be the completion of Creation.

Augustine does not deny the truth of this perspective at least for the elect and from the point of view of God's ultimate purpose. And he certainly does not think of Adam's state in paradise as a stable perfection. At the same time, he tends to look at the story from the perspective of his own involvement in sin and evil. And what strikes him is the absolute abyss between Adam in paradise and the condition of the human race after the Fall. Adam's sin in eating the forbidden fruit only appears to be a small fault. The action itself is not of great consequence, but what matters is that obedience would have been simple both because God's command was easy to fulfill and because "it was given at a time when desire was not yet in opposition to the will" (CG 14.12; PC, p. 571). The horror of the fall lies not in the act of disobedience, but in the evil will, the evil tree from which the fruit of disobedience grew. Augustine distinguishes evil actions from the basic posture of the will that lies behind them, and he argues that pride was the start of Adam's evil will (CG 14.11, 13).[9] Pride, equated with the love of oneself, is at the heart of Adam's fall and represents a conscious rebellion against God's sovereignty. It is, as well, the death of the soul and enables Adam's body to rebel against his soul in concupiscence. By their disobedience of pride Adam and Eve bring upon themselves the penalty of the disobedience of lust (CG 13.3, 13, 15). As they rebelled against God, so their bodies rebel against them. The first death is completed when the soul, separated from God, is separated from the body, which becomes a corpse. And the second death is the reunion of soul and body for eternal torment (CG 13.2–11). Pride, then, carries in its train inevitable physical and eternal death; and it is both these deaths that represent the penalty for Adam's disobedience.

It is the conscious and fully responsible character of Adam's sin that explains its horror for Augustine. He knows of the Irenaean view that Adam was childlike, and he agrees that Adam sinned when he was neither wise nor foolish (OFW III.71ff.). But even in his earlier writings he refuses to employ this perception as a way of extenuating Adam's fault. For Irenaeus and Nyssa Adam's sin, though real, is not surprising because of his immaturity. One expects children to make mistakes. But for Augustine Adam is fully responsible. He knows God's command; it is easy to observe; his desire and his will are not in conflict with one another. And the gratuitous character of Adam's sin gives it a meaninglessness, which is one way of underlining the mysterious and perverse character of sin. Like Augustine and his companions when as children they stole pears, Adam had no need of the forbidden fruit. Augustine's wish in stealing the pears was "only to enjoy the theft itself and the sin" (*Conf.* 2.4; PC, p. 47). And he supposes that Adam's sin must have had the same meaningless perversity of a longing for forbidden and unnecessary fruit. Adam's fall cannot finally be explained, only condemned in the most absolute fashion.

The association Augustine makes between his own experience of sin and his understanding of Adam's, together with warrants that he finds in Scripture, particularly Romans 5:12ff., leads him to the conclusion that all human beings inherit Adam's condemnation.[10] Unlike the angels, who were created individually, human beings all take their origin from Adam. And so (*CG* 13.3; PC, p. 512):

> . . . those first sinners were sentenced to death, with the provision that whatever sprang from their stock should incur the same punishment. . . . Because of the magnitude of that offense, the condemnation changed human nature for the worse; so that what first happened as a matter of punishment in the case of the first human beings, continued in their posterity as something natural and congenital.

This is the bondage to sin and death of which St. Paul speaks, and it is not to be understood merely by the fact that human beings are mortal. It means that all Adam's posterity have lost the capacity to will the good and are headed for the eternal damnation of the second death. The entire race is a mass of perdition, justly condemned by God because of Adam's sin. Augustine's way of telling the story enables him to maintain God's sovereignty and to recognize the full reality of evil within the created order. Adam is fully responsible for his sin and its consequences, and so God cannot be held in any sense accountable by having created him liable to fall. And the disastrous impact of the Fall is really a way of taking the evil we experience with utter seriousness.

This assessment of the Fall and its consequences is, of course, more radical than the view taken of the human predicament by Irenaeus and Nyssa, indeed, by all Augustine's predecessors and contemporaries. But Augustine departs still further from the tradition as he carries the story forward. In fact, he argues, it would have been perfectly just of God to have stopped the story with Adam's fall and allowed the rest of human history to be nothing but a futile plunge towards eternal death. Instead, Augustine argues that God, desiring to exercise his mercy, elects a small and mysterious number of human beings out of the mass of perdition

(*CG* 13.3, 14, 23; 14.1, 26). The elect are destined to make up the ranks of the fallen angels (*Ench.* 29). It is here that Augustine introduces the idea of predestination (*CG* 13.23; PC, p. 538):

> . . . the second death is certainly not the common lot of all men because those are exempt "who have been called in fulfilment of his purpose," those whom he previously "foreknew and predestined." as the Apostle says, "to be fashioned in the likeness of his Son, so that he might be the first-born in a family of many brothers" (Rom. 8:28f.). They have been rescued from the second death by God's grace, through the action of the Mediator.

The election of the saints out of the mass of perdition "was always fixed, by his [God's] predestination, in his eternity and in this co-eternal Word" (*CG* 12.17; PC, p. 493). The strange feature of Augustine's notion of the elect is not the distinction between the saved and the damned. With the exceptions of Origen and Nyssa, the other Fathers were prepared to make the distinction even though it drove against their conviction that God willed the salvation of all. Instead, the pecularity of Augustine's view is that God wills the salvation only of some and that human choices play no role in the distinction between saved and damned.

Augustine's emphasis on God's grace is partly the product of his insistence upon God's sovereignty and partly a reaction to the Pelagian claim that human beings are capable of taking the first steps towards God by themselves. And that same emphasis leads him to redefine human freedom. As he sees it, the trouble with equating choosing and freedom is that our will is necessarily divided against itself even when we make right choices, since to will one good can be to nill another good. The fulfillment of human freedom, then, cannot merely reside in the choice of what is good. The divided will can only be healed when it is made to cleave to the Good; that is, to God. The paradox of a servitude that is perfect freedom represents Augustine's redefinition of true human freedom.[11] Only the elect in the City of God will have this freedom, since they will find the impossibility of sinning. Adam before the Fall could choose both good and evil, while fallen human beings can choose only evil.[12] The saints during their pilgrimage on earth can begin to choose good, but their healing is incomplete. They can still sin; and though their emotions may be righteous, they have no voluntary control over them.

These ideas deserve fuller discussion, but the point I want to make is that only after prevenient grace has elected the righteous are they capable of responding to God. In this light Irenaeus' conviction that the dispensations of God are meant to educate humanity for its destiny makes no sense. For Augustine the Christian story after the fall of Adam can really only be continued by the election of the saints and their response to that election which gains them a place in the City of God. The Old Testament and even the Incarnation have meaning for Augustine only when connected with the mystery of predestination and election. Augustine's attention is not fixed upon the providential course of human history so much as upon the fate of the saved and the damned. I do not mean to suggest that Augustine no longer speaks in terms of the salvation history that finds in the Incarnate Lord the fulfillment of the Old Testament and the anticipation of the new age. But I do wish to argue that his schema tends to rob the story of its meaning, and I need to try to establish the point by discussing his treatment of the Old Testament and of the Incarnation.

Augustine's treatment of the Old Testament in *The City of God* poses a problem that cannot be solved. In 15.1 (PC, p. 595) he implies that the second part of his long treatise is concerned with the two cities, that is "two societies of human beings, one of which is predestined to reign with God for all eternity, the other doomed to undergo eternal punishment with the Devil." His specific reference is to the "final destiny" of the two cities, which he discusses in Books 19–22. He has spoken of their "origins" in Books 11–14, and in Books 15–18 he undertakes "to describe their development from the time when that first pair began to produce offspring up to the time when mankind will cease to reproduce itself" (PC, p. 595). Putting it this way looks as though Augustine is treating the Old Testament historically. Indeed, he establishes a series of epochs in the Old Testament—the infancy of the human race from Adam to Noah, its boyhood from Noah to Abraham, its adolescence from Abraham to David, and its manhood from David to Christ (*CG* 16.43, 24; 15.8). Throughout these epochs the line of the City of God can be traced, and we gain the impression that the City of God is in existence throughout the Old Testament (cf. 15.17, 27; 16.1, 3, 9, 10, 35). On the other hand, the first dedication of the City of God is accomplished by Christ at his Resurrection, while the second dedication is reserved for the age to come (*CG* 15.18–19, cf. 15.8). No answer is given to the question how those before Christ can be citizens of a city not yet founded.[13] Not only does Augustine fail to think through the place of the Old Testament in the salvation history, he also fails to be consistent in recognizing the centrality of the Incarnate Lord for the foundation of the City of God.

Failure to resolve these historical questions suggests that Augustine's interest in the Old Testament lies elsewhere. He puts his conviction as follows (*CG* 16.2; PC, pp. 652f.):

> . . . the writer of these holy Scriptures (or rather the Spirit of God through his agency) is concerned with those events which not only constitute a narrative of past history but also give a prophecy of things to come, though only those things which concern the City of God. For everything that is here said about those human beings who are not citizens of that City is said with this purpose, that the City may show up to advantage, may be thrown into relief, by contrast with its opposite.

Not all the details of the narrative are "symbolical," but just as the plough exists for the ploughshare and the lyre for the strings that make music, so the unprophetic parts of Scripture exist for the sake of what has a deeper meaning. In other words, the Old Testament is best understood as an allegory of the predestinarian structure of Augustine's thought. The Christian story can be reduced to the mysterious operation of God's grace in electing the saints from the mass of perdition.

Equally astonishing and even more problematic is the way Augustine deals with the Incarnation. To be sure, we have already seen that he associates the deliverance of the righteous from the mass of perdition and the foundation of the City of God with the Incarnate Lord. And there can be no doubt that in some sense God's elective and prevenient grace is to be equated with his act in Christ. Nevertheless, election more often than not is spoken of without any reference to Christ. For example (CG 14.1; PC, p. 547):

> Now the reign of death has held mankind in such utter subjection that they would all be driven headlong into that second death . . . if some were not resecued from it by the undeserved grace of God.

This way of describing redemption becomes so habitual that it is hard to remember that Christ is the Mediator and Saviour. It is, as well, puzzling that, while the second part of The City of God deals with the origins, development, and final destiny of the two cities, there is no book and no extended treatment of the Incarnation. We have moved a long way from the Christocentric piety of Irenaeus and Nyssa. For Augustine what matters is God's mysterious dealings with the human soul; and even the Christian story, though it does not disappear, tends to dissolve into the drama of prevenient grace and the saints in the City of God.

THE CHRISTIAN LIFE AS A RESPONSE TO GRACE

Augustine transforms the Christian story so that it becomes a way of talking about God's sovereign and merciful election of the saints. From one point of view he retains the same kind of narrative found in Irenaeus and Nyssa. God creates the world with angels and human beings perfectly ordered. The evil angels, followed by Adam and Eve, fall and introduce evil into the created order. God elects Israel, sends the prophets, and finally his Word becomes incarnate to bring Redemption. And for the saints in the City of God Redemption not only delivers them from the consequence of the Fall—original sin—but also brings them the stable perfection of immortality and perseverance in bliss that God had intended for Adam. The possibility of not sinning is transformed into the impossibility of sinning. From another point of view, however, all that really matters about the story is that it explains the radical character of the human predicament and shows us the mystery of God's elective grace which alone enables the few to begin to respond to him. In other words, the story becomes a way of talking about the precondition for any consideration of the Christian life as something that lies in any measure within our own power. We can look at Augustine's version of the story and be repelled by its denial that we have any say about our own destiny and by its restriction of salvation to the few who are arbitrarily and gratuitously chosen. But we must remember that there is another way of responding. To those who believe they have been elected predestination brings hope and strength. Incapable of helping themselves, they are convinced that God has freed them to begin to turn towards him and to embark on the pilgrimage to the heavenly city.

Augustine's *De Trinitate* shows us what the landscape looks like once we move inside the predestinarian schema. The treatise was written from 399 to 419 and while Augustine was working on *The City of God* (413–27). It makes few explicit reference to the predestinarian views of *The City of God*, but it is fair to argue that it presupposes those views throughout and speaks of the Christian life from the point of view of those who have received prevenient grace.[14] I need to add that even though *De Trinitate* purports to be a discussion of the Trinity, Augustine's preoccupation throughout is with the Christian life. The first seven books are a careful exposition of the Trinity as found in the Catholic faith, together with the soteriological implications of the doctrine. Books 8–15 embark upon the task of understanding the faith that has been expounded. The key to the argument is found in the doctrine of the image of God. If we can know ourselves as the triune image of God, we shall be able to understand the Trinity by analogy. And what Augustine finds is not a static or achieved image of God, but a set of human activities moving towards the destiny of the saints in the City of God, when the triune image will finally be established. In discussing those activities he gives us some idea of his understanding of the Christian response to God's grace.

Book 8 of *De Trinitate* focuses upon love. In seeking to understand the faith he has already expounded, Augustine asks how we can love God. Since we cannot love what we do not know, there must be some innate principle within us by which we can know God and so love him. And this innate principle must be some likeness to God, since only like can know like. Augustine's argument is complex, but his conclusion is based upon defining God as love and the innate and like principle of knowledge that is within us as the image of Love (*DT* 8.11–12; *NPNF¹* 3, p. 123):

> Behold, "God is Love": why do we go forth and run to the heights of the heavens and the lowest parts of the earth, seeking Him who is within us, if we wish to be with Him? Let no one say, I do not know what I love. Let him love his brother, and he will love the same love. For he knows the love with which he loves, more than the brother whom he loves. So now he can know God more than he knows his brother: clearly known more, because more present; known more, because more within him; known more, because more certain. Embrace the love of God, and by love embrace God.

The paradox is that the principle of knowledge that enables us to love God is our capacity to love. Love, then, defines not only God but his image in us.

If love is the image of God, the next question must be whether love is triune and reflects the Trinity. We might speak of the lover, the beloved, and the love that unites them; but since I can love myself and in this way lover and beloved are one, we have only found the place to look for the image of the Trinity. Books 9 and 10, then, represent triadic ways of analyzing love. The image of God, love, can be analyzed as a mind with knowledge and love of itself. Or we can think of mind, knowledge, and love as interrelated activities of the soul and speak of memory, under-standing, and will. There is no need to enter into the details of Augus-tine's exposition.[15] For our purposes only two points need to be made. First, even though love can be analyzed in triadic ways, it remains a single activity, just as the three persons of the Trinity by no means undermine the fundamental unity of God. The unity of the human soul or mind corresponds to the unity of God. The second point is that what we can now know of the image of God in us is an activity. This idea implies that the image will be completed only in the age to come when love will cease to be an activity and will be a constant cleaving to God. God, who is Love, has made us for himself by giving us his image, the capacity to love; and our hearts are restless till that capacity finds its term in perfect fellowship with God.

What Augustine says elsewhere in his writings about love fills in the picture.[16] I can do no more than offer the briefest of sketches, but my point is not so much to give a complete treatment of Augustine's view of the Christian life as to suggest a broad scheme that will put his major themes in some kind of interpretive order. As a human capacity love has both an appetitive and a creative aspect. That is, when I love someone I not only have a desire to be united with the beloved but must also will the beloved's existence apart from me. A balance must be struck between the unitive and the distancing aspects of love. Mere appetite is possession, not love; while merely willing the other's good can scarcely be called love. Moreover, love remains the same whether its object is our neighbor or God. The command to love God and the neighbor is a single command; we love the one in the other. Human love as appetitive and creative, as implying both involvement and detachment, is, as well, an image of God's love, since God remains utterly distinct by nature from his creation and yet cares for it by his providence. Finally, human love can be defined not so much in terms of its character as an activity as in terms of its object. From this point of view, Augustine makes a distinction between "use" and "enjoyment." To enjoy a love means to treat it as ultimate; and, of course, only the love of God can be understood this way. All human loves must be "used," that is, treated not as ends in themselves but as loves that point beyond themselves to the love of God. As a result, the Christian is obliged to order his love under the love of God; and this is what enables him to see the love of God in his love of the neighbor.

To return to *De Trinitate*, Augustine shifts his perspective in Books 11–14 by speaking of the Christian life as knowing rather than loving. The paradox of Book 8 that love is the innate principle by which we know God in order to love him reminds us that loving and knowing are not presented as opposed to or even fundamentally different from one another. They are simply alternative ways of talking about the life of the mind as it grows towards its destiny of becoming the image of God. In any case, Augustine orients his discussion of knowing towards his quest for the image of God. While we cannot speak of "the outer man" as the image of God, the forms of knowledge based on sense perception do possess traces of the Trinity. In perception we find the object seen, vision, and the attention of the mind that fixes images in our mind. Moving a step higher, we find that conception involves three things—

memory of sense impressions that have been placed in the mind, the
internal vision that "sees" the images of earlier perceptions, and the will
that unites the two. But these triads by no means unite us to God. Both
perception and conception are highly fallible, and neither takes us easily
beyond the perceptible world. It is only when we turn to the higher
forms of knowledge that characterize "the inner man" that we can begin
to find the image of God.

In Book 12 Augustine turns to the kind of knowledge available to us
through reason. He distinguishes the lower from the higher reason by the
terms of knowledge and wisdom: "Yet action, by which we use temporal
things well, differs from contemplation of eternal things; and the latter
is reckoned to wisdom, the former to knowledge" (*DT* 12.22; *NPNF¹* 3, p.
168). If knowledge is the active life of virtue, it can share in the image of
God only when it is united to contemplation. And wisdom, as the contemplation of eternal things, is properly speaking the perfect worship,
love, and vision of God. Nevertheless, the capacity to contemplate God
cannot be equated with the exercise of that capacity. And so Augustine
must complete his discussion of the inner man's knowledge by turning in
Book 13 to faith (*DT* 13.26; *NPNF¹* 3, p. 182):

> For we wished to ascend, as it were, by steps, and to seek in the
> inner man, both in knowledge and in wisdom, a sort of trinity of
> its own special kind, such as we sought before in the outer man;
> in order that we may come, with a mind more practised in these
> lower things, to the contemplation of that Trinity which is God,
> according to our little measure, if indeed, we can even do this, at
> least in a riddle and as through a glass.

The first step is remembering the faith. And while this is merely a triad
of the outer man which involves the memory of words, the mental vision
that recollects them, and the will that unites the two, nevertheless, if
someone "holds and recollects what those words signify, now indeed
something of the inner man is brought into action." In other words, the
faith *that* is believed becomes the activity of faith by which the Christian
begins to be able to contemplate God.

In Book 14 Augustine comes full circle. Once faith has become inter-
nalized, it is a remembering, understanding, and loving of God. We have
returned to the triad of Book 10. The conclusion appears this way (*DT*
14.15; *NPNF¹* 3, p. 191):

> This trinity, then, of the mind is not therefore the image of God,
> because the mind remembers itself, and understands and loves

itself; but because it can also remember, understand, and love Him by whom it was made. And in so doing it is made wise itself.

The distinction between the triadic activity of the mind and the proper focus of that activity upon God is what explains Augustine's insistence that a long convalescence is needed for the renewal of the image of God in us. The process will not be completed until the age to come (*DT* 14.23; *NPNF*[1] 3, p. 196):

> For the likeness of God will then be perfected in this image, when the sight of God shall be perfected. And of this the Apostle Paul speaks: "Now we see through a glass, in an enigma, but then face to face" (1 Cor. 13:12). And again: "But we with open face, beholding as in a glass the glory of the Lord, are changed into the same image, from glory to glory, even as by the spirit of the Lord" (2 Cor. 3:18). And this is what happens from day to day in those that make good progress.

What Augustine means is that our growth in the capacity to love and to know God is the process by which God's grace renews his image in us. And the goal of the process is the vision of God.

What does Augustine mean by saying that the destiny of the saints is the face-to-face vision of which St. Paul speaks? The impression conveyed by the use of 1 Corinthians 13:12 at a number of points in *De Trinitate* is that to see God face to face is to perceive his presence in the image of God finally perfected in the elect. The same idea is expressed in the next to last chapter of *The City of God* (*CG* 22, 29; PC, p. 1087):

> ... perhaps God will be known to us and visible to us in the sense that he will be spiritually perceived by each one of us in each one of us, perceived in one another, perceived by each in himself; he will be seen in the new heaven and the new earth, in the whole creation as it then will be. ...

We can, I think, take this idea one step further without doing violence to Augustine's thought. The perfection of the saint's loving and knowing God is the perfection of the image of God in him and the basis for his "vision" of God. But Augustine can identify the human soul, the image of God, with memory (*Conf.* 10.14). And so our loving and knowing has a history. It is as we look back upon that history that we discern God's presence in our lives, a presence that has been perpetual but to which our sin has blinded us.

I think what Augustine means is something like this. Human life for the elect is a long pilgrimage or convalescence. And just as a sentence does not make sense until the period is placed at the end of it, so our pilgrimage does not achieve its meaning until we arrive at our destination. There in the City of God we shall be able to have for the first time a retrospect over our entire life. And so for the first time we shall see that all our loving and knowing was informed by the presence of God. The perfection of our loving and knowing will be accompanied by the perfection of our remembering. And God's presence is the proper object of all three activities. Moreover, we shall not only see our own lives this way, we shall see one another in the same light. The pilgrimage of the Christian life is, then, a constant struggle to remember, to know, and to love. But these activities will find their completion only in the Christian destiny. Then the image of God will be achieved. Then no clouds will obscure our vision of God's presence. The broken lights that characterize our perceptions of God's redeeming work in this present order will be united in the face-to-face vision for which we now yearn.

As I suggested earlier, Augustine's articulation of Christian experience is both like and unlike that of Irenaeus and Nyssa. Like the other two figures I have discussed he finds himself delivered by Christ and made a partaker of Christ's victory. And like them he sees the Victor as the hero of a story that begins with Creation, continues with the election and history of Israel, culminates in the Incarnation, and finds its consummation in the new age. Unlike them, however, Augustine seeks to articulate his own experience. This means, in the first instance, that he is more concerned with salvation than with the Saviour, more interested in the effect of the Christian story than in the story itself. As well, since his experience is of a Christian life that must be distinguished from Christian destiny, his emphasis is upon the Christian hope rather than upon its fulfillment and upon our anticipation of the age to come, not our participation in it. It is for this reason that Augustine's Christian is a pilgrim set upon a journey that has not reached its goal and a convalescent who has received the medicine of salvation but who awaits his final cure in the City of God. These differences tend to separate Augustine from the other Fathers of the Church, but they are precisely the differences that make him seem more familiar to us. The impact of Augustine upon all of Western theology can best be understood by realizing that when we read him, it is as though we have come home.

II

Mended Lives

4

The Family

Fellini implied of his film *The Satyricon* that it was a journey into space.[1] What he meant was that trying to portray Petronius' first-century novel was an exercise in imagination. And it is helpful to remember that reconstructing what life was like in late antiquity is a kind of science fiction; or, we could say, it is a little like what a paleontologist does by taking a few bones and teeth and drawing us the picture of a dinosaur. Our information about the ancient world is similarly incomplete. The literary evidence, of course, derives from what we should call the upper classes, which makes it hard to understand what life was like for the masses. Moreover, it seldom occurs to people to describe the accepted conventions of a society: Commonplaces rarely receive comment. So it is that we must read between the lines to imagine the ordinary conditions of life. But it is not merely that our evidence of the ancient world is partial; our own conventions often create mental blocks for us in trying to understand the ancient world. What would a world be like without the automobile or electricity, to say nothing of the telephone?

Even though we can never be sure of our conclusions, there are ways of doing what Fellini did in his film.[2] I can remember walking through the ruined streets of ancient Ostia, the port of Rome, late on a summer afternoon. What struck me was the obvious difference in scale between that world and ours. It is no large task to walk from one end of Ostia to the other. Even the two major streets (the *cardo* and the *decuman*) seem cramped and narrow. The widest streets in ancient Rome were only twenty-one feet across. And so soon as one leaves the major streets one encounters rabbit warrens of small alleys with buildings crowded in upon one another. The private house was clearly exceptional. We know from a description of Rome carefully compiled under Constantine between 312 and 315 that has been preserved in two later versions (the *Regionaries Notitia* and *Curiosum*) that this was true in Rome. There were only 1,797 private dwellings (*domus*), while there were 46,602 *insulae* or apartment houses. That means a ratio of roughly one house to every twenty-five apartment buildings. The *insulae* were commonly three stories and often were five or six stories. Fires and collapsing buildings were common hazards of urban life.

The impression forces itself upon us that ancient urban life was cramped. Populations were not large by our standards.[3] Rome may have had a million inhabitants in the early fourth century, while Pompeii in the first century seems to have had a population of roughly 20,000. But these populations were compact and local. In a large city, as is to some degree still true today, the operative social unit was the quarter. Rome must almost have been a federation of smaller, more manageable "cities," just as the Empire itself was really a federation of city states throughout the Mediterranean. We forget how the automobile and modern transportation have affected the way we build our cities and suburbs. If life was cramped in the ancient world, the public places of a city supplied some relief. In ancient Ostia it is pleasant to emerge from the twisted back alleys into the forum, the amphitheater, the baths, or the temples. These public spaces gave people room, and it is obvious that much of ancient life took place in the open and in public. Any traveler to the Mediterranean who has walked towards the public square after the afternoon siesta can imagine how a city like Ostia worked.

If the scale of space differed from what we are used to, so did the scale of time. There were twelve hours in the day, but these were equal divisions made between sunrise and sunset. Thus, an hour was shorter in winter than in summer. Moreover, the nine to five day did not exist. We may suppose that people worked, but there were many of the very rich and the very poor who did not. And public spectacles and holidays occupied more of the year's time than we should find reasonable: Marcus Aurelius, toward the end of the second century, limited the number of festival days so that 230 days were left for business. Time would also have been a factor in traveling. In one sense travel was easy during the Empire. To this day one can immediately tell when he has hit upon a Roman road in England by the surprising disappearance of twists and turns. The roads went everywhere, and a system of imperial stations where houses and provisions for a journey were available was established; even so, a carriage could succeed in covering only forty or fifty miles a day. And the sea voyage from Alexandria to Puteoli in Italy took twelve days. It was not a world of instant travel or communication.

The point of what I have said is merely to remind us that the family in late antiquity existed in a physical and social context quite different from ours. And the same thing needs to be said about the family itself. Indeed, there is no word in either Latin or Greek that quite corresponds to our word "family." The *familia* in the Roman world was the household, and that is what the Greek words *oikos* and *oikia* also often mean. And by household we must mean not only husband, wife, and children, but also slaves and clients. Trimalchio, the wealthy freedman satirized by Petronius in the *Satyricon*, had four hundred slaves. This is clearly meant to be a large number, and we cannot suppose that everyone owned slaves. Moreover, many slaves must have been agricultural workers on the large estates in the country. Slaves were commonly freed, particularly by the owner's will upon his death; they could also purchase their freedom. This meant that there was a large class of freedmen; indeed, the early imperial civil service was really the emperor's household, with freedmen holding the important positions. If slaves and freedmen occupied the lowest strata in society, the senatorial and equestrian classes were at the top of the pyramid. And in the provincial cities the members of the municipal curia formed a local aristocracy.

The *paterfamilias* ruled the Roman household. In principle, his authority was absolute over his wife and children, as well as over his slaves. Women were subject to their fathers or, upon marriage, to their husbands. But it should also be noted that in theory sons also possessed no rights of their own to property while their fathers remained alive. Obviously, in practice these customs came to be qualified, and a good deal of autonomy was given to those who in principle remained subject to the *paterfamilias*. Patronage was extremely important, and the relation between client and patron formed the very fabric of society. The patron not only supplied money and some of the physical needs of his clients in return for their support, he also acted as a kind of judge for them. We cannot understand the role of bishops in the ancient Church without seeing that they were the patrons of their people. Hippolytus, for example, writing at the beginning of the third century, tells us that Callistus, who later became bishop, was responsible for helping Pope Zephyrinus take care of the banking needs of the Christians in Rome. The early house churches in Rome and elsewhere were in all likelihood the houses of those who chose to become patrons of the Church. And the early catacombs were often the family cemeteries of such patrons.

One extremely appealing glimpse into ancient family life is afforded by a Roman schoolboy's description of his day's routine, an essay dating to the beginning of the third century and included in one of the bilingual school manuals known as *Hermeneumata Pseudodositheana*.[4] The day begins when the boy summons the slave to open his window and bring his clothes. Then:

> As soon as I have put my shoes on I take a towel—I have been brought a clean one. Water is brought to me in a jug so that I can wash. I pour some of it over my hands and face into my mouth; I rub my teeth and gums; I spit out, blow my nose and wipe it, as any well brought-up child should.

After greeting his parents, he goes to school with his pedagogue. School is interrupted by lunch, and the day ends as follows:

> I must go and have a bath. Yes, it's time. I go off; I get myself some towels and I follow my servant. I run and catch up with the others who are going to the baths and I say to them one and all, "How are you? Have a good bath! Have a good supper!"

We do not meet a modern child in a modern family, but somehow it does not seem absolutely foreign to us. The real difference is that what we should think of as family life is set in the larger context of the household.

MARRIAGE AND THE FAMILY IN THE NEW TESTAMENT

Needless to say, the New Testament writers give us no extended descriptions of the Christian family, and we are forced to read between the lines to come to any conclusions.[5] But the striking feature of what we do find is that there is no one attitude towards the family. There are some passages which betray a hostile attitude and, indeed, a rejection of marriage and of the family. Other statements can be found that suggest the Church has become a new household for Christians. And, finally, several of the New Testament writers uphold the family as a human good and seek to ensure that families bring credit on Christianity by being well ordered. All three of these attitudes reflect differing notions of how the Gospel is supposed to alter and to shape family life. In other words, Christianity brings some sort of change to the family as the early Christians knew it. And whether they had been Jews or Gentiles these Christians knew only a patriarchal society and a family that was a household, including more than parents and children. The puzzling part of what we find is the obvious contradiction between attitudes that now reject, now supplant, and now affirm the family.

In one sense, what appears to be a hostile attitude towards the family may be in the first instance merely a recognition of one possible consequence of following Jesus. Matthew 19:29 has Jesus say: "And every one who has left houses or brothers or sisters or father or mother or children or lands, for my name's sake, will receive a hundredfold, and inherit eternal life." All this needs to mean is that following Jesus sometimes means the renunciation of a person's old life, including his family. In parenthesis we should note that Luke's version of this saying (Lk. 18:29) focuses on the family by substituting "household" for "houses," by omitting "lands," and by adding "wife." But it does begin to look as though the renunciation of one's family is more than merely a possible consequence of becoming a Christian. Christ has come to bring a "sword" of "division" to set the members of a family against one another (Mt. 10:34–39, Luke 12:51–53, cf. 10:21, Mk. 13:12, Micah 7:6). The impact of the Gospel shatters the family and can even lead the unconverted members to hand their Christian relatives over to persecution. The true Christian, therefore, can call no one his father on earth (Mt. 23:9) and must even refuse to bury his own father (Mt. 8:21–22, Lk. 9:59). What begins as a description of the sort of thing that can happen to the Christian comes close to being given the force of a moral imperative. It is not just that one *may* have to renounce one's family. The renunciation becomes an obligation. And there are signs that Matthew, at any rate, approves of a Christian asceticism that would do away with marriage altogether. It is possible to become a eunuch "for the sake of the kingdom of heaven" (Mt. 19:12).[6]

This attitude seems certainly connected with ideas about the new age that must have derived in some measure from Judaism. In the age to come "they neither marry nor are given in marriage, but are like the angels in heaven" (Mk. 12:25, Mt. 22:30, Lk. 20:35). Jesus' answer to the Sadducees not only affirms the reality of the new age after the general resurrection but also defines it as abolishing the need for protection and for the family as he knows it. It is this idea that lies behind the principle St. Paul enunciates in Galatians 3:28: "There is neither Jew nor Greek, there is neither slave nor free, there is neither male nor female; for you are all one in Christ Jesus." This statement almost certainly represents an interpretation of Baptism that St. Paul adopts from the tradition to which he committed himself at his own Baptism, and its meaning has primary reference to the age to come. The conventions of this world order, national, economic, and social, are regarded as dividing people

from one another rather than as uniting them, even though it seems odd
to think of marriage as in principle divisive. But in the age to come all
divisions will be removed and all united in Christ. Thus linked to the
future, the abolition of the distinction between male and female must
have been harmless. But if Christians in some sense already participate
in the new age here and now, what would "neither male nor female"
mean? It is clear from 1 Corinthians 7 that there were those who took
the principle quite seriously and thought that what it meant for them
was not merely an insistence upon the equality of men and women, but
also the abolition of marriage and of sexual intercourse. Thus, to follow
Christ meant to renounce the family altogether. And let me note in
passing that this attitude is rooted in Jewish ideas about the age to come
rather than in Greek ideas about the body and its value.

There is, however, a more positive implication of the principle that in
Christ national, economic, and sexual divisions are overcome. The unity
of believers in Christ establishes the new family of the Church. St. Paul
can speak of himself metaphorically as the father of the Christian communities he founded (1 Thess. 2:11, 1 Cor. 4:14, Gal. 4:19). The unity
that ought to obtain among Christians is emphasized throughout Paul's
letters. By dividing into factions, he warns, the Christians in Corinth run
the risk of denying that they have all been baptized in Christ and have
been given equal participation in the Spirit (1 Cor. 1:10, 12:13). The
"weak" and the "strong" in Rome are exhorted to be united in love (Rom.
14–15). The same insistence on the unity of Christians in Christ pervades John's Gospel, and dominates the Supper Discourses (John 13–17).
The new commandment is that Jesus' disciples love one another as he
has loved them (John 13:34), and the metaphor of the vine (John 15)
shows how Christians are organically bound to one another as branches
of Christ, who is the vine. The family is, as well, a category by which
John expresses the theme of unity in Christ. Towards the end of the
Passion narrative (19:17–30) John tells the story of Jesus' death so that it
may be understood in an "earthly" or a "heavenly" way. From an earthly
point of view Pilate writes the title to indicate the charge on which Jesus
is being executed. The soldiers, as was customary, take Jesus' clothing
and divide it, casting lots for his seamless robe. There follows the moving scene of the dying man making provision for his mother and his
beloved disciple by asking them to treat one another as mother and son.
He thirsts and is given a sponge full of vinegar. He says "it is finished"
and dies. John means us to see, however, that these earthly events have a
heavenly meaning. The title, written in Hebrew, Latin, and Greek, identifies Christ as the universal king, while the seamless robe suggests his
priesthood. His work is to create a new family not based on blood ties,

but on his divine creative command. Once that work has been accomplished, he calls for the cup of death and proclaims the verdict "my work has been perfected."[7]

Of course, the family is only one metaphor for the Christian community, which can be thought of as a temple, a body, or a flock under the true Shepherd. But it is a metaphor that vividly expresses what the early Christians must have experienced. Many of them must have had no place to belong. In particular, we hear of widows and orphans brought under the protection of the Church (Acts 6:1, 1, Tim. 5:3ff., James 1:27). For those who had no family the Church supplied the protection and nurture they would otherwise have lacked. The Church was their family. And even for those who did live in families, the patronage of the Church put them under the *paterfamilias*, Christ. It may be that this is what Mark has in mind in his version of Matthew 19:29, the verse with which I began this discussion. Mark 10:29–30 has Jesus say:

> Truly, I say to you, there is no one who has left house or brothers or sisters or mother or father or children or lands, for my sake and for the gospel, who will not receive a hundredfold now in this time, houses and brothers and sisters and mothers and children and lands, with persecutions, and in the age to come eternal life.

The loss of one's family will be more than made up for by incorporation into the new family of the Church, even though this reward will be attended by persecution. Christians are those who can call one another brother and sister.

To think of the Church as a new family might imply the abolition of the family in any ordinary sense. But it is quite possible to understand the conviction not as a rejection of the family but as an enriching of it. Existing households would not necessarily be broken up; on the contrary, by being united with the greater household of the Church they would find themselves transformed. Several times in Acts Luke tells us of the conversion of entire households (Acts 10:2; 11:14; 16:15; 31; 18:8; cf. 1 Cor. 1:16). Far from breaking these families up, the Gospel aims at confirming them. That this point of view was a common one finds its support in the fact that Hellenistic Jewish "rules for households" (*Haustafeln*) are repeated in Ephesians 5:21ff., Colossians 3:18ff., and 1 Peter 2:18ff. The duties of husbands, wives, children, and slaves are defined in such a way that the household may function in an orderly and decent fashion. To some degree, the theme reflects the Jewish attitude towards the family. In classical Judaism rabbis were obliged to be married, and it is clear that family life is thought to be the norm. As it is put in the

Christian context of the Epistle to the Hebrews: "Let marriage be held in honor among all, and let the marriage bed be undefiled" (Hebr. 13:4). But the rules for households doubtless functioned in another way. Good order in the family would impress unbelievers just as disorder would bring reproach upon the Church. In 1 Peter Christians are told to "keep your conscience clear, so that, when you are abused, those who revile your good behavior in Christ may be put to shame" (1 Peter 3:16).

In one sense the attitude I am describing simply affirms the value of the family and seeks to reinforce the ideals of the wider society for family life. But there is at least one passage in the New Testament that suggests Christians could go further and think of Christ as transforming the family. In 1 Corinthians 7:4 St. Paul argues that the husband rules over his wife's body *and* that the wife rules over her husband's body. The first part of his statement would have caused no surprise, since both Roman and Jewish societies were patriarchal and treated women as inferior. The second part is a radical disavowal of all social norms and precedents of the time. A Christian marriage, then, is distinct because the partners are treated as equals. The conventions of our society, at least as commonly stated, blind us to the shock of St. Paul's view. But there can be no doubt that in the ancient world it would have clarified how Christ transforms human social relations. The context of this view of what a Christian marriage ought to be suggests that St. Paul is worrying with the question of what it means in the present age to anticipate the norm of the age to come that insists "there is neither male nor female." Some of the Corinthians had taken the principle literally, making no distinction between their present and their future participation in the new age. As a result, they repudiated their sexuality, the family, and marriage and lived together as spiritual brothers and sisters. St. Paul does not deny that this is one possible way of affirming the principle, but warns the Corinthians that they are not yet living in the new age in fact and are still subject to "the temptation to immorality" (1 Cor. 7:2) and insists that a Christian marriage is as valid as celibacy as a way of anticipating the new order.

The difficult question, of course, is the way and degree to which the norms of the age to come can transform the social conventions of the old order. People do not cease being Jews or Greeks, males and females simply because of Christian hope. And it is even doubtful that St. Paul in sending Onesimus back to Philemon expects that the two will no longer be slave and master. St. Paul's concern is not with abolishing national identity, marriage, and slavery. Instead, he is concerned that the character of these institutions be seen in a new light. Philemon must receive his slave "no longer as a slave but more than a slave, as a beloved brother" (Philemon 16). The important change effected by Christ has to do with attitudes. What matters is that Christians are brothers and sisters in the family of Christ and not whether they are Jews or Greeks, married, or slaves. In some respects, of course, this conviction betrays itself outwardly. Nowhere is this more clearly seen than in St. Paul's attitude toward women. Their equality in marriage is echoed in their equal participation in Christian worship. Women must be veiled, not as a sign of their inferiority, but to reveal to the evil angels of the old order the honor of their new status in Christ.[8] The only passage in the genuine letters of Paul (assuming he did not write Ephesians) that argues against what I have said is 1 Corinthians 14:34–35. But that passage not only contradicts Paul's recognition elsewhere in the letter that women *do* speak in the church, but it also appears in different places in different ancient manuscripts of the New Testament. And so the order that women be silent in church looks like a gloss added to Paul's text to make his view accord with a less radical one that would subscribe to the patriarchal conventions of Roman society.

In sum, we need to recognize that the New Testament treats no one attitude toward the family as normative. In a sense, regarding the Church as the Christian's true family dominates the picture we can deduce from the different writings. But this does not really settle the question because to treat the Church as one's family might imply either the rejection or the affirmation of one's own family. As well, the ambiguity we have discovered is affected by the double character of the Christian's life in this age. By the facts of the matter the Christian is still living in the old order of things, but by hope and promise he is a new creature in Christ. And exactly what this novelty of life means is not easy to decide. The mending of lives took the form of celibacy, but it also took the form of marriage and family life. As we shall see, the ambiguity does not disappear after the New Testament. The differing attitudes, together with the problem of implementing a new ideal, persist in the Church.

CHRISTIANITY AND ROMAN SOCIETY BEFORE CONSTANTINE

Let me begin by saying something about the way Christianity appeared in the Roman Empire and by arguing that the ambivalent attitude to which reference has been made is reflected in what we can know of the actual impact of Christianity upon marriage and the family. The Roman historian Tacitus, writing toward the end of the first century, argued that the Christians were easy scapegoats for Nero to blame for the great fire of Rome in 64 because they "hated the human race." On this evidence, ordinary Romans perceived the Christians as people who rejected everything that made life human—the theater, the baths, and even the ordinary human ties of society and family. Justin Martyr in his *Second Apology* (ca. 155) gives us a concrete instance of one way Christianity actually broke up a family. A woman who had lived an unchaste life was converted to Christ; and after reforming her own life, she attempted to reform her husband's. Failing in her attempt, she divorced him; the husband became a persecutor of her Christian teacher.

About 170 C.E. the pagan philosoper Celsus attacked Christianity in his book *The True Word*, and it is likely that Justin Martyr was the chief object of his attack. Celsus' arguments against Christianity are in large part theoretical in character, but they include ad hominem attacks against the Christians as uncultured and immoral. Indeed, it would appear that the raw nerve in Celsus struck by the Christians is his loyalty to the *mos maiorum*, to his own cultural heritage. He portrays the Christians as disruptive of the bonds of society, including family ties (*CC* 3.55, Chadwick, pp. 165f.):

> In private houses also we see wool-workers, cobblers, laundry-workers, and the most illiterate and bucolic yokels, who would not dare to say anything at all in front of their elders and more intelligent masters. But whenever they get hold of children in private and some stupid women with them, they let out some astounding statements as, for example, that they must not pay any attention to their fathers and school-teachers, but must obey them. . . . And if just as they are speaking they see one of the school-teachers coming, or some intelligent person, or even the father himself, the more cautious of them flee in all directions; but the more reckless urge the children on to rebel.

The "hatred of the human race" that characterizes the Christians means among other things for Celsus that they disrupt family life.

Origen, writing to refute Celsus in the middle of the third century, does not deny the charge outright, but argues that it cannot apply to virtuous teachers and fathers. His refutation suggests that Christian belief and teaching takes priority over cultural ties, even those of the family. But he does not mean to suggest that Christianity is incompatible with those ties (*CC* 3.56; Chadwick, p. 166):

> But let Celsus show us what prudent father or what teachers who teach noble doctrines we have made children and women to leave. And let him consider the women and children before and

after their conversion to our faith, to see whether the doctrines
which they used to hear are better than ours.

In principle, then, Christianity is not opposed to the family, but it does
hold up a moral and spiritual ideal that is more important than the
family. And Origen implies, as well, that the issue of the family is not
whether it is good in itself, but whether it supports the Christian ideal.
Celsus' charge against the Christians, then, is not so much refuted as
deflected.

This insistence upon the Christian ideal often led in the early Church
to martyrdom. It is here that we can see most clearly the conflict between Christianity and Roman society. To be sure, the early persecutions
seem to have been the result of popular prejudice against the Christians.
This peculiar people was readily blamed for any disaster, whether it was
famine, plague, or the great fire of Rome. By the middle of the third
century popular prejudice against the Christians as haters of humanity
waned; and when Decius in 250 and Diocletian in 303 issued edicts
which had the effect of putting Christians outside the law, their mea-
sures were no longer consistently and rigorously enforced by local officials or supported by so widespread a popular feeling as in the early
period. Yet however sympathetic one may be to early Christianity, it is
impossible to avoid the conclusion that persecution was a natural response to it and that the popular prejudice against Christians had a basis
in fact. The Roman world rightly saw that one possible implication of
Christianity was a rejection of the social order. And there were some
Christians who drew this conclusion with strict logic.

The most obvious example comes from the opening years of the third
century. Perpetua was the daughter of a wealthy man in North Africa,
but became a Christian and was arrested. Her father tried to dissuade
her from confessing Christianity, but Perpetua responded by saying that
she could not be anything other than what she was, a Christian (*ACM*, p.
109):

> At this my father was so angered by the word "Christian" that he
> moved towards me as though he would pluck my eyes out. But he
> left it at that and departed, vanquished, along with his diabolical
> arguments.

Perpetua's father did not give up, but returned with baffled love and
anguished incomprehension. Perpetua pitied him, but remained loyal, "a
bride of Christ."

The martyr attitude was problematic not only for Roman society, but also for the Church. And we find an increasing reaction against those who sought out martyrdom. Clement and Origen in Alexandria strove to cut a middle path between some Gnostic Christians who denied the value of martyrdom altogether and fanatics like the Montanists who rushed to it. The problem was how to maintain a balance between an exclusive loyalty to Christ and the open attitude towards society required by his mission. And, as Gregory Nazianzen puts it in his panegyric on Basil the Great, the rule of martyrdom came to forbid Christians "voluntarily to go to meet it (in consideration for the persecutors and for the weak) or to shrink from it if it comes upon" them (*NPNF*[2] 7, p. 397). More specifically, Origen considers the problem of the martyr's family in his *Exhortation to Martyrdom*, written in 235. He is addressing Ambrose and Protoctetus, and Ambrose has a wife and children. Following Matthew 19:27–29 Ambrose must forsake his family, "breaking apart such bonds and fashioning wings" for himself (*EM* 15; CWS, p. 52). He must hate his wife and children, his brothers and sisters in order to help the ones he hates "by becoming a friend of God through that very hatred and so receiving the freedom to benefit them" (*EM* 37; CWS, p. 69). What Origen means is that Ambrose's example in confessing Christ affords the possibility that his children will be moved by his example and follow it, thereby becoming Ambrose's children and not merely his "seed." That is, martyrdom becomes not so much a rejection of his family by Ambrose as a transformation of it. The Christian ideal creates a new and better family not based on blood ties, and it transforms Ambrose's own family.

What I am suggesting is that the rejection of the family that often characterized Christianity in the age of the martyrs often carried with it the notion of the Church as a new and true family. In one respect the Church was a family not only in theory but in practice. As we have seen, the New Testament shows us that from the earliest times the Church took under its protection widows and orphans, and there seems also to have developed an institutionalization of virgins, single women who found their family in the Church. We cannot be sure exactly what happened, but by the middle of the third century we discover a polemic in East and West against the virgins *subintroductae*.[9] Apparently, single women often lived in clerical households, and the arrangement came to have a spiritual and ascetic meaning. One is reminded of Paul's problem in Corinth. At any rate, two letters attributed to Clement of Rome (fl. 95) but really to be dated in the first half of the third century supply instructions regarding virginity. Needless to say, the author approves of what he regards as a supernatural ideal, but he insists that virginity be accompanied by the other virtues, particularly active works of charity. And he rejects communal living arrangements for male and female ascetics.

Presumably, the letters reflect a widespread practice in the East, possibly Palestine. This is confirmed by the letter from the synod that condemned Paul of Samosata in 268. Paul is accused of fostering the practice of *subintroductae* in Antioch. ". . . even if it be granted he does nothing licentious, yet he ought at least to guard against the suspicion that arises from such a practice, lest he cause someone to stumble" (*HE* 7.30.13; LCL 2, p. 221). In the West Cyprian of Carthage in the middle of the third century takes the same line (Ep. 61; *ANF* 5, p. 357). For men and women to live together in celibacy, lying "in the same bed side by side," is simply asking for trouble.

Although the Church as a novel family could be abused, it could also function not only to provide people with a place to belong but also bring them into a household spiritually tied to the new age and quite literally spread throughout the known world. Some sense of the Church as an ecumenical household breathes through the inscription that Abercius of Hieropolis in Phrygia caused to be placed on his tombstone toward the end of the second century.[10] What he remembers and wants to be remembered by is his trip to Rome. An early Christian pilgrim, Abercius says "everywhere I had associates having Paul as a companion, everywhere faith led the way and set before me for food the fish from the spring mighty and pure, whom a spotless Virgin caught." The veiled language suggests the arcane character of earliest Christianity in which the family of the Church protected believers from the hostile forces of the outside world. And this sense of family identity was more than local. A freemasonry operated by which Christians felt at home in churches throughout the Mediterranean. The mystery religions must have provided the same sort of family feeling at the local level. But it is instructive that in Apuleius' *Golden Ass* when Lucius goes to Rome he must be re-initiated into the mysteries of Isis.[11] The Church, in contrast, developed institutions that enabled it to have an ecumenical unity. By the end of the second century the Great Church throughout the Roman Empire used the same Scriptures, administered the same sacraments, and had the same ministry and Rule of Faith. As we shall see in the next chapter, hospitality functioned at the ecumenical as well as the local level to make real the family character of the Church.

The third attitude found in the New Testament also finds expression in the writers before Nicaea.[12] Marriage and the family are affirmed as good, and high ideals are established for family life. In some respects, the Church reacts against Gnosticism and its denial of the goodness of the material creation. For most Gnostics the sexual act was to be abhorred, and by abolishing procreation they effectively abolished marriage. While the Church never disavowed the ideal of virginity, it resisted

the extreme asceticism of some Gnostics. And, if the Church Fathers are
to be believed, they also rejected libertine forms of Gnosticism that undermined the family in another way. As Tertullian puts it: "Heretics do
away with marriages; psychics accumulate them" (*On Monogamy, ANF*
4, p. 59). What he means is that the Montanists, of whom he had
become one, follow the golden mean between the abolition of marriage
by the Gnostics and the permission of second marriages for widows and
widowers granted by the Catholic Church (the "psychics").

The usual attitude of the Church towards marriage at the beginning of
the third century is expressed by Minucius Felix as follows (Octavius 31;
ANF 4, p. 192):

> But we maintain our modesty not in appearance, but in our heart
> we gladly abide by the bond of a single marriage; in the desire of
> procreating, we know either one wife, or none at all.

Christians define their attitude in opposition to a profligate age, and it is
largely the reaction to the times that explains Christian insistence upon
chastity. If marriage is good, celibacy is usually thought better. But
marriage is clearly the condition of the majority of Christians, and we
find a constant attempt to impose discipline. The marriage bond is
exclusive and lifelong, and any breach of it is regarded as adultery. A
second marriage is permitted only when the first spouse has died. Administering this discipline, however, obviously became difficult, and we
hear from both Hippolytus and Tertullian that Callistus, the bishop of
Rome (217–222), introduced new rules regarding marriage. Hippolytus
puts it polemically (*Ref.* 9.8; *ANF* 5, p. 131):

> And he [Callistus] first invented the device of conniving with men
> in regard of their indulgence in sensual pleasures, saying that all
> had their sins forgiven by himself. . . . Also he permitted females,
> if they were unwedded, and burned with passion at an age at all
> events unbecoming, or if they were not disposed to overturn their
> own dignity through a legal marriage, that they might have
> whomsoever they would choose as a bedfellow, whether a slave or
> free, and that a woman though not legally married, might con-
> sider such a companion as a husband.

The first point indicates that Callistus has instituted a penitential system
to readmit adulterers to the communion of the Church. The second
reflects a change in the old rule we find in Hippolytus' *Apostolic Tradition* that a man could take a slave as wife. Hipploytus objects to Callis-

tus' granting of the same privilege to a free woman.[13] The main point I wish to make, however, is that these developments indicate a concern to affirm marriage and to maintain high ideals even if doing so means dealing pastorally with those who fall short of them.

THE IMPERIAL CHURCH IN THE FOURTH AND FIFTH CENTURIES

From the year 312 when Constantine triumphed by the sign of Christ's cross the Church occupied a changed position in Roman society. Imperial patronage led eventually to the establishment of the empire as officially Christian in the time of Theodosius the Great (+395). But the changed position of Christianity by no means resolves the ambiguity of Christian attitudes towards the family. Indeed, the government itself gave legal recognition to the Church's emphasis on celibacy.[14] An imperial edict of 320 reads as follows (Theodosian Codex VIII.xvi.1):

> Those persons who were considered celibates under the old law shall be freed from the threatening terrors of the statutes and shall live just as if supported by the bond of matrimony in the number of married men, and all men shall have equal status with respect to accepting what each is entitled to. Nor indeed shall any person be considered childless, and the disabilities attached to that term shall not harm him. We apply this provision also with respect to women, and we release all of them indiscriminately from the legal compulsions imposed like yokes on their necks.

This edict represents a drastic reversal of earlier legislation. Under Augustus and his successors the Papian-Poppaean laws encouraged marriage and the propagation of children and penalized the unmarried and childless. It was extraordinary for the Empire to abandon its attempt to foster the family. And for this reason the law supplies us with good evidence for the strength of the Christian ideal of virginity together with that ideal's implied rejection of the family.

Of course, in the fourth century and afterwards the hostile attitude of Christianity towards society is to be seen most clearly in monasticism. Originating in Egypt, possibly in a small way before 300, the monastic movement is very much the product of the fourth century. The motives and purposes of these ascetics were, of course, complex and mixed. Positively, their aim was to live the Christian life fully, to make war upon the Devil in his own desert stronghold, to live the life of angels, true philosophers, and martyrs. Negatively, the movement was in part a protest against the now public character of the Church and the consequent loss of moral rigor and purity. And at the level of unworthy motivation, there were those who fled to the monasteries as refuges from the civic obligations incumbent upon peasants bound to the land and local aristocrats compelled to discharge expensive and ruinous "liturgies" or civic obligations.

One of the chief requirements of the monastic life was the renunciation of all earthly ties. According to John Cassian in the early fifth century and Benedict in the sixth, the new monk was obliged to strip off all his possessions, including the clothes on his back; he was not to have anything of his own. Obedience to the abbot also involved the renunciation of the family. In his *Institutes* (4.27) John Cassian tells the story of Abbot Patermucius. By "dogged persistence" he had persuaded the monks to receive himself and his little boy into their monastery against the rules.[15] Once admitted, however, father was separated from child. Moreover, the child was deliberately mistreated by being ill-clothed and by being beaten in the presence of his father as a test of Patermucius' obedience. The result, according to Cassian, was that (*Inst.* 4.xxvii, *NPNF*[2] 11, p. 228):

> . . . he no longer regarded him as his own son, as he had offered him equally with himself to Christ; nor was he concerned about his present injuries, but rather rejoiced because he saw that they were endured not without profit, thinking little of his son's tears, but anxious about his own humility and perfection.

The final test came when Patermucius, a new Abraham sacrificing his Isaac in obedience, was required to throw his son into the river to drown, a fate from which the child was saved by prearrangement with some of the monks.

If from one point of view monasticism in the fourth and fifth centuries represented an "angelic" life that rejected marriage and the family together with other earthly ties, from another perspective monasteries can be understood as surrogate families. Basil the Great in the second half of the fourth century drew up rules for monasteries that were designed to harness the monastic movement to the Church and to purify it. These rules have continued to influence Christian monasticism both directly and indirectly through their impact on John Cassian and Benedict. Basil decisively rejected any completely solitary definition of the Christian life. The solitary life, he says, ". . . is plainly in conflict with the law of love, which the apostle fulfilled when he sought not his own advantage but that of the many, that they might be saved" (*LR* 7; Clarke, p. 163). The communal life was meant to revive the paradigm of the early Jerusalem

Church described in Acts, where all things were in common. The children who came to the monasteries Basil envisaged, whether as students or in anticipation of becoming monks or nuns, "should be trained in all godliness as common children of the brotherhood" (*LR* 15; Clarke, p. 175). The implication is that the Christian community is a new family, and the communal ideal of early Christianity found concrete expression in the monasteries. As well, Basil's *Rule* includes provisions designed to minimize monasticism's disruptive effect on society. Novices are not accepted in circumstances that would mean hardship for their families. Financial obligations must be discharged; slaves cannot become monks without the permission of their masters; married men must seek their wives' permission to enter the monastery.

It was, of course, not only the monasteries that became families for Christians. To some degree the local churches must have retained their character as Christian families. In what we know of the lives of John Chrysostom, Jerome, and Augustine we find that Christians gathered round these dominant figures as though they were the *patresfamilias* of households.[16] And Basil the Great's monastery in Pontus was not only located on a family estate but consisted in some degree of members of his own family. Pelagius was active in Rome among the old aristocratic families, and it seems reasonably clear that the power they had exercised as pagans continued when they became Christian.[17] And even in a more general way the Church continued to present itself as the new family to which Christians belonged. The idea is a constant theme in John Chrysostom's baptismal homilies, given in the late fourth century. Baptism is a wedding whereby the believer is married to Christ and his Church (*Bap. Instr.* 1.1; ACW 31). Baptism makes us brothers and sisters of one another and overcomes the distinctions of language and wealth (*Bap. Instr.* 3.6–7, 8.1–2; ACW 31). Rich and poor alike receive the same gifts (*Bap. Instr.* 11. 21; ACW 31, p. 167):

> . . . for in Christ Jesus there is neither male nor female, there is no Scythian, no barbarian, no Jew, nor Greek; not only is there no difference of age or nature, but even every diference of honor is canceled out; there is one esteem for all, one gift, one brotherhood binding us together. . . .

The familial unity of Christians is primarily realized in the worship of the Church. And we may question how far it translated itself into the daily lives of worshippers. The very size of churches in the Christian Empire suggests that there must have been some loss of family feeling in communities that were no longer small and coherent. Nonetheless, the ideal remains, and we need not suppose it had no effect on the realities of people's lives.

In a third respect the post-Constantinian Church retained the divergent emphases of early Christianity's attitudes towards the family. It affirmed the importance of marriage and taught a strict view of its moral obligations. John Chrysostom's sermons in the latter part of the fourth century provide numerous examples of the way in which the Church sought to affirm high standards for marriages.[18] Of course, he assumes the subservience of the wife. To the husband he says, "Govern your wife, and thus will the whole house be in harmony" (Hom. 20 on Eph.). At the same time, a true marriage is thought to involve mutual affection, a rejection of riches, and an affirmation of the Christian ideal: "If any marry thus, marry with these views, he will be but little inferior to solitaries; the married but little below the unmarried" (Hom. 20 on Eph.; *NPNF*[1] 13, p. 151). What Chrysostom is arguing is that the ideal Christian life found most clearly expressed in monasticism can also be lived in the world and in a family. If in one respect the life of the family falls short of the highest goal, in another respect it is to be honored above the monastic life. That is, the ideal Christian marriage and family is something achieved in the midst of great difficulty and grave temptation. The pilot who guides his ship through storm and tempest is more to be respected than the one who plies the tiller in a safe harbor.

We must not, however, romanticize this ideal of the Christian family. A. H. M. Jones remarks that it is strange that after Christianity came to predominate in the Roman Empire "the general standards of conduct should have remained in general static and in some respects to have sunk." His judgment is (*Later Roman Empire*, p. 979):

> If the moral code taught by the Church was not notably higher than that of pagan philosophy, it was preached with far more vigour to a far wider audience, and was backed by the sanction of eternal punishment in the next world.

Jones suggests that one reason for this failure was that the Church's standards were impossibly high, and the ideal was not a practicable one. At the same time, this broad judgment probably needs to be qualified by saying that in some cases the ideal view must have taken hold. Much more could be said both regarding the theoretical approaches taken to the family in the Christian Empire and regarding the actual conditions in which people lived. But the general conclusion seems clear enough. The ambiguous attitudes towards the family we find in the New Testament and in the early period persist after Constantine's recognition of the Church. The polar extremes of renunciation and affirmation of the family may be found. And the theme of the Church as a new family to some degree embraces those extremes by allowing Christians to see their new family either as a rejection of their old or as an enrichment and support of it. Let me conclude my discussion by raising the question of how these attitudes are related to the Church's theology.

THE CHRISTIAN IDEAL

The thesis I should now like to develop is that what the three attitudes I have sought to describe have in common is a more or less coherent religious and spiritual ideal. And the attitudes diverge from one another insofar as the ideal is thought to be opposed to society or transforming of it. Of course, we must not think of this ideal in a systematic way; nor can it be argued that there was any one definition of the Christian life in the early Church. Nevertheless, there are certain trends and broad characteristics that can be found. From the beginning Christianity was both a way of life and a message of salvation. That is, it taught an ethic showing us how to use our freedom, but it also proclaimed that God in Christ had brought us deliverance. The development of early Christian thought attempted to give articulation to these two points, and it explored their interrelationship.

In general, the Fathers insist that the ethical aspect of Christianity be made subservient to its spiritual message.[19] And if, at one level, we are obliged to work out our own salvation by living the good life, at a more important level, that is possible only because of what God has done and is merely a first step towards perfection. As we have seen, using themes that ultimately derive from Greek philosophy, the Church Fathers argue that salvation involves the perfection of the mind's governance of the body and its passions. On the one hand, the task is a moral one. The Christian must overcome and transform the passions, for example anger or lust. And the perfection of this task involves not only the stable acquisition of virtue, but also that perfect control of the body which renders it incorruptible in the resurrection of the dead. On the other hand, to use Irenaeus' language, it is the vision of God mediated by Christ in Creation, in Scripture, in the Incarnation, and in the sacraments of the Church that empowers the mind to do its task. The moral dimension finds its place in the broader context of a religious vision.

In addition, the growing vision of God comes to be thought of in Platonizing categories that derive from the *Symposium* and the *Phaedrus*. God created the soul with an appetite for himself, and as the Beloved he awakens that appetite and draws us to himself. The patterns implied by this view are first elaborated by Origen in the third century. Like Gregory of Nyssa he regards Solomon's three books as an allegorical statement of the fundamental configuration of the Christian life. Proverbs represents moral instruction, a preliminary aspect of the soul's pilgrimage that enables it to purify its vision and move towards the contemplation of God. Ecclesiastes concludes with the judgment that the entire created order is "vanity"; and this, says Origen, implies that an intellectual contemplation of our world teaches us its contingency and enables us to see that God exists and has informed the creation with his activity and presence. The last aspect of the Christian life is represented by Song of Songs. Here the believer finds union with the Word of God in love and the face-to-face vision of God. The unitive stage is regarded as our ultimate destiny; but to the degree that it is foreshadowed in this life, it is not an end in itself, but rather empowers the soul for the active and virtuous life. A balance is struck between contemplation and action. Origen treats this ideal as the true meaning of martyrdom and of prayer, and it exercises enormous influence on what could be called the ideology of monasticism elaborated by the Cappadocians, Gregory of Nyssa in particular.

Obviously, much more could be said of these themes; but for our purposes the point to be made is that they sometimes find their focus in a Christian ideal of virginity. In the late third century Methodius of Olympus wrote his *Symposium*.[20] The treatise is meant to be at once a Christian version of Plato's dialogue and a discussion of the Christian ideal. The fundamental theme is virginity, and the various speakers are the virgins who share in the banquet at Arete's estate, high in the mountains in a garden facing east and under the shade of a chaste tree. The Word Incarnate is the "Archvirgin," and his virginity is described not only as chastity but also as that by which "He preserved his flesh incorrupt." In other words, virginity is a symbol of the perfect control of the mind over the body and its passions. This control expresses itself not only in moral virtue but also in a physical incorruption that is equated with the risen life of the new age. Virginity is gradually redefined so as to mean the physical and moral incorruption that makes a person "like God." Likeness to God, a phrase borrowed by Methodius and others from Plato, "means to banish corruptibility" (1.5; ACW 27, p. 47). Christ, then, as the Archvirgin, is the first principle for this pattern of salvation.

In the eighth speech Methodius introduces a further theme pointing out the very word "virginity" is closely related to the expression "near God." *Partheneia* is almost *partheia*, "and this is significant of the fact that virginity alone makes divine those who possess her and have been initiated into her pure mysteries" (8.1; ACW 27, p. 105). The speech goes on to expound the process of divinization not in physical or moral terms, but by emphasizing the contemplative dimension of the Christian life. Employing the myth of the *Phaedrus*, Methodius argues that by removing incontinence the soul is enabled to soar (8.2; ACW 27, p. 106)

> . . . up into the supramundane regions of this life, see from afar things that no mortal has gazed upon, the very meadow of immortality bearing a profusion of flowers of incredible loveliness. And there they are ever and always contemplating the sight of that place. And hence they care nothing for the things which the world thinks good—riches and fame and family trees and marriage ties.

Methodius can describe this destiny by an allegorical interpretation of Song of Songs, where the marriage is of virgin souls with Christ. Virginity, then, has moral, physical, and spiritual dimensions and corresponds to the Christian ideal of salvation. It must be added that Methodius' tendency to treat chastity as not only physical and moral but also spiritual enables him to regard chastity as a possibility in marriage. Virginity remains a higher form of life, but its spiritual ideal may be found in marriage as well as apart from it.

The equation of virginity with salvation, as well as the Christocentric emphasis of Methodius, also find expression in Gregory of Nyssa's treatise *On Virginity*.[21] He associates virginity with the incorruptibility of God, the impassible begetting of the Son, the pure Virgin birth of the Incarnate Word, the purity of the Holy Spirit, and the presence of God. This enables him to describe virginity as salvific (*On Virg.* 2; NPNF[2] 5, p. 345):

> . . . virginity . . . while it remains in Heaven with the Father of spirits, and moves in the dance of the celestial powers . . . nevertheless stretches out hands for man's salvation . . . while it is the channel which draws down the Deity to share man's estate, it keeps wings for man's desires to rise to heavenly things, and is a bond of union between the Divine and human, by its mediation bringing into harmony these existences so widely divided.

Virginity, then, is in the first instance a way of speaking of God's saving grace. And the human response is to embrace the virgin life and so seek God's presence. That task is to begin with a moral one, and the transformation of lust to love, passion to virtue. Moreover, like Methodius, Nyssa regards the completion of the process as a rendering of the body incorruptible. In other words, virginity finds its completion in the resurrection of the body after this life.

Nyssa's emphasis in the treatise, however, is upon the contemplative dimension of the process. He speaks of lifting our longings "to that height which sense can never reach" (*On Virg.* 11; *NPNF*[2] 5, p. 356):

> The beauty noticed there will be but as the hand to lead us to the love of the supernal Beauty whose glory the heavens and the firmament declare, and whose secret the whole creation sings.

The pattern of the ascent of the soul in love to God in response to his love is elaborated by themes that derive from the *Symposium* and *Phaedrus* of Plato. The soul climbs through lesser beauties to Beauty itself. This progress results in a begetting that takes place in the good, and the soul gains wings for its ascent. Nyssa's doctrine is rich in nuances, and there are a good many tensions that might be explored. For example, the contemplative ideal is integrated with the notion of salvation as incorruption by arguing that the vision empowers the soul to govern the body and render it incorruptible. But sometimes Nyssa seems to regard contemplation as the goal rather than a means to the resurrection life. Suffice it to say, however, that virginity is used to focus both the themes that revolve around incorruption and those comprised by contemplation. In short, it stands for Nyssa's profound analysis of the Christian destiny.

In a sense, virginity becomes a metaphor for the ideal Christian life. Like Methodius, Nyssa never cuts the ties with virginity in a moral or physical sense; but he does recognize that the ideal it symbolizes can to a degree be realized in marriage. Chapter 8 of the treatise is a defense of marriage and concludes (*NPNF*[2] 5, p. 353):

> But our view of marriage is this; that while the pursuit of heavenly things should be a man's first care, yet if he can use the advantage of marriage with sobriety and moderation, he need not despise this way of serving. . . .

This judgment is made poignant by Nyssa's lament that his own marriage has in one sense cut him off from virginity (*On Virg.* 3; *NPNF*[2] 5, p. 345). And yet the clear implication of the treatise as a whole is that as an ideal there is another sense in which Nyssa is committed to virginity and has embarked on the virgin life.

Thus though the ideal of which Nyssa speaks is elaborated in terms that appear to reject marriage and the family, it is nevertheless capable of being used to transform marriage. Moreover, Nyssa does not lose sight of the communal character of the Christian ideal. Although he does not tend to find that character exemplified in marriage, it is important to remind ouselves how he conceives it. His doctrine of the Trinity is decisive in this respect. If humanity is the image of the Trinity, then just as God is a single, ineffable nature with individuation (Father, Son, and Spirit), so humanity is a single, ineffable nature with individuation. That is, the terms of "human nature" and "image" apply, properly speaking, only to the whole plenitude of the human race. And we are individuals not as separate centers of consciousness, but as relations in the one human nature, indeed, in the human nature of Christ. Nyssa's theology attempts to balance the antinomies of individual and corporate, as well as those of grace and freedom, contemplation and action, Church and world. And in principle, virginity acts as a symbolic locus for an analysis of all these tensions.

Augustine will provide one last illustration of the themes attaching to the Christian ideal in its relation to the family. He can regard that ideal as opposed to all earthly ties. In the *Confessions* when speaking of his mother's concern that he not die unbaptized, Augustine betrays his hostility to his father by saying that Monica ". . . did all that she could to see that you, my God, should be a Father to me rather than he" (*Conf.* 1.11; PC, p. 32). Examples could be multiplied, but the point is simply that Augustine was capable of seeing the Christian life as a rejection of his own family. At the same time, particularly in his mature writings, Augustine saw the Christian life in family terms. One has the impression that the Platonizing pattern illustrated by the famous "thou hast made us for thyself, and our hearts are restless till they find their rest in thee" begins to yield to rather a different view. Especially in *The City of God* the Christian life begins to appear less as an ascent to God than a pilgrimage towards the future consummation of his City. In Book 15.16 Augustine explains that forbidding the marriage of relatives is meant to extend marriage as fully as possible, allowing it to function as a way of uniting all people by social ties. And in Book 19 he uses the Stoic idea of "appropriation" in a modified form to argue for the social character of human nature. To the fundamental human instinct of self-preservation is appropriated the preservation of family, friends, cities, and finally the whole race.[22]

Although he approaches the point very differently from Nyssa and does so by taking account of marriage directly, Augustine agrees with Nyssa with respect to the corporate character of the Christian destiny. To be sure, he is thinking of a city rather than a family, but the difference is not so great as to prevent our arguing that the Christian destiny is a familial one (*CG* 22.29; PC, p. 1087):

> . . . perhaps God will be known to us and visible to us in the sense
> that he will be spiritually perceived by each one of us in each one
> of us, perceived in one another, perceived by each in himself.

Augustine has moved somewhat beyond Methodius and Nyssa. Like
them he assumes that the Christian destiny will involve incorruption and
the resurrection of the body, and like them he argues that it will result in
the perfection of our vision of God. Without losing these themes, however, Augustine goes on to give pride of place to the community. Our
vision of God will be one of God's presence in ourselves and in one
another. Is it too much to say that the perfected City of God is also the
perfected family of God?

Some support to the suggestion just made may be found in Augustine's
description of the mystical experience he and Monica shared in Ostia not
long before her death. They were conversing about the eternal life of the
saints, and together they were lifted outside themselves (*Conf.* 10.10; PC.
p. 197):

> And while we spoke of the eternal Wisdom, longing for it and
> straining for it with all the strength of our hearts, for one fleeting
> instant we reached out and touched it.

At least a hint may be found of the way in which the family is transformed by the Christian vision. Augustine puts it more soberly and theo-
logically when he speaks of love. Only God is the proper object of love; all
other loves are of value only to the degree that they are ordered under
the love of him. This means that the family, and indeed any human
relationship, can never be regarded as an end in itself. At the same time,
human loves receive their meaning and value when ordered by the love
of God. They are transfigured by him and are vehicles through which we
may find him. And so we find a warrant in Augustine for the notion that
the Christian ideal can transform the meaning of the family.

Conclusion

Let me suggest that what we have discovered in this brief examination of
the family in the early Church is the attempt in varying ways to put an
ideal into practice. The ideal finds expression in the theological broken
lights that are related in one way or another to the versions of the
Christian story investigated in part one. And what these broken lights
focus upon is the unity of all people in Christ. The victorious Saviour
establishes the basis for a new humanity perfectly in harmony with God

and perfectly united as a single body. Of course, as a destiny the new humanity waits for its consummation in the age to come. It is there that the ideal will coincide with reality and will result in perfected vision and a transfigured physical order. But as a description of what the Christian life is, at least in principle, the unity of the new humanity is a vision meant to mend and to shape the lives of Christians. And the mending and shaping takes place in a good many different ways.

If there is any least common denominator, however, it is the conviction that the Church is a family. Sometimes very specific conclusions are drawn, and we can think of widows, orphans, and virgins who find in the Church the ordinary benefits of living in a household. And at this level, as we have seen, abuses are possible and the ideal can succumb to merely human understandings of the family. The institution of virgins *subintroductae* had to be abolished for this reason. In another concrete respect the new humanity found expression in the life of the Church through hospitality, an aspect we will examine in the next chapter. Perhaps the most important experience of the new humanity in the corporate life of the Church resides in its public worship. There the ideal is constantly proclaimed and ritually enacted. Of course, this actualization of the new humanity must have been more vivid in the earlier period when the Christian communities were small and Christians were probably known to one another as individuals. But even when the Church became the predominant religion of the Empire and its liturgy attended by multitudes there must have been a sense of solidarity that truly expressed the new family of Christ.

Granted that in differing ways to experience union with Christ the Archvirgin was also to participate in Christ's family, the problem remained how to relate one's life in this family to one's life as an individual. There were those, as we have seen, who thought that belonging to the new humanity excluded the family life of the old humanity. And there can be little doubt that the early Church in general held up celibacy as somehow a higher form of life. On the other hand, the Church never abandoned the notion that the new humanity could be compatible with the family in the ordinary sense of the word. Chrysostom's attitude does not seem eccentric when he argues that the Christian (and monastic) ideal can be practiced in a marriage and a family. However much these polarities betray tensions and difficulties in living out the ideal, we can conclude that there was and is no one way in which human lives are mended.

The tensions that have been observed point towards two larger issues we must keep in mind as we explore the Christian life in the early Church. One is the problem of the relationship between a general ethical

theory of love and what ethicists are beginning to call "special relations."
That is, it would be possible to define Christian love in such a way that
particular bonds of love would be inappropriate. And thinking through
how to avoid this conclusion poses a good many theoretical difficulties.
A second larger issue has to do with the Church's relationship to society.
Are we to think of the Church as a household distinct from "the world"
or as one open to it? To put the issue in terms of the topics to be
considered in the next two chapters, is hospitality to be confined to the
Church and is Christian citizenship in the heavenly Jerusalem to be
opposed to citizenship on earth? These questions ought not to be understood as the posing of problems to be solved but merely as the stating of
issues constantly to be addressed by Christians as they strive to live the
new humanity in the particular social circumstances in which they find
themselves.

5

Hospitality

Lucian was a pagan satirist writing in the second century, and one of his targets was Peregrinus, a religious teacher whom Lucian regards as a charlatan. Peregrinus ended his career by setting himself on fire at the Olympic games of 165. For our purposes the interesting part of Lucian's account is his description of Peregrinus' brief career as a Christian. Peregrinus rose rapidly in the Christian hierarchy and was ultimately arrested for his confession of the faith (*Peregrinus* 12–13; Casson, pp. 368f.):

> Once he was behind bars, the Christians, who considered this a catastrophe, moved heaven and earth to get him free. When this proved to be impossible they went all out to do everything else they could for him. From the crack of dawn on you could see gray-haired widows and orphan children hanging around the prison, and the bigwigs of the sect used to bribe the jailers so they could spend the night with him inside. Full-course dinners were brought to him, their holy scriptures read to him, and our excellent Peregrinus . . . was hailed as a latter-day Socrates. From as far away as Asia Minor, Christian communities sent committees, paying their expenses out of the common funds, to help him with advice and consolation. The efficiency the Christians show whenever matters of community interest like this happen is unbelievable; they literally spare nothing. And so, because Peregrinus was

in jail, money poured in from them; he picked up a very nice income this way. You see, for one thing, the poor devils have convinced themselves they're all going to be immortal and live forever, which makes most of them take death lightly and voluntarily give themselves up to it. For another, that first lawgiver of theirs persuaded them that they're all brothers the minute they deny the Greek gods (thereby breaking our law) and take to worshipping him, the crucified sophist himself, and to living their lives according to his rules. They scorn all possessions without distinction and treat them as common property; doctrines like this they accept strictly on faith. Consequently, if a professional sharper who knows how to capitalize on a situation gets among them, he makes himself a millionaire overnight, laughing up his sleeve at the simpletons.

From a hostile witness this testimony is remarkable and indicates that to an outsider the most obvious mark of the Christians was their concern to care for one another. Lucian, of course, regards this attitude as proof of their folly. And while we cannot suppose that Christians always treated one another as brother and sister, Lucian's description enables us to say that Christians came close enough to attaining this ideal to be noticed for it. Hospitality characterized the family life of the Church.

If Christians were a hospitable people, the two questions asked at the end of the last chapter can nonetheless be raised. Did the common life of the Church come into conflict with the special relations of Christians to one another within the Church? And did the Church's charity extend beyond its confines to the wider society? No one answer can be given these questions. Yet on the whole it should be clear from what we have learned about the family that special relations continued to exist alongside the duties of Christians to the family of the Church. The issue that is raised will appear in fourth and fifth century monasticism, where we find an ambiguous attitude towards special relations within the monastic community. The second question proves a perennial issue.[1] When Tacitus observes that the Christians hate the human race, he gives us another pagan insight into early Christianity. The Christians often appeared to care only for one another and not for those outside the faith. They were brothers and sisters because they were Christians and not because they were children of God in virtue of their creation. At the same time, while charity does seem to have begun at home, it clearly often extended to the unbelieving neighbor. These questions, together with the issue how the Christian ideal shaped and informed hospitality, must be kept in mind as we examine some of the evidence from the New

Testament, the age of the martyrs, and the imperial Church of the fourth and fifth centuries.

HOSPITALITY IN THE NEW TESTAMENT

There is, of course, nothing specifically Christian about hospitality; but the frequent association of hospitality with almsgiving strikes our modern sensibilities as somewhat peculiar. Even Romans 12:13 ("Contribute to the needs of the saints, practice hospitality") appears to make the association. What explains it is that the first Christians simply continued the religious duties to which they had been accustomed as Jews. That is, however much Christianity came to mean the repudiation of the Jewish law with its observances of circumcision, the sabbath, and the food laws, the pious duties of prayer, fasting, and almsgiving remained incumbent upon the Christian. Tobit 12:8 in the Apocrypha shows us that these three activities were thought central to the righteous life by Jews. And in Matthew's Sermon on the Mount we find the same point of view. The giving of alms represents one dimension of hospitality, and the only difference Matthew makes between Christians and the "hypocrites" is that Christians must give alms in secret (Mt. 6:2–4; cf. Lk. 11:41, 12:33).

The giving of alms is tied to Christian attitudes towards wealth, and Luke's point of view is the most interesting one we find in the New Testament.[2] Luke's tendency is to sharpen Christ's words about the rich and to make poverty a necessary mark of following him. For example, it is not the "poor in spirit" whom Jesus blesses but "the poor." And the blessing finds a corresponding curse on the rich (Lk. 6:20, 24). The ideal portrait of the Jerusalem church Luke presents in Acts expresses his basic point of view. He affirms the duty of giving alms (Acts 3:2–10; 9:36; 10:2, 4, 31; 24:17), but understands that duty in a special way. He puts it this way (Acts 4:32):

> Now the company of those who believed were of one heart and soul, and no one said that any of the things which he possessed was his own, but they had everything in common.

The narrative that follows makes it clear that Luke is not thinking of some early form of communism. Instead, the concern of Christians for one another expresses itself in a voluntary way as the richer Christians sell their lands and houses so that they may give alms to the needy (Acts 4:34–37, cf. Lk. 12:33). The sin of Ananias and Sapphira is not that they failed to sell all they had, but that they lied about the amount of money they were giving (Acts 5:4).

Other dimensions of hospitality find expression in the New Testament. Luke's account of the Jerusalem church limits hospitality to the local community and identifies it with caring for the poor. Hospitality in this sense is what gives concrete reality to the fellowship of the church. But hospitality can also mean caring for Christians from other churches. It is evident that St. Paul, for example, was often given hospitality by being the guest of Christians in the different communities he founded (Philem. 22, Rom. 16:23). The command to entertain strangers from other Christian communities occurs several times in the New Testament. Hebrews 13:2 exhorts its readers to practice hospitality as a form of "brotherly love" (Hebr. 13:1), and Romans 12:13 treats it as contributing "to the needs of the saints." 1 Peter 4:9 commands Christians to "practice hospitality ungrudgingly *to one another*" (see also 3 John 5). The requirement that a bishop be hospitable (1 Tim. 3:2, Titus 1:8) should probably be understood in the same way. And the rule that apostles and teachers be given food, drink, and presumably shelter when they come to town fits the same general pattern (1 Cor. 9:4–14, 1 Tim. 5:18). Hospitality is not merely the charitable giving of alms, it also functions to establish unity in the Church at both the local and the ecumenical level.[3]

It is remarkable that we do not find any clear evidence that hospitality should be practiced by Christians toward unbelievers. There is a tendency to restrict it to the Church, just as "love" in the New Testament is more often than not confined to believers. Nevertheless, there are at least two passages that may suggest that Christians are expected to be hospitable to those outside the faith. The first is Matthew's parable of the sheep and the goats (Mt. 25:31–46). It is "the nations of the world" who are summoned to judgment, and despite the usual interpretation of the parable as a reference to Christian behavior, it looks very much as though what Matthew has in mind is the way unbelievers treat Christians. Those outside the faith are to be judged by whether or not they have been hospitable to Christians. And, we may argue, if pagans are expected to be hospitable towards Christians, surely Christians must be at least as virtuous. The second passage is Romans 12:13 taken in its full context. The verse itself does not envisage hospitality beyond the Church, but as the following verses show, the attitudes Christians must have toward one another must also characterize their treatment of unbelievers, even of their persecutors. For their part Christians are to "live peaceably with all" (Rom. 12:18).

HOSPITALITY IN THE AGE OF THE MARTYRS

What we have found in the New Testament remains true in the second and third centuries. Hospitality expresses itself as a charitable caring for the physical needs of Christians and, increasingly, of non-Christians. And it functions to bind the Church together locally and ecumenically. The evidence now to be examined also suggests that the Church's hospitality became increasingly institutionalized and was administered to a large degree by the bishops. It also implies that hospitality began to function in an apologetic fashion towards the outside world. Not everyone was impressed, as Lucian's reaction shows us, but there must have been those who either benefitted from Christian charity or were moved by Christians having all things "in common." The example of Christian community life was probably more persuasive to unbelievers than the proclamation of the Christian message. It is impossible to resist the conclusion that at one level the Church grew rapidly more because its common life acted as a magnet attracting people than because the Christians were effective in their public preaching.

Almsgiving remains one form of hospitality that Christians are expected to practice. In *2 Clement*, which is probably a homily from the first half of the second century, giving alms is regarded as better than prayer and fasting, the other two traditional religious duties. It is the love that covers a multitude of sins (*2 Clement* 16:4; cf. 1 Peter 4:8). Hospitality in this sense is not merely a virtuous act but functions to atone for sin.[4] The *Didache*, very early in the second century, treats almsgiving as characteristic of "the Way of Life" and cites the words of Jesus to prove the point and to explain how alms should be given (*Didache* 1.5; cf. Luke 6:30, Mt. 5:26). No one may receive alms unless he is needy, and the giver of alms must take care to bestow his gifts wisely, assuring that they are given according to "the Gospel of the Lord" (*Didache* 15.4). The way *Didache* puts the command suggests that hospitality can be problematic. It is difficult to be sure it is effective, and it can function to encourage irresponsibility. But with these qualifications it remains a Christian duty.

Two passages from *The Shepherd of Hermas*, written in Rome in the first part of the second century, include entertaining strangers as part of hospitality.[5] Caring for widows, orphans, and the destitute is linked with redeeming "from distress the servants of God" and being "hospitable" (*Mandate* 8.10; *Ap. Frs.*, LCL 2, p. 105). In *Similitude* 9.27 the allegorical meaning of the tenth mountain "where were trees sheltering some sheep" is (*Ap. Frs.*, LCL 2, p. 285):

> Bishops and hospitable men who at all times received the servants of God into their houses gladly and without hypocrisy; and the bishops ever ceaselessly sheltered the destitute and the widows by their ministration, and ever behaved with holiness.

Neither of these passages envisages hospitality extending beyond the Church, and both of them refer to two different sorts of hospitality, sheltering the destitute in the local community and entertaining visiting "servants of God." The union of charity with the function of hospitality to bind the Church together at the local and the ecumenical levels preserves what we found in the New Testament evidence.

The ecumenical dimension of hospitality is a theme to be found in *1 Clement*, a letter from the Roman to the Corinthian church to be dated about 96. The Corinthian church is praised for its hospitality (*1 Clem.* 1.2), and the examples of Abraham, Lot, and Rahab are cited to show how the virtue is rewarded (*1 Clem.* 10.7, 11.1, 12.1, 3). The passages take on special meaning when we remember the purpose of *1 Clement:* A dissension has arisen in the ministry of the Corinthian church, and the Romans write a letter urging the Corinthians to restore unity. Hospitality is one of the virtues thought capable of doing this. It is significant that the unity of the local church is presented as bound up with the ecumenical unity of Christian churches throughout the Mediterranean. The fellowship of the Church is by no means that of a club that excludes people from membership. Quite the contrary, it is a unity open to Christians from other places. An inclusive ideal of community life is affirmed, and we may suppose that implementing this ideal was no easier in the ancient world than in ours. Indeed, the more one reflects upon the association of unity and hospitality, the more one begins to suspect that the unity envisaged is a novel one, opened outward rather than closed in upon itself.

It becomes obvious that hospitality understood this way is liable to abuse and can actually threaten the fellowship of the local church. We find evidence that this was so by the early second century in the *Didache.* The rules in chapters 11 and 12 suggest that there is still a peripatetic Christian ministry of teachers, apostles, and prophets (cf. 1 Cor. 12:29, Eph. 4:11). These charismatic leaders traveled from one community to another and, as we have seen, had the right to be cared for by the local communities. The problem, of course, was what to do about false teachers and about those who abused the hospitality of the Church. The *Didache* requires that apostles and prophets be tested by the truth of their message and by their behavior. But the rule boils down to a simple way of handling the problem (*Didache* 11.4–5, 12; 12.2; *Ap. Frs.*, LCL 1, pp. 327ff.):

> Let every Apostle who comes to you be received as the Lord, but let him not stay more than one day, or if need be a second as well; but if he stay three days, he is a false prophet. . . . But

> whosoever shall say in a spirit "Give me money, or something else," you shall not listen to him. . . . If he who comes is a traveller, help him as much as you can, but he shall not remain with you more than two days, or, if need be, three.

Rules always suggest the problems people are obliged to meet. And it is clear that hospitality, though it was supposed to foster ecumenical unity, could sometimes prove inimical to the local community. We also hear in the *Didache* of prophets and teachers who decide to settle in the local community (*Didache* 13). It seems likely that the problem of false prophets was the major factor in the disappearance of a peripatetic Christian ministry. By the middle of the second century we know only of local officers, and the development of the three-fold ministry of bishops, priests, and deacons is virtually complete. The bishops become increasingly the agents of the Church's exercise of hospitality, and the deacons are given the task of assisting them in their work. And, of course, the bishops are given an ecumenical function by maintaining communication with one another. Hospitality is one form of that communication, as we can see in the letters of Ignatius, the bishop of Antioch, who was entertained by the churches and bishops of Asia Minor on his way to martyrdom in Rome at the beginning of the second century.

Despite the problematic character of hospitality, it continues to be enjoined upon Christians. Early in the third century Clement of Alexandria thinks of it as the fulfillment of Christ's commands. The parable of the sheep and the goats in Matthew 25 is interpretated as implying rules that Christians must follow (*Instr.* 3.12; *ANF* 2, p. 293):

> Come to me, ye blessed, inherit the kingdom prepared for you from the foundation of the world: for I was hungry, and ye gave me meat; I was thirsty, and ye gave me drink; I was a stranger, and ye took me in; naked, and ye clothed me; sick, and ye visited me; in prison, and ye came unto me.

Clement thinks of hospitality entirely as a moral virtue, a charity by which needy people are cared for. He attacks people who will exercise hospitality to their pet animals but not to other people. They (*Instr.* 3.4; *ANF* 2, pp. 278f.)

> . . . overlook the chaste widow, who is of far higher value than a Melitaean pup, and look askance at a just old man, who is lovelier in my estimation than a monster purchased for money. And though maintaining parrots and curlews, they do not re-

ceive the orphan child; but they expose children that are born at home, and take up the young of birds, and prefer irrational to rational creatures. . . .

The moral duty of hospitality, then, is basic to the Christian life. And Clement nowhere suggests that it should be limited only to Christians.

In the middle of the third century Cyprian of Carthage supplies us with evidence that gives us a glimpse into specific aspects of the hospitality Clement simply recommends as a virtue. Cyprian fled Carthage in 250 when the Decian persecution began, but he continued to guide the Church by his letters, some of which have been preserved. In letter 35 he instructs the presbyters and deacons to continue caring for the widows, the sick, the poor, and strangers by using the money he has left with "Rogatianus, our fellow-presbyter." What we must imagine is a fund for hospitality administered by the bishop through his deputies. At one level, the charity of the Church has become institutionalized (cf. letter 4). One particular form this hospitality takes is ministering to the needs of the confessors in prison (letters 4 and 36). We may be reminded of Peregrinus, who was so well cared for by the Christians while he was imprisoned. A second specific form of hospitality is the use of the Church funds to redeem Numidian Christians taken captive by barbarians (letter 59). However much the Church and its officers are responsible for administering hospitality, individual Christians are exhorted by Cyprian to practice the virtue. In Book 3 of his *Testimonies against the Jews* Cyprian cites Scripture to give a sanction for almsgiving and hospitality. Passages from both testaments demonstrate the importance of caring for one another. One gains the impression that Cyprian is thinking primarily of hospitality among Christians.

Some idea of Cyprian's understanding of the meaning of hospitality is given by his eighth treatise, *On Works and Alms*. He begins by pointing out that "by almsgiving we may wash away whatever foulness we subsequently [after Baptism] contract" (*ANF* 5, p. 476). The theme noted in 2 *Clement* takes pride of place in Cyprian's thinking. A religion that emphasizes holiness and yet recognizes the virtual inevitability of post-baptismal sins finds in hospitality a means of atonement. It is a kind of second Baptism that "once again bestows the mercy of God." The rest of the treatise moves away from this theme, but treats almsgiving as something that gives Christians merit and gains them a heavenly reward. Almsgiving and the care of the poor are duties commanded by God himself in Scripture, and Cyprian cites a large number of proof texts that include Matthew's parable of the sheep and the goats and Luke's account of the Jerusalem church where all held everything "in common" (Treatise 8.23, 25; Mt. 25:31–46, Acts 4:32). Hospitality is the true fast of which Isaiah speaks (Treatise 8.4; Isa. 58:1–9), and Cyprian appeals to Tobit's listing of the three duties of prayer, fasting, and almsgiving (12:8–9). He also thinks of almsgiving as a spiritual liturgy. Just as "the Gentiles" offer the gifts of their public works (liturgies) and by the display of their munificence seek to please "proconsuls and emperors," so Christians offer their gifts with "God and Christ as the spectators of the gift." And the reward they gain is not "a four-horsed chariot or a consulship" but "life eternal" (Treatise 8.21; *ANF* 5, p. 482).

One point that Cyprian make deserves special comment. Hospitality is a duty that takes precedence over one's family responsibilities; no one can be excused from it (Treatise 8.16; *ANF* 5, p. 480)

> . . . for the benefit of his children; since in spiritual expenditure we ought to think of Christ, who has declared that He receives them; and not prefer our fellow-servants, but the Lord, to our children, since He Himself instructs and warns us, saying, "He that loveth father and mother more than me is not worthy of me, and he that loveth son or daughter more than me is not worthy of me" (Mt. 10:37).

The duty of hospitality is a duty to Christ, and it is more important than one's earthly duties. Cyprian thinks of hospitality in the context of a religion of rewards and punishments, but treats it as a spiritual virtue to be exercised for religious reasons, arguing that the family life of the Church has priority over one's own family responsibilities.

In Book 7 of his *Ecclesiastical History* Eusebius gives us a glimpse of what was happening in Alexandria when Cyprian was active in Carthage about 250 and in the following decades. Two stories suggest that as in Carthage so in Alexandria the hospitality of the Church was to some degree institutionalized and administered by the bishop. Eusebius cites a letter of Dionysius, bishop of Alexandria, that gives an account of the plague which began in Alexandria about 250. The persecution of Decius was followed by war and famine "which we bore along with the heathen" (*HE* 7.22; LCL 2, p. 185). After a brief respite the plague came, the worst disaster of all, "but, no less than the other misfortunes, a source of discipline and testing." The Church passed the test, since most Christians (LCL 2, pp. 185ff.)

> . . . in their exceeding love and affection for the brotherhood were unsparing of themselves and clave to one another, visiting

> the sick without a thought as to the danger . . . tending them in
> Christ, and so most gladly departed this life along with them. . . .

A reference to presbyters and deacons suggests that the Church helped to
organize this response to the disaster, and Dionysius states that the
conduct of the heathen was quite the opposite of that of the Christians.

A second story Eusebius tells us concerns the conduct of Dionysius'
successor as bishop of Alexandria, Anatolius (*HE* 7.32). War broke out
again in Alexandria when the emperor Aurelian about 270 took back
Alexandria for the Empire. The Greek quarter of the city was besieged,
while the rest of the city was allied with the Romans. Anatolius negotiated
with the Roman general and the Greek authorities in Alexandria and
secured the release of the civilian population from the siege. In this way he
rescued not only Christians but innocent pagans as well. If we read this
story in the light of what is generally known about the period, some
tentative conclusions may be drawn. It looks as though the Christian
Church in Alexandria was effectively organized and administered by the
bishop. The Church was, in effect, an empire within the Empire or at least
a city within the city. It also seems clear that the municipal and imperial
authorities in Alexandria lost their effectiveness because of civil war and
the imperial anarchy of the third century. What is significant is that the
Church in the person of its bishops stepped into the breach and successfully dealt with the affairs of the city. Again we must remind ourselves of
the central importance of patronage in late antiquity. The remarkable
feature of Eusebius' story is that Anatolius acted as a patron for pagans as
well as Christians. As early as the last third of the third century we find a
precedent for the patriarchal authority of the bishop of Alexandria that we
find in full flower with Athanasius and Cyril in the following centuries.
Christians began to care for pagans even before Constantine, and the
hospitality exercised was in part that of the institution.

HOSPITALITY IN THE CHRISTIAN EMPIRE

Since at its most fundamental level hospitality is a moral virue that should
characterize the Christian life, the homiletical literature of the early
Church is where we may first look to discover how hospitality is regarded
by Christians in the fourth and fifth centuries. Cyril of Jerusalem delivered
his catechetical homilies in the middle of the fourth century, and one of
his concerns is to make clear to those seeking Baptism the moral demands
they must meet. Fasting, prayer, and almsgiving remain central religious
duties for the Christian (4.37). Moreover, commenting on John the Baptist's sermon in Luke 3:7–14, Cyril argues that clothing and feeding the

poor are to be understood as the "fruits of repentance" demanded by John the Baptist and the Gospel (3.8). Almsgiving is also to be understood as one of the fruits of the Spirit that believers receive in Baptism (16.12). Thus, hospitality is not only something required as a sign of the repentance that prepares people for Baptism, it is also a virtue that flows from the grace given in the sacrament.

Somewhat later in the fourth century John Chrysostom frequently preaches the necessity of hospitality. He has in mind both alms given to the poor and the entertainment of strangers. The first aspect, in particular, can be related to his constant polemic against the misuse of riches. It was this attitude that ultimately caused his fall from power, his exile, and his death. When he became patriarch of Constantinople in 398, he began a campaign to remove abuses in the Church and to mobilize its resources to help the poor. His success at reform made him powerful enemies not only in ecclesiastical circles but also at the imperial court. His prophetic voice was finally silenced. It is with all this in mind that we hear his exhortations to hospitality. To give of one's wealth to the poor is not really to give what is one's own (Hom. 2.18 on the Statues; *NPNF*[1] 9, p. 350):

> I have often smiled when reading wills that said, let such a man have the ownership of these fields, or of this house, and another the use thereof. For we all have the use, but no man has the ownership.

Indeed, it is only by giving our riches to the poor that we can truly possess them, since when used this way they purchase a heavenly reward. God did not bestow wealth equally partly because it is unimportant and not common to all like air, water, fire, and sunshine and partly because the right use of it trains us in virtue. As well, almsgiving atones for our sins (Hom. 2.19–20 on the Statues, Hom 14.2 on 1 Tim.).

If the right use of wealth is important according to Chrysostom, so is the right motivation for using it well (Hom. 14.2 on 1 Tim.; *NPNF*[1] 13, p. 454):

> Observe, the hospitality here spoken of [1 Tim. 5:9f.] is not merely a friendly reception, but one given with zeal and alacrity, with readiness, and going about it as if one were receiving Christ Himself.

To entertain strangers is to receive Christ in fulfillment of his own words in John 13:14 and Matthew 10:40, and as soon as one looks at it this way, it becomes important to perform hospitality oneself. Chrysostom's remarks are addressed to the wealthy, who could, if they chose, place the burden of giving hospitality on their servants. But even the example of Abraham argues against doing this. Abraham had three hundred and eighteen servants, and yet he and Sarah ministered to strangers with their own hands (Gen. 18, Hom. 14.2 on 1 Tim.; Hom. 45.3 on Acts; Hom. 2.15 on the Statues). And unlike Abraham we know that it is "Christ whom we take in" (Hom. 21 on Rom.). The wrong or an inadequate motivation in giving hospitality is also betrayed by the tendency of Christians to let the Church's institutions bear full responsibility for the poor and strangers. Chrysostom exhorts Christians to give alms themselves and not simply pay "those who preside in the Church" so that they may distribute the money (Hom. 14.3 on 1 Tim.). Moreover, they are not to send strangers to the Church's hostel but take them into their own homes (Hom. 45.4 on Acts; NPNF^1 11, p. 276):

> "Why, has not the Church means" you will say? She has: but what is that to you? that they should be fed from the common funds of the Church, can that benefit you? If another man prays, does it follow that you are not bound to pray?

Chrysostom in no way opposes the institutionalization of charity, but he is unwilling to see this as a way of relieving individual Christians from their own duty to exercise hospitality. And the virtue must be motivated by thinking of the poor and the stranger as Christ.

Augustine in the early fifth century has essentially the same point of view as Chrysostom. Almsgiving, together with prayer and fasting, is a fundamental religious duty (On Man's Perfection in Righteousness 18), but it is of no avail without "a true and catholic faith in God" (Against Two Letters of the Pelagians 3.14; NPNF^1 5, p. 408). The righteous are distingushed from the unrighteous not by their works but by their faith. This is why almsgiving forgives our sins only in a qualified way and only if the alms are accompanied by the greatest alms of all, forgiving our debtors and loving our enemies. Moreover, only those elected by God out of the mass of corruption are able to have this right motivation (Ench. 72–77). Augustine presses beyond the position taken earlier by Cyprian and Chrysostom. He does not deny that hospitality can forgive our sins after Baptism, but he insists that true hospitality is possible only for the elect and only if they are motivated by a forgiving love. While it is possible to be uncomfortable with the way Augustine relates his ideas to his predestinarian schema, it is important to see that he is concerned to press beyond a merely moralizing understanding of hospitality, just as

Chrysostom is concerned to avoid the limitations of the institutionalization of the Church's hospitality.

As early as Cyprian we discover that the hospitality of the Church was
organized and administered by the bishop. Little is known until the sixth
century of the finances of the Church, but it is reasonably clear that
monies were held both by bishops and by other institutions within the
Church.[6] Much of the Church's wealth was expended in caring for the
poor and for strangers. The Constantinian Revolution did not change this
in principle, but a vast difference was made by the sudden influx of
resources granted by imperial patronage and by the gifts of the wealthy
who sought to imitate the emperor. The rents of the lands that Constantine gave the Church of Rome amounted to more than four hundred
pounds of gold a year. While it is notoriously difficult to give monetary
equivalents for ancient sums, it is obvious that the leaders of the Church
found themselves dazzled and astonished by the sudden transformation,
if not from rags to riches, at least to a wealth no one could possibly have
foreseen. Abuses, of course, were common. Half a century after Constantine Pope Damasus of Rome lived in such grandeur that one of the pagan
senators of Rome cynically remarked that he would be happy to become
a Christian were he made bishop of Rome.[7] The story of John
Chrysostom illustrates the difficulty honest and zealous bishops had in
resisting the pressures to worldly pomp and power. Chrysostom would
have none of it, and his ascetical behavior as patriarch seems to have
caused as much antipathy toward him as his vain attempts to reform the
Church. All this needs to be said lest we romanticize what happened in
the fourth and fifth centuries.

The other side of the picture, however, is that the resources of the
Church were used for hospitality on a scale that cannot be exaggerated.
Eusebius, in his *Life of Constantine*, portrays the emperor as the very
model of Christian hospitality. He cared for widows, orphans, the poor,
and virgins. "It was scarcely possible to be near him without receiving
some benefit, nor did it ever happen that any who had expected to
obtain his assistance were disappointed in their hope" (*LC* 1.43; *NPNF*[2]
1, p. 494; see also 4.28, 440). Constantine was, as well, rivalled by his
mother Helena (*LC* 3.44). One form that imperial hospitality took was
the establishment of hospitals and hospices for the care of the poor and
strangers. Details of this enterprise are not available, but we do know,
for example, that at Alexandria in 416 the number of hospital attendants
(*parabalani*) was reduced to five hundred. We can be sure that this
reflects the establishment of hospitals in the major cities and that the
Church began to function as an arm of the state in administering public
welfare.

The emperors were not alone in establishing and endowing hospitals. Bishops and even private Christians followed suit. The most notable example of episcopal concern for hospitality may be found in Gregory Nazianzen's *Panegyric on Basil the Great*. Part of Basil's work in Caesarea of Cappadocia, where he became bishop in 370, was to care for the poor.[8] Nazianzen tells how he succeeded in rivalling Moses and Elijah by persuading those who were hoarding grain to open their stores during a famine (*Pan. on Basil* 34–36). But the great contribution of Basil was more enduring (*Pan. on Basil* 63; *NPNF*[2] 7, p. 416):

> A noble thing is philanthropy, and the support of the poor, and the assistance of human weakness. Go forth a little way from the city [Caesarea], and behold the new city, the storehouse of piety, the common treasury of the wealthy, in which the superfluities of their wealth . . . are stored, in consequence of his exhortations, freed from the power of the moth, no longer gladdening the eye of the thief, and escaping both their emulation of envy, and the corruption of time.

The reference is to the great hospital and hospice Basil built on the outskirts of Caesarea, better in Nazianzen's view than the seven wonders of the world. Wealthy lay people also sometimes founded hospitals. We know that Paulinus of Nola, when he was governor of Campania about 380, built a hospice for the poor at Cimitile.

One of the letters of Julian the Apostate, written in 362, gives some idea of the extent and impact of the Church's institutional hospitality. Soon after he became emperor in 361, Julian decided to withdraw imperial patronage from the Church and bestow it upon the old pagan religions. In his time it must have seemed the repression of an upstart religion and an innovation in the state. But in retrospect it looks as though Julian vainly tried to turn the clock backwards. And Julian's restoration of paganism clearly borrows certain features from the Church's organization. Letter 84, written to Arsacius, the pagan high priest of Galatia, outlines the steps to be taken in establishing paganism (Bidez 1.2, pp. 144–47). The pagan priests must be careful in performing their duties and exemplary in their lives. But since what has recommended Christianity ("atheism") most to people is "hospitality towards strangers," Arsacius is to establish "numerous hospices" in the cities. Moreover, all are to be received, since the Christians care not only for their fellow believers but for pagans as well. Julian's hostile witness enables us to see how central to the Church and to society in general Christian hospitality had become. The pagans could not fall behind the

Christians in hospitality if they expected to be able to recommend their faith to the world.

Another way in which Christians offered hospitality under the Christian Empire was through the monasteries. All the evidence suggests that entertaining strangers was a feature of Christian monasticism from its beginnings in the late third and early fourth centuries. And the Rules of Basil the Great and of Benedict build hospitality in this form into the very structure of the monastic life. One particular form this took involved pious Christians who toured the monasteries to learn more about the ascetical life. Basil himself puts it this way (Ep. 223; LCL 3, p. 293):

> . . . having read the Gospel, and having perceived therein that the greatest incentive to perfection is the selling of one's goods and the sharing of them with the needy of the brethren, and the being entirely without thought of this life, and that the soul should have no sympathetic concern with the things of this world, I prayed that I might find some one of the brethen who had taken this way of life, so as to traverse with him this life's brief flood.

And so Basil visited monks in Egypt, Palestine, Coele-Syria, and Mesopotamia and learned from their asceticism. Similar motives led Christians like Jerome and Rufinus to avail themselves of monastic hospitality. Chrysostom exhorts the people of Antioch to visit the monks in the mountains nearby to learn from them how the Christian life should be lived.

Pilgrimages began to be taken for more straightforward reasons, and by the end of the fourth century it became a common pious duty to visit the holy places in the East and particularly in Jerusalem. Toward the end of the fourth century a lady named Egeria, probably from Galicia in the Spanish peninsula, wrote an account of her pilgrimage. What she says about her reception at Mt. Sinai is typical (*Itinerarium* 5.12; SC 21, pp. 116f.):

> Of course, I ought always to give thanks to God in everything. And I wish not only to speak of the honor He has given me, though unworthy and undeserving, of visiting all those places I did not deserve to see, but also of all those holy men, whom I can never thank enough, who deigned to receive me in my lowliness in their monasteries or at least took me to all the places I wanted to see because of the Holy Scriptures.

The hospitality of the monasteries often made pilgrimages possible, though we cannot suppose that pilgrims did not also stay elsewhere.

Indeed, Gregory of Nyssa takes a dim view of pilgrimages largely because it often required offenses to modesty: " . . . as the inns and hostelries and cities of the East present many examples of licence and of indifference to vice, how will it be possible for one passing through such smoke to escape without smarting eyes?" (*On Pilgrimages, NPNF*[2] 5, pp. 382f.).[9]

The *Institutes* and *Conferences* of John Cassian, written at the beginning of the fifth century, afford us glimpses of how hospitality appeared to those actually practicing the monastic life. Cassian, a disciple of Evagrius Ponticus and a friend of John Chrysostom, was well acquainted with monasticism as it had developed in the East during the fourth century, and he became one of the founders of Western monasticism when he settled in Marseilles and established monasteries there. At one level he thinks of hospitality within the monastery as an imitation of the first Jerusalem church where all regarded their possessions as held "in common." Book 7 of *The Institutes* outlines the monk's battle against the spirit of covetousness. The evil is not one that attaches to human nature as such, and for the monk it originates "only from the state of a corrupt and sluggish mind, and often from the beginning of his renunciation being unsatisfactory, and his love towards God being lukewarm at its foundation" (*Inst.* 7.1). For this reason Cassian insists that whoever enters the monasteries must renounce all possessions. There can be no "mine" and "thine" in the monastery. Two examples from Scripture help define how this shall be (*Inst.* 7.17, cf. *Inst.* 2.5). The example of the early Jerusalem church and of Paul's collection from the Gentile churches for the poor in Jerusalem show what the renunciation of covetousness and the true hospitality of a Christian community are (*Inst.* 7.18; *NPNF*[2] 11, p. 254):

> . . . if we want to obey the gospel precept, and to show ourselves the followers of the Apostle and the whole primitive church . . . we should by no means aim at looking after our own interests, but should seek out the discipline and system of a monastery, that we may in very truth renounce this world . . . and should look for our daily food, not from any store of money of our own, but from our own labours.

It is not enough to give up one's possessions; the very desire for them must be eradicated. And this is possible only by remaining in the common life of the monastery where all are obliged to care for the others.

Thinking of hospitality in terms of the monastery itself raises the question whether to have all things in common makes all the monks the same. Cassian's insistence that the monk can have nothing of his own and must "remember nothing of [his] kinsfolk or . . . former affections" implies the stripping away of one's personal identity (*Inst.* 4.36; *NPNF*² 11, p. 231). We might suppose that all associations are forbidden in the interest of the monk's commitment to the monastery, but Cassian recognizes the importance of particular friendships within the monastery and does not think of them as necessarily incompatible with the common life of the monks. The issue is a corollary of what we have already seen as the problematic relationship between loyalty to one's own family and loyalty to the family of the Church. Cassian's "First Conference of Abbot Joseph" (*Con.* 16) is on friendship. Abbot Joseph speaks of many different kinds of friendship and argues that only a perfect spiritual friendship is lasting. Built upon a renunciation of the world and victory over the passions, this friendship unites monks in the eternal spiritual ideal that represents the goal of the monastic life. The conference goes on to consider whether such friendships undermine the common life of the monastery and argues for a negative answer on the basis of Christ's special love for the beloved disciple (*Con.* 16.14; *NPNF*² 11, p. 454):

> But this love of one in particular did not indicate any coldness in love for the rest of the disciples, but only a fuller and more abundant love towards the one, which his prerogative of virginity and the purity of his flesh bestowed upon him.

The classical ideal of friendship is in this way given a warrant in Scriptures and in Christ's own example. A special relation can actually assist one's progress towards perfect holiness.

To digress from Cassian, the Platonic echoes in this idea can be heard more clearly in Gregory Nazianzen's account of his friendship with Basil the Great during their school days in Athens. It was there that the two friends "felt the wound of mutual love" (*Pan. on Basil* 17–19; *NPNF*² 7, p. 401):

> And, when, as time went on, we acknowledged our mutual affection, and that philosophy was our aim, we were all in all to one another, housemates, messmates, intimates, with one object in life, of an affection for each other ever growing warmer and stronger. Love for bodily attractions, since its objects are fleeting, is as fleeting as the flowers of spring. . . . But love which is godly and under restraint, since its object is stable, not only is more lasting, but, the fuller its vision of beauty grows, the more closely does it bind to itself and to one another the hearts of those whose love has one and the same object. This is the law of our superhuman love.

As "one soul inhabiting two bodies" (*Pan. on Basil* 20; *NPNF²* 7, p. 402) the friends made progress in a Christian life defined in some degree by the ideal of love sketched by Diotima in Plato's *Symposium*. The Platonic ideal of love becomes the bond uniting Christians to one another and to their Lord. Nazianzen's account of his own experience illustrates the principles expounded by Cassian in conference 16.

Returning, then, to Cassian, we need to take one final step. If hospitality can be identified with the common life of the monastery, a fellowship that aims at reproducing the earliest Christian community found in Luke's description of the Jerusalem church, it can actually be enhanced by special friendships, provided they are spiritually pure. And, as well, the spirit of hospitality extends outwards. Just as the intimate character of friendship, paradoxically, remains fully open to the life of the community, so the community defines its fellowship as, paradoxically, open to the stranger. This is monastic hospitality in its most obvious sense, and in Cassian's writings we can see something of how hospitality looked to those offering it. Hospitality takes precedence over ascetical discipline (*Inst.* 5.23; *NPNF²* 11, p. 242):

> But when any of the brethren arrive they rule that we ought to show the virtues of kindness and charity instead of observing a severe abstinence and our strict daily rule: nor should we consider what our own wishes and profit or the ardour of our desires may require, but set before us and gladly fulfil whatever the refreshment of the guest, or his weakness may demand from us.

Cassian illustrates this principle by a story of Abbot Archebius, who deceived his guests by feigning to leave his cell so that they might inhabit it and by building a new cell for himself (*Inst.* 5.37). What is most striking about Cassian's point of view is that he recognizes the tensions among friendship, the common life of the monastery, and the entertainment of strangers, but nonetheless insists that the three aspects of the monastic life are not only compatible but necessary for the living out of the Christian ideal. I should even suggest that the remarkable aspect of Christian ideas about hospitality revolves around relating it to the common family life of the Church in such a way as to insist that the Christian community must be turned outwards as well as inwards.

HOSPITALITY AS A SPIRITUAL IDEAL

Discussion of hospitality in the early Church has revealed a number of problems and dangers. Obviously, hospitality could be abused. This is the way Lucian understands what happened to Peregrinus, who made a small fortune for himself out of Christian hospitality. That Lucian is by no means incorrect in his assessment of what often happened is indicated in the Christian sources. We have seen that false prophets were a major problem in the earliest period and may certainly suppose that people benefited from Christian hospitality when they were not in need. We cannot identify a modern welfare system with ancient Christian hospitality, but there can be no surprise that any form of hospitality is subject to abuse. There were, however, other problems in the early Church. We have seen something of the ambiguity that attached to establishing the common life of the Christian family. Did that life allow for special relations and did it remain open to the stranger and the unbeliever? There is no single answer to the questions. Instead, we find a set of tensions whether we think of the family or of hospitality or, as we shall see, of citizenship. Sometimes the common life of the Church came into conflict with other commitments and with the outside world. But sometimes it helped to order and to shape private associations of individual Christians and the public role of the Church in society. This tension can appear in the context of a larger one between the orientation of the Church to the new age and its location in this one. We can think of the two tensions as two questions. Was the Church to be holy and separate from the surrounding society or catholic in its openness to society? And was the Church to be otherworldly or this-worldly in its basic orientation?

With respect to hospitality the second of these questions can be related to two dangers that have appeared in the evidence we have examined. There was the real risk that in applying the ideal of hospitality to the realities of this world, the spiritual ideal would be lost. One form that this could take was the institutionalization of hospitality. Chrysostom has this risk in mind when he exhorts his hearers not to suppose that the Church's charity renders their own unnecessary. To the degree that the Church's work becomes merely institutional, it ceases to be Christian. In the writings of Cyprian and Augustine we see another sort of danger. Hospitality can be moralized as well as institutionalized. While both writers recognize the view that almsgiving can atone for sin, they both argue that the deed itself without the proper motivation is of no avail. Concentrating on the motive for hospitality is a way of trying to prevent its becoming no more than a moral act, insufficient in itself even to constitute a moral person. There is the risk that hospitality may be cut off from the spiritual impetus that makes it Christian. And it is only this impetus that can give hospitality its proper function. The virtue is meant to be not only the fulfillment of the religious command to care for the poor and the stranger but also one that defines the Christian family in its inward and outward aspects. Inwardly, hospitality binds the Church together as a community of love; outwardly, it furthers God's purpose that all be made one in Christ.

If hospitality mended lives both for those who gave it and for those who received it, it was because the broken lights of theology informed and defined it. We cannot argue that there are particular theological themes that define hospitality, but we have already seen that when the Fathers discuss the subject they do have Scripture, the example of Christ, and religious convictions in mind. And if there is one least common denominator, it is the vision of a new humanity in Christ. Implicitly in Irenaeus' theology and explicitly in Nyssa's we have seen that this humanity is meant to be all-embracing. The Body of Christ is what defines individuals, and the social character of human nature is tied to specifically Christian themes such as the new Adam and the perfected image of God. Hospitality can really be equated with the bond of love that unites all Christians in the new humanity of Christ and that, in principle, brings all people into the Church. For this reason, it is possible to say that patristic understandings of love correlate with the practice of hospitality. Making the correlation preserves hospitality as a spiritual ideal and prevents it from becoming nothing more than an institutional or moral good.

One of John Chrysostom's sermons illustrates the point I am making, since he integrates hospitality with the social nature of humanity and with love. He is commenting on St. Paul's panegyric on love in 1 Corinthians 13 and begins by arguing that "God from the beginning contrived ten thousand ways for implanting love" in us. What he has chiefly in mind is that we all spring from Adam as from one source and so are bound mutually together. This is evident at one level in the ties that bind members of a family to one another. But God (Hom. 34 on 1 Cor.; *NPNF*² 12, pp. 204f.)

> . . . devised also another foundation of affection. For having forbidden the marriages of kindred, he led us out unto strangers, and drew them again unto us. For since by this natural kindred it was not possible that they should be connected with us, he connected us anew by marriage, uniting together whole families by the single person of the bride, and mingling entire races with races.

Our need for one another presses us beyond families to establish cities and nations and, finally, to commerce among the nations. Chrysostom's argument reflects the Stoic idea that a recognition of self-preservation as the fundamental human instinct actually defines humanity in a cosmopolitan way. To preserve oneself requires preserving one's family, one's city, one's nation, and ultimately all of human society. It is instructive that Chrysostom identifies the social character of human beings with love as a natural gift capable of actualizing this character. And it is implicit in his argument that the new Adam, Christ, fulfills God's promise in Creation. Moreover, in expounding his vision of all humanity united in love, Chrysostom ends by focusing upon the rich and the poor. They have need of one another, and the rich must remember to use their wealth as Abraham did, "for all strangers and for all in need." He and Job provide examples of a hospitality that binds rich and poor together. And so it becomes clear that hospitality is a crucial dimension of the love that orders and unites the human race.

While Chrysostom's emphasis is upon the horizontal dimension of hospitality as the dynamic binding of the new humanity together, Gregory of Nyssa focuses upon the vertical dimension. That is, the new humanity for him is primarily to be understood as our growth into the corporate humanity of Christ which stands as the term of the process leading towards the new age and the restoration of all things. Hospitality can be understood as a part of this growth. In his sermon on the Baptism of Christ Nyssa speaks of baptismal regeneration as the putting on of the new humanity (*NPNF*^{2} 5, p. 523):

> But there is certainly need of some manifest proof, by which we may recognize the new-born man, discerning by clear tokens the new from the old. And these I think are to be found in the intentional motions of the soul, whereby it separates itself from its old customary life, and enters on a newer way of conversation.

Zacchaeus provides him with one example of what he means (Luke 19:1–10). The tax collector made "fourfold restitution to those whom he had unjustly damaged, and the rest he divided with the poor—the treasure which he had before got by ill means from the poor whom he oppressed." Hospitality, then, becomes a sign of regeneration and the fruit of Baptism. And as a moral virtue it stands at the threshold of the Christian life that is meant to go on from the ethical to the intellectual and spiritual stages. Although we cannot argue that Nyssa gives hospitality so important a place in his view of the Christian life as Chrysostom, we can certainly see that he relates it to his broader understanding and so preserves its spiritual meaning. It is not unfair to elaborate his discussion of why God created humanity last (*On the Making of Man* 2) by saying that just as God behaved as the perfect host by preparing everything for his guest, so his image reflects that perfect hospitality.

One furthur implication follows from the attempt to maintain the relationship between hospitality and the Christian vision. True hospitality will only be found when the dream comes true in the age to come. The forms that hospitality takes in the present point beyond themselves to a Christian destiny. The problems and difficulties encountered make it clear that our present hospitality is imperfect. Nevertheless, it does participate in or anticipate the perfected hospitality of our destiny. For Nyssa participation is the key, and hospitality, like the other virtues, plays a role in enabling us to find the presence of our destiny in the present. For Augustine, in contrast, hospitality can only anticipate the future. Prayer, fasting, and almsgiving constitute the righteousness of this life "in which we pass through our course hungering and thirsting after the perfect and full righteousness" (*On Man's Perfection in Righteousness* 18; *NPNF*[1] 5, p. 164). The love that motivates the religious duties of the present does, however, anticipate the time when it will be "increased and fulfilled,—contemplating in full vision what it used to see in faith, and acquiring in actual fruition what it once only embraced in hope" (19).

The lives mended by hospitality, then, are mended because the broken lights of theology preserve the spiritual meaning of the virtue, which becomes the mark of the family life of the Church. The community, in turn, is oriented to and united with Christ, and in this way the corporate aspect of salvation is lived out. But in that living out tensions emerge. Looking back to the preceding chapter, we can see an ambiguity attaching to the relation between the hospitable life of the Christian community and the family. And in the next chapter we shall see a similar ambiguity connected with Christian attitudes towards the state. In chapter nine I shall turn more specifically to monasticism as a concrete attempt to realize the Christian ideal of the hospitable family open to the world. And in chapter ten I shall examine some of the ways in which the ideal is reassessed when the Roman Empire collapses in the West before the barbarian invasions of the fifth century. From all of these points of view the tensions are more obvious than their resolution. The Christian finds himself faced with conflicting loyalties—to his family, his friends, his city, and his Church, to his life in this world, and to his future and eternal destiny. Perhaps the tensions ought not to be resolved, but should be accepted as a dynamic that presses the Christian forward in his life toward the final point at which broken lights will yield to full vision and mending will be completed.

6

Alien Citizens:
A Marvelous Paradox

The *Epistle to Diognetus* purports to be a Christian response to pagan curiosity about a cult that enables its adherents "to set . . . little store by this world, and even to make light of death itself" and to display a "warm fraternal affection" for one another. In chapter 5 the Christian stance toward earthly cities is described as a marvelous paradox (*Ep. Diogn.* 5.4; LCL 2. p. 358):

> . . . though they are residents at home in their own countries, their behaviour there is more like that of transients; they take their full part as citizens, but they also submit to anything and everything as if they were aliens. For them, any foreign country is a homeland, and any homeland a foreign country.

Part of what this means is that Christians, though in most respects no different from others, have renounced certain widespread practices of the Roman world. For example, "they marry and beget children, though they do not expose their infants." More profoundly, they exemplify the Pauline paradox of strength perfected in apparent weakness (2 Cor. 6:1–10). The *Epistle to Diognetus* finds no better way to put it than to suggest that Christians bear the same relation to the world that the soul does to the body. Diffused throughout the cities of the world, Christians are in one sense imprisoned and rejected by them, but in another sense hold them together and remind them of a heavenly destiny.

The marvelous paradox of Christians as alien citizens is one that finds roots in the New Testament and constant expression in the writings of the early Church.[1] And yet to find a precise way of defining the paradox either as a theory or as a description of practice is a frustating task. The *Epistle to Diognetus* scarcely supplies us with an elaborated theory. And, since the document is Melchisedek-like, bereft of any certain social setting, we have no way of understanding the practice to which the author alludes save to imagine in very general terms what it might have been like to be a Christian in a Roman city in the second century. But the problem is one that transcends understanding the *Epistle to Diognetus*. To define the paradox and to consider how to practice it was and continues to be the task of Christians at all times and in all places. In what follows I should like briefly to examine the theme of alien citizenship as it appears in select but representative figures of the ancient Church, and in two rather different contexts, the ante-Nicene Church and the imperial Church of the fourth century.

I

The Church of the first three centuries displays a bewildering inconsistency in its stance towards the culture around it. One thinks of the martyr Polycarp, confident of a higher judgment than Caesar's, dismissing the crowd by saying in irony, "Away with the atheists!" But one also thinks of Origen explaining Christianity in the salon of a pagan dowager empress. The Roman government is sometimes regarded as the obscene beast of Revelation, but Christians could also regard it as an order in which they had a stake. They were proud of their aristocratic martyrs and magnified (when they did not invent) their share in supporting the Empire. The Christians of the Thundering Legion had preserved Marcus Aurelius' army in a tight place.[2] And it was this philosopher king to whom Melito of Sardis addressed his claim that Christianity, which began in the reign of Augustus, was "an omen of good to your empire, for from that time the power of the Romans became great and splendid" (*HE* 4.26.7). Tertullian of Carthage and Clement of Alexandria, both writing in the early third century, seem to represent the two poles of the early Church's inconsistency. Tertullian tends to reject the Roman world; Clement, to embrace it. There is truth to this conclusion, but a closer look will demonstrate that both begin by seeking to understand the marvelous paradox of alien citizenship.

Tertullian addresses his *Apology* to the rulers of the Roman Empire. He begins by noting that Truth—to be understood, of course, as Christianity—"knows she is but a sojourner on the earth, and that among strangers she naturally finds foes" (*Apol.* 1; *ANF* 3, p. 17). The strangers, however, are not necessarily foes; and what Tertullian says has the possibility of being construed as a statement of the marvelous paradox. Christians, though aliens, can also be Romans and, in any case, benefit the Empire and its cities. At least this is where Tertullian begins (*Apol.* 42; *ANF* 3, p. 49):

> . . . we . . . are accused of being useless in the affairs of life. How in all the world can that be the case with people who are living among you, eating the same food, wearing the same attire, having the same habits, under the same necessities of existence? We are not Indian Brahmins or Gymnosophists, who dwell in woods and exile themselves from ordinary human life.

Christians participate in the economic and social life of the Empire and benefit it as much as anyone else. Moreover, Christians by their behavior support the moral order of society. Though wrongly accused of infanticide, they alone do not expose their children. It is the pagans who stand convicted of the very crimes they seek to fasten on Christians.[3] Tertullian's claim is that, since no one is truly a Christian who fails to meet the moral demands of his faith, "we . . . alone are without crime" (*Apol.* 45; *ANF* 3, p. 50). Not only has "virtue put some restraint on the world's wickedness," but Christian prayers have also averted God's wrath and mitigated disaster.[4] Finally, the Christian sojourners pray for the strangers' Empire, because in God's providence it has been ordained to restrain evil and to delay the end of the world (*Apol.* 32, 39).

While Tertullian recognizes that Christians are a part of society, his emphasis is upon the other side of the paradox. The strangers among whom Christians live more often than not turn out to be foes. He connects opposition to Christians to the rapid growth of the Church. Indeed, he goes so far as to claim that Christians come close to constituting "the majority in every city."[5] "We are but of yesterday, and we have filled every place among you—cities, islands, fortresses, town, market-places, the very camp, tribes, companies, palace, senate, forum—we have left nothing to you but the temples of your gods" (*Apol.* 37; *ANF* 3, p. 45). Even if we discount Tertullian's rhetoric, the impression remains that Christianity was a growing and alien power within ancient society. The reaction of pagans was no different than in the time of Nero. Christians were regarded as "enemies of the human race, rather than of human error" (ibid.), and the common opinion treated Christians as scapegoats responsible for floods and droughts, pestilence and famine.[6] It is this aspect of the matter that drives Tertullian beyond the paradox of alien citizenship. Though he begins by recognizing that Christians are both involved in and disengaged from society, he ends by welcoming the charge that Christians are enemies of pagan society and by insisting that they must break all ties with a world totally corrupted by idolatry.

Tertullian's project, then, is consciously like Noah's. His city, indeed his entire world, is doomed. The doom is evident in the pervasive presence of idolatry. The Christian encounters idols not merely in the temples but in the baths, the marketplace, the theater, the circus, the arena, and in private as well as public associations.[7] The problem is not so much how to find a place to stand in Roman society but how to escape involvement in it. The urban life of late antiquity effectively removed privacy as an option. No one could easily escape being a part of the urban life around him. For Tertullian's Christian, life is seen as a desperate attempt to escape the pollution and filth surrounding him on all sides. Christians must avoid not only the temples but all public amusements. They may not be idol makers or astrologers, panders or gladiators; idolatry, with its attendant immorality, has so corrupted other professions that Christians are also forbidden to become teachers, soldiers, or civil servants.[8] The ark of the Church alone provides a refuge, and even there the Christian runs the risk of being washed overboard before gaining access to the majestic spectacle of the universal conflagration in which all God's enemies are consumed.[9] Only the pure may board the ark, and in his Montanist years Tertullian understands purity to consist in obedience to the new moral and ascetical demands revealed by the Spirit through dreams, visions, and prophetic ecstasies.

Tertullian's attitude towards philosophy illustrates the same initial acceptance but final rejection of the marvelous paradox of alien citizenship that may be found in his attitude towards society; in the end, the paradox cannot be maintained. Tertullian begins by accepting Justin Martyr's solution to the problem of the relation between Christian and pagan truth. From one point of view there is continuity. Both by reading the Old Testament and by using their reason the Greek philosophers caught glimpses of the truth. The soul is naturally Christian, and its kinship with the Word of God enables it to find truth. On the other hand, there is discontinuity. What the philosophers saw dimly and partially has now been revealed in Christ clearly and fully. Truth is the same wherever it may be found, and all truth is Christ's. But it is only in the Incarnate Word that we find truth complete and available to all.[10] Tertullian begins with Justin's paradox of continuity and discontinuity, but he ends by moving beyond the paradox and rejecting philosophy altogether.[11] The philosophers disagree with one another because each treats his partial glimpse of the Truth as the whole and draws mistaken conclusions. They teach immorality. Socrates was possessed by a demon. One can only conclude that Athens has nothing to do with Jerusalem.[12]

It is Tertullian's attitude towards martyrdom that more than anything else demonstrates that however much he pays lip service to the marvelous paradox, he ends by failing to maintain it. The martyr in prison has in reality been delivered from the prisonhouse of the world.[13] Like the desert for the prophet, prison enables the martyr to exhibit fully his alien character. In principle, the Christian has never been part of the city in which he lived. In martyrdom the process of severing the social ties to that city is completed. Tertullian may well have edited *The Martyrdom of Perpetua and Felicitas*. Even if he did not, he would have agreed with its understanding of martyrdom. For Perpetua her prison is a palace. Embracing it involves a total and cruel rejection of her father, her family, and her city. This attitude, which contradicts the *Epistle to Diognetus'* marvelous paradox, is widespread in early Christianity. Eusebius tells us of five Christians martyred in the Diocletian persecution in Egypt. When the governor asks them who they are, they give the names of prophets. And when asked their city,[14]

> [The spokesman] answered that Jerusalem was his country (no doubt thinking of that of which Paul has spoken, "There is a free Jerusalem on high, which is our mother," and, "You have come to Mt. Sion to the city of the living God, the heavenly Jerusalem"). And he had this in mind. But [Firmilian], casting his thoughts lower, upon this earth, and inquiring closely and curiously what this might be, and where it lay . . . he answered, "It was a city to be the homeland only of the righteous, for none but those should have a share in it; and it lay toward the east, toward the rising sun." And so again he philosophized about those matters. . . .

For Tertullian, as for many other early Christians, the paradox fails. The alien character of Christianity dominates. The only city that matters is the heavenly Jerusalem.

Clement of Alexandria, a contemporary of Tertullian's, in some respects echoes the Latin writer's insistence that Christians are strangers and sojourners who inhabit cities but despise "the things in the city which are admired by others" and live "in the city as in a desert" (*Strom.* 7.12; *ANF* 2, p. 545). The Christian's city is heaven, not Athens, Argos, or Sparta; and his lawgiver is God, not Solomon, Phoroneus, or Lycurgus (*Ex.* 10). But the theme is transformed by Clement into an approximation of the marvelous paradox of the *Epistle to Diognetus* (*Strom.* 4.26; *ANF* 2, p. 441):

> But I shall pray the Spirit of Christ to wing me to my Jerusalem. For the Stoics say that heaven is properly a city, but places here on earth are not cities; for they are called so, but are not. For a city is an important thing, and the people a decorous body, and a multitude of men regulated by law as the church by the word—a city on earth impregnable—free from tyranny; a product of the divine will on earth as in heaven. Images of this city the poets create with their pen. For the Hyperboreans, and the Arimaspian cities, and the Elysian plains, are commonwealths of just men. And we know Plato's city placed as a pattern in heaven.

Christians are still thought citizens of the heavenly Jerusalem, but their citizenship on earth, though alien, is a true citizenship. The heavenly life can in some sense be lived on earth, a life freed from tyranny. Moreover, this alien citizenship fulfills the dreams of the Greeks. The Stoics, the poets, and Plato should be able to see in the Church the commonwealth for which they yearned. Like Tertullian Clement thinks of this novel citizenship as a deliverance. But unlike him he treats it as a deliverance not merely *from* the world but *for* the world. Heavenly citizenship requires not the dissolution of social ties but their transformation.

Clement's understanding of idolatry is crucial to his espousal of the paradox. Humanity once possessed "the truly noble freedom of those who lived as free citizens under heaven (*Ex.* 1; *ANF* 2, p. 172). But idolatry placed its yoke on the entire created order and turned humanity "from heavenly life, and stretched [it] on the earth, by inducing [it] to cleave to earthly objects" (*Ex.* 2; *ANF* 2, p. 178). Idolatry in its many different manifestations is "the fountain of insensate wickedness" (*Ex.* 3; *ANF* 2, p. 184). Failing to know the good involves failing to do the good, and idolatry explains the human predicament. In these opinions Clement is simply giving expression to themes that are commonplace not only in early Christian writings but also in Judaism. But he goes one step further by associating idolatry with custom. The ancestral customs of the Gentiles are idolatrous chains that bind humanity in superstition, ignorance of the truth, and licentiousness (*Ex.* 10). Custom, then, must be avoided like Charybdis or the island of the sirens (*Ex.* 12; *ANF* 2, p. 205):

> Sail past the song: it works death. Exert your will only, and you have overcome ruin; bound to the wood of the cross, thou shalt be freed from destruction: the Word of God will be thy pilot, and the Holy Spirit will bring thee to anchor in the haven of heaven."

Like Ulysses bound to the mast, Christians are freed from the lethal effects of the old songs of custom and idolatry and able to join in the harmony of the New Song, the harmony that ordered Creation and now brings the order of Redemption.

Two further themes involved in Clement's appeal to flee custom distinguish his attitude from Tertullian's. Like Tertullian he insists that Christians must be aliens, that they must break their connection with idolatry and with their ancestral customs. But the appeal to do this is a general one. All humanity is urged to embrace the freedom of the New Song. Moreover, breaking with custom does not mean a break with the world: " . . . we do not abolish social intercourse, but look with suspicion on the snares of custom, and regard them as a calamity" (*Instr.* 2.1; *ANF* 2, p. 239). In other words, the social ties of late antiquity are condemned only to the degree that they are tainted with idolatry. Once freed from that bondage, they can be used and transformed. The detailed instruction of the *Paedagogus* and the point of view of *Who is the Rich Man that is Saved?* both focus upon this theme. All things can be rescued from bondage and transformed to their proper value by being made God's. Just as the grasshopper's song completed and perfected Eunomus' ode, so the revelation of God's Word transfigures human society. The Christian becomes a citizen as well as an alien, and Clement would agree with Origen that (*CC* 8.74; Chadwick, pp. 509f.)

> Christians do more good to their countries than the rest of mankind, since they educate the citizens and teach them to be devoted to God, the guardian of their city; and they take those who have lived good lives in the most insignificant cities up to a divine and heavenly city.

The marvelous paradox is asserted by the Christian Platonists of Alexandria.

Clement's attitude towards Greek philosophy seems designed to maintain the same paradox, though it may be that it runs the risk of losing the paradox in too positive an assessment of philosophical truth.[15] Like Tertullian he follows the schema we first encounter in Justin Martyr. The philosophers derived their truth either from the Old Testament or from "certain scintillations of the divine Word" in their minds.[16] This means that they spoke truth. Discontinuity, however, is attached to the derivative and partial character of philosophical truth. Like Prometheus the philosophers have stolen "a slender spark, capable of being fanned into flame" (*Strom.* 1.18; *ANF* 2, p. 320). Like the Bacchae, who tore Pentheus asunder, they have divided the body of truth (*Strom.* 1.13). Because of this the multitude fears philosophy as children are terrified of masks (*Strom.* 6.10). But the fear is unnecessary, because Christian truth turns

the slender spark to blazing truth and unites again the torn body of
truth. Moreover, Clement agrees with Philo that philosophy is the handmaid of right religion. It was a pedagogue to the Greeks as the Law was
a pedagogue to the Jews.[17] Philosophy continues to be a handmaid to
truth by providing tools for the defense of the Christian faith. Jerusalem
is not contrasted with Athens. Instead, "because of the Word the whole
world has now become Athens and Greece" (*Ex.* 11; *ANF* 2, p. 203).
Clement's attitude is the warrant for Christian Platonism and the basis
for his attempts to articulate the Gospel in the lingua franca of his day.
As with any remythologizer, the risk is that the alien character of Christian truth will be lost.

Clement, as well, softens the alien character of martyrdom. Its perfection is not so much the completion of a Christian's alienation from
society as the exhibition of "the perfect work of love" (*Strom.* 4.4; *ANF* 2,
p. 411). From one point of view martyrdom becomes a metaphor for the
Christian life. Its obedience springs neither from fear of punishment nor
hope of reward, but from love. And the shedding of faith as spiritual
blood is more important than the mere shedding of blood. Christians are
not to seek outward martyrdom for its own sake and so "give themselves
up to a vain death, as the Gymnosophists of the Indians to useless fire"
(*Strom.* 4.4; *ANF* 2, p. 412). Inner martyrdom is required, a governing of
the passions so that the impassibility which makes us as like God as
possible is gained (*Strom.* 4.22–23). Clement does not go so far as to
agree with the Gnostics that outward martyrdom is to be rejected (*Strom*
4.9; *ANF* 2, p. 422):

> Those who witness in their life by deed, and at the tribunal by
> word, whether entertaining hope or surmising fear, are better
> than those who confess salvation by their mouth alone. But if one
> ascend also to love, he is a really blessed and true martyr.

Clement values martyrdom, but only if it is the authentic expression of a
Christian life. One should not avoid martyrdom when it comes, but
neither should one seek it out, since doing so makes one an active "ac-
complice in the crime of the persecutor" (*Strom.* 4.10; *ANF* 2, p. 423). A
via media between fanaticism and Gnosticism is established, and martyrdom becomes not so much the final alienation of the Christian as the
completed expression of a citizenship of love.

Both Tertullian and Clement in their attitudes toward society, Greek
philosophy, and martyrdom begin by recognizing the marvelous paradox
of alien citizenship. And both regard this novel citizenship as a deliverance. At the same time, both have a tendency to let the paradox dissolve.

Tertullian ends by insisting on the alien character of Christianity. In practice as well as in principle the Christian life dissociates people from the social ties of ancient society. Athens is rejected for the heavenly Jerusalem, and the martyr becomes a sign of perfected alienation from the prisonhouse of the world. In contrast, Clement's view of deliverance treats it as one not only from the world but for the world. Released from its bondage to custom and idolatry, society is free to be transfigured. The whole world becomes Athens, and the martyr expresses perfected love. The deliverance becomes a reordering of the earthly commonwealth, and the stage is set for the imperial Christianity of the fourth century.

II

The victory of Constantine at the Milvian Bridge in 312, together with his consequent patronage of the Church, must be regarded as a revolution. Yet like all revolutions it was in one sense the product of complicated forces already at work in society, and it held implications for the future that were unforeseen. It is difficult enough to understand Constantine's conversion; it is virtually impossible to describe accurately its relation to Christianity as a social phenomenon in the ancient world. It seems most reasonable to understand Constantine's conversion as his gradual commitment to the Church, culminating in his deathbed baptism.[18] Presumably, he began by understanding Christ as another manifestation of Sol Invictus, and the imperial patronage of Christianity did not immediately mean the suppression of paganism. Indeed, Christianity can scarcely be regarded as the official religion of the empire until Theodosius the Great's edict of 380, promulgating the emperor's wish that all his subjects be Christian. Moreover, Constantine's motives in espousing Christianity were related to the accepted idea of the pax deorum. To appease the God of the Christians was to gain his power in the ordering of the Roman world. That Constantine could be convinced of this must in some way be related to his recognition of Christianity's power in human lives. At any rate, we are dealing with an emperor's decision to bet on one case of what Peter Brown calls "spontaneous combustion arising from friction within a system of widely shared ideas."[19] The sort of vision we have found in Clement of a divine deliverance capable of reordering society erupted in a variety of contexts in the third and early fourth centuries. And it was a vision capable of supplying an ideology for Constantine's political and religious settlement. We find two examples of the ideology in Eusebius of Caesarea's *Panegyric on Constantine* and in Lactantius' *Divine Institutes*. And, to anticipate a conclusion, the vision of alien citizenship, to the degree that it became an ideology for Rome, lost its paradoxical character. The danger implicit in Clement's position became explicit.

Shortly before Constantine's death Eusebius delivered a panegyric in celebration of the thirtieth anniversary of the emperor's accession. His theme is one God, one Empire (*Panegyric* 16; *NPNF*[2] 1, p. 606):

> ... when that instrument of our redemption, the thrice holy body of Christ . . . was raised, at once for the abolition of ancient evils, and in token of his victory over the powers of darkness, the energy of these evil spirits was at once destroyed. The manifold forms of government, the tyrannies and republics, the siege of cities, and devastation of countries caused thereby, were now no more, and one God was proclaimed to all mankind. At the same time one universal power, the Roman empire, arose and flourished, while the enduring and implacable hatred of nation against nation was now removed.

It should be noted that the ideal is no longer the city but the universal commonwealth identified by Eusebius with the Empire. Clement's vision of a transfigured social order is identified with the political order, and Christians lose their alien character. Needless to say, Eusebius' description is exaggerated; but it is not merely rhetorical.

Eusebius compares the present to the past (*Panegyric* 8; *NPNF*[2] 1, p. 592):

> ... peace, the happy nurse of youth, extended her reign throughout the world. Wars were no more, for the gods were not: no more did warfare in country or town, no more did the effusion of human blood, distress mankind, as heretofore, when demon-worship and the madness of idolatry prevailed.

Civil war had indeed been replaced by peace and order, and Eusebius' verdict, while exaggerated, clearly has a basis in fact. What is more important, however, is his explanation of the restored pax Romana. It is the suppression of polytheism and idolatry that has restored order. Warfare was the legacy of the pagan city. By proclaiming one God, the possibility of uniting all cities under a single commonwealth was established. The pax Dei replaces the pax deorum. Constantine's victorious rule is regarded as the completion of a process whereby all nations are united "in one harmonious whole" under the one God of the Christians. The Constantinian order has a spiritual as well as a political dimension. Victory over the barbarians corresponds with the triumph over those spititual barbarians, the demons, whom pagans worshipped as their gods (*Panegyric* 6–7). The imperial fostering of Church building projects, together with the plundering of the pagan temples, is an outward sign of this spiritual victory (*Panegyric* 8, 9, 17). Constantine is God's vicegerent in securing for the world this sacralized order.

One set of ideas by which Eusebius explains this order is drawn from the solar religion employed in the imperial cult in pagan days by Elagabalus and Aurelian as well as by Constantine. Eusebius begins his oration by cleverly protecting this language from misunderstanding. The celebration is in honor of "the Great Sovereign himself," and it becomes clear that this King is God, to whom the emperor addresses his praises, and whom "the all-radiant sun" obeys. The panegyric continues by describing God's providential governance of the whole created order, a governance administered by "His only begotten pre-existent Word, the great High Priest of the mighty God." The Word is (*Panegyric* 1; $NPNF^2$ 1, p. 583)

> ... that Light, which transcendent above the universe, encircles the Father's Person, interposing and dividing between the eternal and uncreated Essence and all derived existence: that Light which, streaming from on high, proceeds from that Deity who knows not origin or end, and illumines the super-celestial regions, and all that heaven itself contains, with the radiance of wisdom bright beyond the splendor of the sun.

This rich—and Origenist, if not Arianizing—description of the Word depicts him as the true Sol Invictus. Constantine is his "friend," acting as interpreter to the world of God (*Panegyric* 2; $NPNF^2$ 1, p. 583). The emperor, then, is the *comes* of God's Word; and, as such, he, too, can be described as the sun "like his Divine example."[20] The four Caesars form a quadriga whereby Constantine is enabled to illumine the whole of the Empire. Invested "with a semblance of heavenly sovereignty," the emperor "frames his earthly government according to the pattern of that Divine original" (*Panegyric* 3; $NPNF^2$ 1, p. 584).

The hierarchical structure that is established, by which sovereignty is passed from the Father through his Word to Constantine, enables Eusebius to apply the solar theology both to the Word and to the emperor. But it is important to note that the structure itself is one that derives from Eusebius' Origenist theology. He can use that theology in an unadulterated form by employing Origen's doctrine of the image of God. The Word is that image, and human beings are created "after" the image of God in virtue of their souls. Specifically, Constantine's "reason

152

BROKEN LIGHTS AND MENDED LIVES

he derives from the great Source of all reason" (*Panegyric* 5; *NPNF*² 1, 585). The peculiarity of Eusebius' argument is that Constantine is presented as the perfect example of (ibid., p. 586)

> . . . a Victor in truth, who has gained the victory over those passions which overmaster the rest of men: whose character is formed after the Divine original of the Supreme Sovereign, and whose mind reflects, as in a mirror, the radiance of his virtue.

Constantine, then, is the paradigmatic example of a human being created after the image of God and, consequently, the perfect moral exemplar on the human level. The perfect sovereignty he exercises over himself enables him to exercise sovereignty over everyone else. The complicated and eclectic themes that Eusebius weaves together as an ideology for the Christian Empire converge in defining the emperor as the figure who binds together the heavenly with the earthly city, thereby effecting a sacralized ordering of the whole world.[21] The risk this view takes is obvious. The alien character of Christian citizenship is for all practical purposes abolished, and it is possible for the "kingdom of our Lord and of his Christ" to be *reduced* to "the kingdom of the world" (Rev. 11:15).

Lactantius, the tutor Constantine employed for his family, presents us in the *Divine Institutes* with a platform for the Christian Empire not unlike Eusebius'. To be sure, his treatise is Latin not Greek, and it depends far more on Cicero and Stoicism than upon Plato for its theoretical structure. Nevertheless, like Eusebius he insists upon the combination of right worship of the one God with the establishment of universal peace and justice. These notion he finds in Cicero's *Republic:*[22]

> . . . the same law, everlasting and unchangeable, will bind all nations at all times; and there will be one common Master and Ruler of all, even God, the framer, arbitrator, and proposer of this law.

This ideal will put an end to the war of city against city. The commonwealth to be established will be based upon a union of religion and wisdom, piety and equity.

In a sense Lactantius describes the Constantinian Empire not only as the realization of the Ciceronian ideal, but also as the restoration of the original order of Creation. The reign of Saturn was characterized by recognition of a single God and of his providence. This right religion enabled human beings to seek "all things in common" (*Div. inst.* 5.5;

ANF 7, p. 140). Once the worship of the one God was taken away, however, and idolatry substituted for it, immorality abounded. More particularly, " . . . the common intercourse of life perished from among men, and the bond of human society was destroyed" (*Div. inst.* 5.5; *ANF* 7, p. 141). With the loss of the knowledge of God wisdom became separated from religion. The state of human affairs prior to the Christian revelation, then, is described as one of fragmentation in which the vertical bond of humanity to God is broken, with the horizontal bond of human beings to one another being broken in a variety of ways as a consequence. Lactantius' implication is that the function of the Christian state is to restore the age of Saturn.

In Book 5 of the *Divine Institutes* Lactantius speaks of this restoration under the rubric of justice. Following his classical sources, particularly Cicero, he regards justice as uniting all the virtues (*Div. inst.* 5.15) and as the equivalent of the chief good for humanity (Epitome 34). His analysis focuses upon "piety and equity" as the essential and focal aspects of justice. The former orders human relationships to God; the latter, to one another. Christianity enables the Ciceronian dream to come true, because it alone teaches true piety. And by regarding all human beings as spiritually equal, it teaches true equity for the first time (*Div. inst.* 5.16; *ANF* 7, p. 151). Justice, understood in this fashion, is the perfect union of religion and wisdom. Lactantius, in Book 7, goes on to speak of the Christian hope of the resurrection and of the millennium when "the sacred city shall be planted in the middle of the earth, in which God Himself the builder may dwell together with the righteous" (*Div. inst.* 7.24; *ANF* 7, p. 219). But he does not long for this and instead implores the preservation of Rome, the city that "sustains all things" and restrains the end of the world (*Div. inst.* 7.25; *ANF* 7, p. 220). The Christian eschatology merely decorates the bare bones of Lactantius' argument, and his conclusion resembles that of Cicero in the *Dream of Scipio* (*Div. inst.* 7.27; *ANF* 7, p. 223):

> . . . let us serve God with unwearied service, let us keep our posts and watches, let us boldly engage with the enemy whom we know, that victorious and triumphant over our conquered adversary, we may obtain from the Lord that reward of valour which He Himself has promised.

The emphasis is upon the sacralized order of the Empire rather than upon its eschatological fulfillment.

Eusebius and Lactantius define the Christian Empire as a sacralized order, but we must turn to the homilies of John Chrysostom to catch a glimpse of how some Christians sought to put the ideology into practice. In one sense, Chrysostom retains the paradox of alien citizenship. The Christian's city, properly speaking, is the heavenly Jerusalem:[23]

> . . . seeing we are by nature sojourners, let us also be so by choice; that we be not there sojourners, and dishonoured, and cast out. For if we are set upon being citizens here, we shall be so neither here nor there; but if we continue to be sojourners, and live in such wise as sojourners ought to live in, we shall enjoy the freedom of citizens both here and there.

It is the conclusion of Chrysostom's exhortation that begins to take us beyond the paradox. The real point of what he says is that our earthly citizenship ought to be so informed by our heavenly that it is transfigured, contributing to the sacralized order of the Christian Empire. He makes the point repeatedly. In his introductory homily on St. Matthew's Gospel he dismisses Plato's "ridiculous Republic" and argues that the apostles teach us of the true Republic of God (Hom. 1 on Mt.; *NPNF*[1] 10, p. 5). Since that city is no dream, but a heavenly reality, we can participate in it during this life and so find "wealth and poverty, freedom and slavery, life and death, our world and our polity, all changed" (ibid.). And in explaining Christ's claim "My Kingdom is not of this world" (John 18:36), he says Christ makes the denial "not because He doth not rule here, but because He hath His empire from above, and because it is not human, but far greater than this and more splendid" (Hom. 83 on John; *NPNF*[1] 14, p. 311).

The transfigured citizenship of which Chrysostom speaks depends upon Christ, but its effect is to bind humanity together in a harmony that goes far to characterize Redemption but is also related to God's intention in Creation. In his homily on 1 Corinthians 13 Chrysostom weaves together the themes of love, the unity of the human race in Adam, the family, and the city (Hom. 34 on 1 Cor.). He employs the Stoic theme (*oikeiôsis*) that the individual appropriates to his love of self the love of family, nation, and universe. These natural forces are "pledges of concord" implanted by God in us.[24] The love for one another that God has created in us explains the institutions of the family and the city. And, by implication, it is the universal commonwealth of Christ that brings God's intention in Creation to its perfection.

There is a tension in Chrysostom's understanding of this universal commonwealth. On the one hand, all those who are citizens of the heavenly Jerusalem are equal. Christ exhorts all to come to him (Mt. 11:28f.) in Baptism, and there are no longer differences between slave and free, rich and poor (*Bap. Instr.* 1.27; ACW 31, p. 33). On the other hand, this spiritual and sacramental equality by no means abolishes the hierarchical ordering of society, where, however transformed, these differences remain. Nevertheless, the impact of the spiritual ideal may be found in the realization that the different orders of society need one another and should mutually support one another. The rulers in cities are obliged in principle to ensure this sort of harmony by protecting the weak from the strong (Hom. 23 on Rom.; *NPNF¹* 11, p. 513). And all Christians who are able are repeatedly exhorted to give alms and to care for the poor. At one level, as we have seen, this enterprise is a public one undertaken by the Church in its hospitals and hostels. The importance of this work cannot be exaggerated. We know that Basil the Great's hostel outside Cappadocian Caesarea acted as a magnet for the establishment of a new quarter of the city.[25] And Julian the Apostate, as we have seen, in his short-lived attempt to establish an imperial paganism, saw the necessity of founding pagan hostels that would rival the Christian ones and would, like them, assist people regardless of their religious commitments (Ep. 84; Bidez 1.2, p. 145). Chrysostom, of course, approves of this work. But he preaches against treating it as a substitute for private almsgiving and care of the poor and strangers (Hom. 45 on Acts; *NPNF¹* 11, pp. 276f.). His polemic against ill-used wealth and his exhortations to give alms are a striking feature of his homilies (Hom. 52 on Mt.; *NPNF¹* 10, pp. 324ff.). These works of mercy are the highest form of asceticism, better than virginity itself.[26] Despite discouragement regarding popular response to his preaching (Hom. 88 on Mt.; *NPNF¹* 10, p. 523), Chrysostom clearly believes that caring for the poor and outcast manifests the universal commonwealth of Christ and the transformed citizenship of this world.

The new citizenship of which Chrysostom speaks is, as well, informed by an ascetical and moral perfection that may be seen most clearly in monasticism. Particularly in the homilies on Matthew, the monks outside Antioch are held up as models of Christian citizenship. Their monasteries are "the city of virtue" (Hom. 72 on Mt.; *NPNF¹* 10, p. 438). As Athanasius says of Antony, "the desert was made a city by monks, who left their own people and registered themselves for the citizenship in the heavens" (CWS, pp. 42f.). Shifting the metaphor slightly, Chrysostom regards the monks as "shining lamps in every part of the earth . . . walls . . . set about the cities" (Hom. 72 on Mt.; *NPNF¹* 10, p. 439). The monastic life is understood not to be a special form of life, but the actualization of heavenly citizenship on earth. The Antiochenes are urged to visit the monks and bring their way of life back to the city (Hom. 55 on Mt.; *NPNF¹* 10, p. 344):

> For even one dwelling in a city may imitate the self-denial of the
> monks; yea, one who has a wife, and is busied in a household,
> may pray, and fast, and learn compunction. . . . The self-denial
> that is practised in the deserts, let us bring into our cities.

What Chrysostom means by this is made clear by his detailed exhortations concerning the theater, the baths, family and social duties, and
economic obligations.[27] His vision is of an urban life purified and transformed by the monastic ideal.

The theme engages his attention to such a degree that he can even
regard the monks as second-rate Christians because they have not tested
their ideal in the turbulent waters of urban life. Their ideal is affirmed,
but its full value is realized only when put into practice in difficult
circumstances. For this reason, Chrysostom, ordinarily an admirer of
monasticism, can attack the monks (Hom. 6 on Eph.; *NPNF*[1] 13, p. 78):

> They, who were living virtuously, and who under any circum-
> stances might have confidence, have taken possession of the tops
> of the mountains, and have escaped out of the world, separating
> themselves as from an enemy and an alien and not from a body
> to which they belonged.

The movement should be in the opposite direction. Though one can
learn to steer the ship of his life in the quiet harbor of the monastery, the
true test comes when the ship enters the stormy seas of the earthly city.[28]
The ambivalence in Chrysostom's attitude towards monasticism is easily
explained. He is committed to the ideal as the Christian ideal, but he is
concerned that its transforming power not be lost. His vision is of a
sacralized society. That vision has obvious corollaries with the ideology
articulated by Eusebius and Lactantius, and it lies behind a prophetic
preaching that aims at realizing that ideology in practice.

The most difficult question to answer is what result was achieved by
Christians like Eusebius, Lactantius, and Chrysostom. Of course, the
Empire had become Christian; and this meant that the Christian Church
became a central, powerful, and wealthy institution in late antiquity. It
is possible to argue that the Church served the cause of *Romanitas*,
breathing new life into the old forms.[29] It is more difficult to argue that
ordinary citizenship was transformed in any obvious or far-reaching
way. We may remember that A. H. M. Jones, in examining the question,
expresses surprise that "the general standards of conduct should have
remained in general static and in some respects to have sunk."[30] The
closest he can come to an explanation of this astonished conclusion is

that the Christians set their ideal so high that it could not be realized and was, consequently, not attempted by most. It is difficult to disagree. Perhaps, however, the conclusion could be elaborated by suggesting that the ideal itself had become corrupted by losing touch with the paradox of alien citizenship. The ideal became a transformed citizenship and so implied that heaven had been or could be brought to earth. The message of deliverance yielded to a message of reordering, most often reducing heaven to earth rather than drawing earth toward heaven.

The alien character of Christian citizenship is affirmed by preachers like Chrysostom, but it ceases to be an essential part of the message. There are, to be sure, some counterweights. Monasticism, for example, which develops in the post-Constantinian period, looks very much like a protest against a Church gone public and an attempt to retain the spirit of the martyrs. But as a protest movement, it soon lost its power by being co-opted by the Church. The work of Athanasius, the Cappadocians, and even Chrysostom tamed monasticism and limited its witness to the alien character of Christian citizenship. Ecclesiastical resistance to imperial control of the Church and to the heretical emperors also can be regarded as a counterweight. The tightening up of catechetical requirements can be added to the picture. But none of the counterweights sufficed to maintain the paradox of alien citizenship.

It is tempting to conclude that, however viable as an ideal, alien citizenship cannot be put into practice, at least on a social scale. Tertullian felt obliged to insist upon the alien character of Christianity, but his program could not be implemented save by martyrdom, because only martyrdom could sever the social ties linking the Christian to earthly society. Clement tended to emphasize the other side of the paradox, but this ran the risk of losing the message of deliverance in that of a new order. And the Christian Empire, by claiming to realize his dream, succeeded only in creating a new social order that was more earthly than heavenly. On the other hand, perhaps a dialectic is at work. Indeed, the very impossibility of realizing the paradox may be its genuine value. Let me briefly examine a theme in Augustine's thought as a way of elaborating this suggestion.

Without entering into any full discussion of Augustine, the central point can nonetheless be made that he restates the *Epistle to Diognetus*' marvelous paradox of alien citizenship. In Book 19 of *The City of God*, written a few years before his death in 430, Augustine raises the question of the chief good for human beings. That chief good is to be regarded as social and understood as the perfect union of peace and everlasting life (19.11). The concluding section of the book (21–28) is a considered discussion of Scipio's definition of a commonwealth in Cicero's *Republic* and an attempt to show how peace is and is not a characteristic of human society in this life. Scipio's definition is that the commonwealth is "the weal of the people," and by "people" he means a multitude "united in association by a common sense of right and a community of interest" (CG 19.21; PC, pp. 881ff.). Crucial to this understanding is the notion of justice, and Augustine like Lactantius understands justice to involve worship of the true God and his rule over "an obedient City" (CG 19.23; PC, p. 890):

> . . . in consequence the soul rules the body in all men who belong to this City and obey God, and the reason faithfully rules the vices in a lawful system of subordination; so that just as the individual righteous man lives on the basis of faith which is active in love, so the association, or people, of righteous men lives on the same basis of faith, active in love, the love with which a man loves God as God ought to be loved, and loves his neighbour as himself.

This definition, with its roots in Cicero and in Scripture, is for all practical purposes the same as Lactantius'.

Augustine, however, refuses to conclude that the Christian Empire fits this definition of a commonwealth. He rejects the prevailing view that saw the Empire as a sacralized order and an instrument of God designed to bring all humanity to Christ.[31] Only the City of God, the future destination of the pilgrim saints, will fulfill the ideal. Augustine begins by insisting upon the alien character of the Christian City. But he argues that the two cities are mixed in this life, and this conclusion means that the Empire can in one sense foreshadow the City of God. The people of God can "make use of the peace of Babylon" (CG 19.26; PC, p. 892). They can be citizens on earth as well as aliens. The paradox is that the Christian saint possesses the peace of the City of God in a double fashion; in this life, "by faith"; in the world to come, "by open vision" eternally (CG 19.27; PC, p. 892). The paradox really describes an attitude towards the Christian life. This life with its associations and duties must be taken seriously, and in one way Augustine gives a primacy to the world of our experience. We must be citizens. Nevertheless, our experience is that of a pilgrim or a convalescent; it takes on its true meaning only when related to our destiny in the City of God. And so we are aliens.

As an attitude Augustine's statement of the paradox makes a certain amount of sense. What is less clear is its meaning in practice. Indeed, in the fifth century we can begin to see the same polarities found in Tertullian and Clement. The sack of Rome by Alaric in 410 was not only the occasion for Augustine's *City of God*, it also sent shock waves throughout the whole Empire. Jerome in Bethlehem asked what was safe if Rome perished. It became increasingly clear during the fifth century that the order of Christian Rome had collapsed in the West. Deliverance once again became the theme of Christian writers. Salvian of Marseilles looked at his world toward the middle of the fifth century and raised the anguished question why God should allow his people to suffer and to be conquered by barbarians. He gives as his answer: "[God] suffers us to endure these trials because we deserve to endure them" (*De gub.* 4.12; Sanford, p. 119). This judgment is supported by a detailed indictment of Roman Christian society. The moral Salvian draws is that we must be Christian in deed as well as word, and his model is an ascetical one. The servants of God show us what we must do. Repentance, withdrawal from the evils of society, and growth in holiness alone hold up the hope of deliverance. Salvian's program is not unlike Tertullian's. And it does seem that in the early middle ages the monasteries supplied the arks in which many Christians sought to live through the cataclysm of the West's collapse.

Clearly, however, Salvian's was not the only point of view. Rutilius Namatianus, returning in 416 to a Gaul devastated by the Visigoths, sees the situation as a challenge to rebuild. His loyalty is to Rome—"what was only a world you have made a city" (*LPIR*; PC, p. 122). And the city must be rebuilt. He shudders upon seeing monks; whether mad, evil, or ill, they are to be condemned for abandoning the human world. Namatianus was probably not a Christian, but there were many Christians who agreed with him. Like Clement of Alexandria, they thought of deliverance as not merely from the horrors of their day but as one for their society. One need only think of Sidonius Apollinaris and his work. It was Christians like these that used the Church and, particularly, the monasteries as a means for restoring order to Europe. The monastery supplied deliverance, but it became an ordering prinicple in building medieval Europe. From the point of view of the student of early Christianty, there is a sense of *déjà vu*. These themes will be explored more fully in chapter eight.

The conclusion I wish to draw is that the paradox of alien citizenship can never be successfully put into practice on a social scale. All the figures that have been discussed state the paradox as an ideal. But in trying to actualize it, they break it. In a context where the Christian message was understood as one of deliverance, there were those like Tertullian who ended by seeing only the alien character of the Christian life. But there were also those like Clement, who saw deliverance as a gift to the world. Inevitably, this attitude ended by changing the message of Christianity from one of deliverance to one of ordering, of sanctifying the world. And so the alien character of Christianity was lost. In Augustine's time the collapse of the Empire in the West meant that there Christianity was once more obliged to speak its message as one of deliverance. And the pattern repeated itself: Deliverance sometimes meant withdrawal from the human city, but it became in time a way of re-ordering it. Nothing stands still in human history; the revolution of today becomes the establishment of tomorrow and invites a further transformation of the city.

Two qualifications of what must seem a negative conclusion can be made. The problem is that if the paradox of alien citizenship cannot be put into practice, where does its value lie? The first qualification that addresses the problem revolves around the value of the tension produced by attempts to live out the paradox. A dialogue is created, and it can be argued that the Church is strongest when the dialogue is full. For example, the perplexing problem of the apparent but ambiguous success of Christianity by the beginning of the fourth century can only be resolved by appealing to the dialogue. Martyrdom and an alien Christianity made the Church a cause, exacting single-minded and exclusive loyalty. But it is hard to believe that this alone explained the rise of Christianity. Equally decisive was the fact that the Church learned to speak the language of its society. In other words, at its best in the pre-Constantinian period the Church managed to combine exclusive loyalty to a religious ideal with the ability to proclaim its message intelligibly to all. The paradox of alien citizenship engendered a dialogue, and the dialogue proved persuasive.

A second qualification of my conclusion is to argue that the paradox of alien citizenship has a value quite apart from its actualization. I should not wish to say that actions and lives are unimportant. But the motivation involved seems to me crucial. There surely is no one way of living the Christian life. Even the same circumstances evoke widely differing lives, and the seed of Christian conviction produces widely differing blossoms. But what is common, or should be, is the Church's vision of alien citizenship. Monk and priest, ruler and private citizen alike have the possibility of living their varied lives in the light of this common vision:[32]

> Jerusalem the golden
> With milk and honey blest,
> Beneath thy contemplation
> Sink heart and voice opprest.

The contemplation of that city works upon the human heart and enables the Christian to be an alien citizen whatever his circumstances, whatever his calling.

To put it all another way, the vision of alien citizenship is really the vision of Christ's victory and the establishment of the new family of the Church by that victory. But the vision is precisely that; it is not direct sight. The broken lights of theology are attempts to expound dim and partial apprehensions of the vision. To some Christ's victory appeared to be a deliverance from the life of the old order of things; to others it was a triumph that promised a reordering of the world. And in thinking of the family created by Christ's victory some focused upon the promise of the new order; others on the demands made by it. As a promise the Church was meant to offer the new humanity to all, and there is an implicit universalism in the viewpoint of most of the Fathers of the Church. Nevertheless, in the West the catholic aspect of the Church came to be qualified by an insistence on its holiness. Tertullian's emphasis remains in Cyprian's view and is ingeniously combined with the catholic note in Augustine's later thought, as we have seen. Perennial issues are raised in complicated ways. The tension between Church and society, Christ and culture goes hand in hand with the tension between the Christian hope and its effect in the present. Nevertheless, the tensions produced by these differing aspects of the Christian vision require growth in the Christian life and are what produce the mending of lives. The ordinary Christian, as well as the martyr, the monk, and the bishop, was in principle shaped by the Christian vision. In the next chapter I wish to examine monasticism as an attempt to make that vision a reality by establishing a framework in which the Christian life can be lived. And in the final chapter I shall turn to ways in which the Christian ideal moulded responses to the crisis of the fifth century in the West.

7

The City Set on a Hill

 It was probably during his third exile (355–62) that Athanasius wrote the *Life of Antony*. Driven from Alexandria by the imperial authorities, the patriarch took refuge with the monks in the Egyptian desert. It may well be that during this time Athanasius forged the alliance between monasticism and the see of Alexandria that remained a force in the Church for hundreds of years. The *Life of Antony* was probably written partly to further this alliance, but it is, as well, a treatise recommending the monastic life to Christians. Certainly, this is the way it functioned as it was widely circulated both in Greek and in a Latin translation. Antony died at an advanced age in 356, and his life supplied an excellent basis for describing early Egyptian monasticism. After the death of his parents he was left at eighteen or twenty years with full responsibility for the family property and for his younger sister. Almost immediately his reflections on the demands of the Christian life were brought to focus by hearing read in church Christ's command to the rich young ruler to sell his goods and give to the poor. Taking the command literally Antony began his movement towards becoming a hermit. He gradually withdrew from his native village and lived in the tombs outside it. Then, going further into the desert, he took up his dwelling in an abandoned fortress.

At this stage in Antony's life, Athanasius tells a story that reveals his understanding of monasticism. Antony barricaded himself in the fortress. There was water available within, and twice a year people left him loaves of bread. Antony "was hidden within as in a shrine" (*LA* 12; CWS, p. 41). Those outside overheard Antony's warfare with the demons. After twenty years (*LA* 14; CWS, p. 42),

> . . . some of his friends came and tore down and forcefully removed the fortress door. Antony came forth as though from some shrine, having been led into divine mysteries and inspired by God. This was the first time he appeared from the fortress for those who came out to him. And when they beheld him, they were amazed to see that his body maintained its former condition, neither fat from lack of exercise, nor emaciated from fasting and combat with demons. . . . He maintained utter equilibrium, like one guided by reason and steadfast in that which accords with nature.

It is not hard to see that Athanasius is describing Antony according to the ideal of the new humanity. The "purity" of his soul or reason has been attained by his progress in the spiritual life and is what has enabled him to gain perfect mastery over his body. The themes that we have already seen entering into early Christian descriptions of salvation find expression in a transfigured Antony. Moreover, this example of the new humanity persuades many to embrace the monastic life so that "the desert was made a city by monks, who left their own people and registered themselves for the citizenship in the heavens" (*LA* 14; CWS, pp. 42f.).

Athanasius' point of view is typical of the fourth century in that monasticism is treated not as a special form of the Christian life but as the actualization of what was in principle a life demanded of all Christians.[1] As we shall see in a moment this was not the earliest understanding of monasticism. In broad terms what happened in the course of the fourth century was that Church leaders like Athanasius harnessed what began as a protest movement to the service of the Church. Part of what this involved was bringing the monks under episcopal authority in one way or another. But, as well, harnessing monasticism meant the creation of a theoretical understanding of it that brought its ascetical and moral discipline into relation with the Church's theology. In this way theology sought to shape the monastic life, and the project of leaders like Athanasius, Basil the Great, and John Chrysostom was to establish a full living out of the Christian life that put its theological principles into practice. There is a self-consciousness about this project that is lacking in Christian approaches to the family, hospitality, and citizenship. At the same time, we shall discover the same ambiguities and tensions found in examining those other dimensions of the Christian life.

The Origins and Character of Early Monasticism

Let me begin by saying something of the origins and character of Christian monasticism in order to show how the movement ran the risk of competing with the Church rather than informing and leavening it. The important point to make is that, while there were obviously "monks" before the Constantinian revolution, it was only after the Church began to be fostered by the Empire that we can speak of a monastic movement. Only in the fourth century do the monks make the desert a city. Nevertheless, the origins of the movement may be traced to the martyr Church of the first three centuries and even to influences not specifically Christian. If we understand Philo of Alexandria's references to the Therapeutae of the first century seriously and literally, we must suppose that there existed in Judaism ascetic communities bearing a striking resemblance to later Christian monasteries. The discovery of the Dead Sea Scrolls and reconstructions of the life of the Qumran community make it all the more likely that there were precedents in Judaism. As well, we cannot altogether exclude the possibility of Oriental and Indian influences. The Indian gymnosophists were well known in late antiquity, and there is a striking resemblance to their practices especially in Syrian monasticism.[2] The Syrian monks often stood in cold water, refused to sleep, and spent years living atop pillars. Their asceticism went far beyond the renunciation of property, meat, wine, and the bath. The last of these abstentions seems odd, since to us it is curious that asceticism and filth were associated in the ancient mind; but neglect of the body clearly was thought to be central to the soul's progress. Finally, in thinking of Oriental influences, we must add the possibility that by the end of the third century Manichaean monasticism played a significant role by giving Christians something to rival.

There were, however, specifically Christian antecedents of monasticism. As we have seen, there is a strand of extreme asceticism in the New Testament, where the Christian life often requires an absolute renunciation of the world, including the family and possessions. Widows and virgins seem to have become almost orders within the earliest churches, and in this way an ascetical ideal was held forth to all. Tertullian's disciplinary writings, as we have seen, insist upon strict rules for Christian holiness.[3] Most important of all, martyrdom often embodied the ascetical ideal of the early Church. Again and again we find two themes in the fourth-century descriptions of monasticism that hark back to the earlier period. The monks are thought to be reviving the practice of the Jerusalem church in Acts, where Christians held all in common. And the monk embraces a martyrdom in his cell. From this last point of view monasticism consciously took the place of martyrdom and so represented a protest against the surrounding culture and against the Church itself, which had become identified with that culture. "An old man said: 'The monk's cell is the furnace in Babylon in which the three children found the Son of God' " (LCC 12, p. 93).

In one sense, then, monasticism was a flight from the world. In *The Sayings of the Fathers* we find a typical view (LCC 12, p. 40):

> When Abba Arsenius was still in the palace he prayed the Lord saying: "Lord, show me the way to salvation." And a voice came to him: "Arsenius, run from men and you shall be saved." He went to become a monk, and again prayed in the same words. And he heard a voice saying: "Arsenius, be solitary: be silent: be at rest. These are the roots of a life without sin."

Arsenius renounced power and position as well as riches to embark on the road to perfection. Leaving the world behind often also meant abandoning books and classical culture (LCC 12, p. 78). The dispute between the Origenist and the anthropomorphite monks in the early fifth century revolved around whether monasticism could include the life of the mind. Moreover, the rejection of the world sometimes includes refusing to have anything to do with the Church. Palladius in his *Lausiac History*, written early in the fifth century, tells several stories of monks who sometimes exercise priestly and episcopal functions without benefit of ecclesiastical ordination (*Lausiac Hist.* 34, 53, 58; ACW 34, pp. 133, 139). And we hear of monks who refuse ordination.

The Sayings of the Fathers preserves a story that vividly illustrates the character of monasticism as a protest against the Church. A young monk has lived in a cave for six years without seeing anyone. The devil disguises himself as an elder, pretending to have a nearby hermitage he has not left for eleven years. The devil says to the young monk (LCC 12, p. 89):

> "I tell you, brother, we do no good sitting like this in our cells. We cannot receive the body and blood of Christ, and I am afraid that he will cast us away if we separate ourselves from that sacrament. But I tell you, brother, three miles from here is a monastery with a presbyter. Let us go there every Sunday, or every other Sunday, and receive the body and blood of Christ, and return to our cells."

The young monk succumbs to this demonic temptation and only realizes what he has done when the elder who accompanied him to church mysteriously disappears. Obviously, we cannot speak of monasticism as utterly divorced from the life of the Church, since even in this story there is a monastery where the liturgy is regularly performed. But the attitude behind the story is no more than an exaggeration of a suspicion of the imperial Church that ran deep in early monasticism. To flee the world in some degree meant fleeing the Church, and it was only this flight that enabled the monk to make war on the devil in his desert stronghold.

One point needs to be added to this assessment of monasticism as a flight from the world. If there were religious reasons for renunciation, there were also social and economic factors. As the Roman Empire emerged from the anarchy of the third century a despotism was gradually established. Imperial control over the social and economic life of the people was increasingly totalitarian. Peasants, for example, were bound to the land where they had been born. They could not escape tilling the soil of their birthplace, and taxation as well as the vagaries of nature often made it impossible for them to eke out a living. In the cities the upper-class members of local curias or councils were required by law to perform the public works (liturgies) that they had once offered voluntarily and in this way were often brought to bankruptcy by financial obligations they could not avoid.[4] There can be little doubt that these factors contributed to swell the ranks of the clergy and the monasteries, and as a result we can by no means suppose that the monastic ideal was wholeheartedly embraced by all who professed to be monks and nuns. Palladius, almost inadvertently, gives us an insight into the realities of monasticism in his description of the monastery of women in Antinoe ruled by Amma Talis (*Lausiac Hist.* 59; ACW 34, p. 140). The sixty young women loved their abbess "so much that no lock was placed in the hall of the monastery, as in others, but they were held in check by their love for her." The locked doors bear witness to the mixed motivation that must have characterized early monasticism.

The sometimes hostile stance of monasticism towards the Church and the mixed motivation for withdrawal from the world were not the only problematic aspects of early monaticism. As well, there was the question whether the solitary life could be regarded as Christian. As we shall see, Basil the Great forbids total solitude, and even in Athanasius' account of Antony as the first hermit we find that Antony's isolation is by no means complete. He is attended by other Christians, and even pagans seek him out as a holy man capable of responding to their questions. Pachomius (ca. 290–346) seems to have been the first to establish a common life for monks, who became known as coenobites. John Cassian's nineteenth Conference addresses the question of the relative merit of the coenobite's and the hermit's ways of life. "Each perfection . . . is partial, not complete. . . . The hermit cannot achieve contempt for material possessions, the coenobite cannot achieve the pure prayer of the contemplative" (*Con.* 19.9; LCC 12, p. 284). The view that he ultimately takes is that only those who have received long training in the common life should seek the hermit's vocation. The norm for monasticism quickly became the community life of the coenobites even though hermitism never completely disappeared.

One last problematic feature of early monasticism deserves comment. The ideal Christian life that marked the aim of the monk included moral virtue and spiritual contemplation as well as asceticism. But the relation of these three elements was not always as clear as it might have been. In particular, there was the risk that ascetical practices might become ends in themselves. In *The Sayings of the Fathers* Abba Evagrius recognizes this (LCC 12, p. 109):

> A wandering mind is strengthened by reading, and prayer. Passion is dampened down by hunger and work and solitude. Anger is repressed by psalmody, and long-suffering, and mercy. But all these should be at the proper times and in due measure. If they are used at the wrong times and to excess, they are useful for a short time. But what is only useful for a short time, is harmful in the long run.

In other words, the ascetical life must be the means by which the monk conquers vice and acquires virtue. Abba Agatho makes the same point by comparing a human being to a tree: Bodily discipline, like the leaves of the tree, is necessary, but the fruit is what counts and is identified with the "inner man" or the mind (LCC 12, p. 107). Fasting and other disciplines should be used to overcome lust and anger (ibid., pp. 50, 69). These exhortations suggest not only the danger of embracing asceticism without using it correctly but also the possibility that too much fasting, for example, may produce anger.

The relation between asceticism and the spiritual life was also problematic and betrayed itself in what can be called the Pelagian theme. The notion that human beings could make the first steps towards God, who would then come to their assistance, pervades early monasticism. In the *Life of Antony* it appears in narrative form. Antony wrestles with demons all night, and only then does the Lord come to his aid. Antony reproaches his Lord with deserting him at the beginnings of his torments, and the Lord replies (*LA* 10; CWS, p. 39):

"I was here, Antony, but I waited to watch your struggle. And now, since you persevered and were not defeated, I will be your helper forever, I will make you famous everywhere."

The risk, of course, is that the monk may suppose he can win the victory by himself and so become one of a small elite that outstrips other Christians in the pursuit of perfection.

BASIL THE GREAT AND MONASTICISM

It must have been with these problematic aspects of early monasticism in mind that Basil the Great set about ordering the movement for the Church in Cappadocia.[5] Gregory Nazianzen's account in his *Panegyric on Basil* puts it this way (*Panegyric* 62; *NPNF*[2] 7, pp. 415–16:

> . . . he [Basil] reconciled most excellently and united the solitary and the community life. . . . He founded cells for ascetics and hermits, but at no great distance from his cenobitic communities, and, instead of distinguishing and separating the one from the other, as if by some intervening wall, he brought them together and united them, in order that the contemplative spirit might not be cut off from society, nor the active life be uninfluenced by the contemplative, but that, like sea and land, by an interchange of their several gifts, they might unite in promoting the one object, the glory of God.

Three themes emerge from Nazianzen's description. Basil unites the solitary with the common life of the monastery, insists that contemplation be balanced by the active life, and thinks of his enterprise in terms of the glory of God. Let me explore these themes as they appear in Basil's *Longer Rules*.

Basil's emphasis is upon the communal nature of the Christian life, and the *Rules* are less tolerant of solitude than Basil apparently was in practice (*LR* 7; Clarke, p. 163):

> Now the solitary life has one aim, the service of the needs of the individual. But this is plainly in conflict with the law of love, which the apostle fulfilled when he sought not his own advantage but that of the many, that they might be saved.

Allusions to 1 Corinthians echo in Basil's description of the common life, and he appeals to St. Paul's use of the body metaphor in chapter 12 to define it. We are members of one body, with Christ as our head and the Holy Spirit binding us together. There are, as well, practical implications of this unity. Since no one is self-sufficient, a community more easily supplies what people need for life. Without others in close contact with him a man will often not recognize his own failings and sins. Virtues like humility cannot be cultivated or expressed in the solitary life. And "when a number live together a man enjoys his own gift, multiplying it by imparting it to others, and reaps the fruits of other men's gifts as if they were his own"(*LR* 7; Clarke, p. 165). Far from being eliminated, individuality finds its full expression in the community.

Basil uses the metaphors of the family and the city to describe the ideal of the monastery. Renunication is necessary if the ideal is to be obtained; like the merchant in the parable who sells everything to obtain the pearl of great price (Mt. 13:45f.), so whoever wishes to obtain the Kingdom must sacrifice his family as well as his riches and fame. This renunciation is "a removal of the human heart to the citizenship in heaven" (*LR.* 8; Clarke, p. 169). Nevertheless, Basil gives commonsense directions about how this renunciation is to be made. "An accurate survey" of the prospective monk's possessions is to be made, and they are to be disposed of carefully (*LR* 9; Clarke, p. 170). Slaves who seek to join the monastery must be returned to their masters just as Paul sent Onesimus back to Philemon (*LR* 11). Married men may be received immediately only if their wives approve; otherwise, an attempt is made to gain the wife's consent before the married man can enter (*LR* 12). These provisions make some attempt to soften monasticism's divisive effect on society so that the family and city of the monastery may not undermine the earthly family and city more than is necessary. The emphasis remains, however, on the prior importance of the community which is thought to be one that "keeps the stamp of those Saints told of in the Acts" who had all things in common (*LR* 7; Clarke, p. 166). It is clear that Basil is thinking of this new family as the city set on a hill that cannot be hid.

The second of the themes that can be disengaged from Nazianzen's description of Basil's work has to do with the character and function of the monastery. The dialectic between contemplation and action is worked out in the hospitality of the monastery. The most obvious form this takes is the entertainment of guests, and detailed advice is given regarding the kind of food that should be offered, all of which is summarized by the principle: "Let this be the limit of our hospitality, what is required by the needs of each visitor" (*LR* 20; Clarke, p. 186). Another form hospitality takes is the reception of orphans into the family of the monastery (*LR* 15). Basil thinks it appropriate that the monasteries have schools not only for the orphans and for children dedicated to the monastic life, but also for others. Boys and girls both join the life of the monastery, though they must take their room and board separately from one another and from the monastery proper. The contemplative aspect of the Christian life is preserved, but is balanced by a movement towards the world. Like Chrysostom, Basil thinks of the monastery as a light shining into the surrounding world, persuading people towards the ideal of the Christian life. The monastic ideal is meant to be a leaven in the Church and in all of society.

The third theme I noted in Nazianzen's panegyric has to do with the glory of God. Basil himself makes the same point in his description of the continence in food and drink required of the monk (*LR* 17; Clarke, p. 181):

> For I think that no words touch the heart of him who is intemperate in eating or move him to alter his habits so much as merely meeting the continent man. This, I think, is the meaning of eating and drinking to the glory of God; so that even at the table our good works shine forth to the glorifying of our Father who is in heaven.

The monk not only makes himself subject to God, but persuades others to the same subjection and so assists the process by which all things find their fulfillment in perfect harmony with God. The whole of Basil's view of the Christian life is implied by the idea of glorifying God. From one point of view, progress depends upon the right exercise of human freedom: "For as firm flesh and clear skin characterise the athlete, so the Christian is betokened by emaciation of body and paleness, which is the bloom of continence, showing that he is truly an athlete of Christ's commandments" (ibid.). The contrast with Athanasius' description of the transfigured Antony suggests that Basil has the realities of the monastic life in mind. More important, however, is the emphasis the metaphor places upon human moral efforts. At the same time, however much continence is the product of human freedom, it also "betokens a man who has died with Christ" and we may suppose is equally the product of God's grace.

The first major point I should like to make about the themes we find in Basil's *Longer Rules* is that they find their full significance in Cappadocian theology. Basil's theology differs in no crucial respects from Nyssa's, and so we can appeal to the description given of Nyssa's theology in chapter two. Each of the themes that finds concrete expression in Basil's *Rules* for the monks also finds theological articulation in central convictions of Nyssa. And, as I argued in chapter two, this is no accident, since

Nyssa's theological task can from one point of view be regarded as the creation of an ideology for monasticism. The broken lights of theology are made to mend lives by setting up the specific structures that will enable the Christian life to be lived as fully as possible. We must remember that for the Cappadocians, the monastic life, far from being a special one, is merely the complete actualization of the manner of life required by the Gospel; Basil's *Rules* are as much rules for all Christians as they are for monks.[6]

The place we have seen given to the individual in Cappadocian monasticism correlates with Nyssa's understanding of the individual. By thinking of individuality in terms of relationship, Nyssa suggest that the more fully Christians are related to one another in Christ, the more they realize their true identity. As relations of the one human nature of Christ, which is the image of God, all human beings are meant to find their perfection in the completed and perfected image of God. This destiny is in some measure a present possibility when the members of the monastic community bring their gifts to the service of one another. The balance Basil attempts to strike between the coenobite and the hermit is one that is defined by the image theology we find in Nyssa's thought. If we ask how we are to imagine or to understand Nyssa's corporate understanding of human nature, we must think of the monastery where all hold everything in common, using and possessing one another's gifts.

The second theme we have examined obviously correlates with Nyssa's treatment of the dialectic between contemplation and action. What are three stages of the Christian life from the point of view of human destiny become three aspects of it when thought of in the present. The ethical aspect acts as a preliminary to the intellectual and spiritual aspects, and so virtue leads to vision. But, of course, the movement is also in the opposite direction. Vision leads to virtue. Concretely, of course, it is the monastery's hospitality that introduces into its routine the movement toward the world that constitutes the life of virtue. The balance struck by the Cappadocians is soon afterwards lost, however, when Evagrius Ponticus and the Pseudo-Dionysius both begin insisting that contemplation represents a higher form of the Christian life. This development places monasticism in a special position and loosens the tight connection between the monastic and the ordinary Christian life. For the Cappadocians, however, the dialectic between contemplation and action engenders an open attitude toward the relationship of Church and world and of Christ and culture.

Finally, the theme of the glorification of God points in the direction of the large structures by which Nyssa defines the Christian life. Our freedom must be used to move toward God and perfect glorification of him.

But that very freedom is itself the gift of God's grace, is exercised in the context of God's providence, and is elicited from us by God, the Beloved. To the dialectics of the individual and the community and of contemplation and action we must add the dialectic of grace and freedom. Theological tensions in Nyssa's thought correlate very well with tensions that characterize the monastic life. It is, to be sure, more difficult to find grace in *The Longer Rules;* but it seems reasonable to suppose that Basil remains committed to a view that would take grace quite seriously.

A second major point must be made about the themes found in Basil's *Longer Rules*. At first it looks as though what we are dealing with is an attempt to take theological ideas and use them as a basis for establishing monasteries. To the degree that this is so, monasticism represents the clearest and, indeed, the only social form that claims to be a direct actualization of Christian convictions. In the case of the family, hospitality, and citizenship, by contrast, Christian belief merely alters and even ratifies existing institutions. While there is some truth to this way of explaining it all, there are two problems with putting it this way. First, as I have suggested, monasticism existed even before this explanation of it gained currency. That is, we cannot really argue that theological themes simply generate Christian monasticism out of thin air, as it were. Instead, theology functions to shape an existing movement by supplying it with a theoretical platform designed to remove ambiguities and solve problems. Thus, even though the correlation between theology and life is more obvious in the case of monasticism than in the other areas of the Christian life we have examined, we cannot suppose that a social phenomenon did not exist before theology began its shaping work.

A second reason for denying that monasticism springs from theology in a direct fashion is that it solves none of the problems we have already identified in speaking of the family, hospitality, and citizenship. Sometimes monasticism took a negative stance towards the surrounding culture, including the Church, and so embodied the hostile attitudes we have found some Christians holding toward the family and the state. On the other hand, the monasteries were sometimes open and related to the outside world. Moreover, just as in the fourth century we find a tendency for Christians to regard their beliefs as a power capable of transforming and sacralizing society, so the view taken of monasticism by the Cappadocians and John Chrysostom saw in it a light that was meant to pervade the whole world, an example meant to bring society towards perfect subjection to Christ. As the monastic life began by providing a particular form of deliverance, a way of escape, so it ended by becoming an ordering principle for a renewed and transformed society. This was the role of monasticism in the imperial Church of the fourth and fifth centuries; and, as we shall see, it became again the role of monasteries in the Latin West during the early Middle Ages. That part of the story begins with the work of John Cassian at the beginning of the fifth century.

JOHN CASSIAN

In 386 on the eve of his conversion St. Augustine received a visit from Ponticianus, an African and an imperial civil servant. Discovering Augustine's copy of St. Paul's Epistles, Ponticianus (*Conf.* 8.6; PC, p. 167)

> . . . began to tell us the story of Antony, the Egyptian monk, whose name was held in high honour by your servants, although Alypius and I had never heard it until then. . . . After this he went on to tell us of the groups of monks in the monasteries, of their way of life that savours of your sweetness, and of the fruitful wastes of the desert. All of this was new to us. There was a monastery at Milan also, outside the walls, full of good brethren under the care of Ambrose, but we knew nothing of this either.

A quarter of a century later Claudius Rutilius Namatianus left Rome to return to his native Gaul, devasted by marauding barbarians. His was a work of restoration, and he took a dim view of those who had abandoned hope by engaging in the monastic enterprise (*LPIR*; PC, p. 233):

> Midway between the island and the mainland we
> 	passed Capraria, a dreary place, where
> there are men who shun the light and call themselves "monks."
> 	They have taken their name from the Greek which
> means "alone" because they wish to live with no one;
> 	they fear fortune, whether good or evil.
> Would a man live in misery to escape it?
> 	Because of their fear, they shun what is good.
> Such reasoning is the raving of a madman.

The surprise of Augustine and the hostility of Namatianus almost certainly reflect the fact that toward the end of the fourth century monasticism was a novel phenomenon in the West. We know something of the work of Martin at Tours, of Honoratus at Lérins, and of Paulinus at Nola.[7] But our fullest evidence comes from the writings of John Cassian. He was not only a pioneer in introducing the monastic life to the West, he was also a living link with the major centers and leaders of monasticism in the East.

John Cassian was probably born in the Roman province of Scythia
Minor, though Provence has also claimed him. As a boy or young
man he and an older friend and countryman, Germanus, were admitted to the monastery near the Cave of the Nativity in Bethlehem.
Intrigued by an Egyptian visitor to Bethlehem, who turned out to be
the famous monk Abba Pinufius, Cassian and Germanus determined
to visit the Egyptian monasteries. Only an oath to return freed them
from the Bethlehem monastery, and they began their spiritual grand
tour. It appears likely that they left before Jerome's arrival in Bethlehem about 386. Once in Egypt Cassian must certainly have become
involved in the dispute between the anthropomorphite and the Origenist monks.[8] His lot was cast with those who disavowed a simple and
literalist understanding of Scripture and the Christian faith in favor of
an Origenism that was certainly speculative and probably theosophical
in character. Indeed, it seems likely that at Cellia Cassian became a
disciple of Evagrius Ponticus, the leading Origenist theologian. Evagrius had been made a reader by Basil the Great and a deacon by
Gregory Nazianzen. Consequently, he had ties with the Cappadocian
Fathers, who had rescued what they could of Origen's thought. Not
long after Evagrius' death Theophilus, the Patriarch of Alexandria,
condemned the Origenists and expelled the Tall Brothers from Cellia.
It is not impossible that Cassian accompanied the Origenist leaders in
their flight. At any rate, we find him around 401 being made a
deacon in Constantinople, where John Chrysostom was patriarch.
Some three years later he was in Rome, where he became a friend of
Leo the Great, the future pope for whom he later wrote a refutation
of Nestorius' opinions. Within five years of the sack of Rome in 410 by
Alaric the Visigoth, Cassian was in Marseilles, where some years later
he wrote his *Institutes* and *Conferences*.

This bare outline of Cassian's career illustrates a striking characteristic
of the Church of his time. It was in some ways a small world, and the
leaders of the Church were bound to one another in friendship and in
enmity by ties that were personal as well as religious. Cassian brought
with him to Marseilles his experience of Egyptian and Palestinian monasticism, and in the *Conferences* we are in much the same world as that
recorded in the *Life of Antony*, the Pachomian literature, and *The Sayings
of the Fathers*. But he also brought with him the allegiance to Evagrian
monasticism, to the broader tradition represented by Cappadocian
Origenism, and to the zeal of Chrysostom, who sought to make the
monastic life a light for the world. His written works are concerned to
integrate these two commitments, and he follows his master Evagrius in
attempting to bind the ascetical and moral aspects of monasticism to-

gether with a more speculative and spiritual ideal, that is to unite the
"practical" with the "theoretical" or contemplative.

Cassian's *Institutes* and *Conferences*, written in the first quarter of the
fifth century, are to be regarded as a response to the request of Bishop
Castor of Apt (near Marseilles) for assistance in establishing a monastic
community in his diocese (*Inst.* pref.; *NPNF*[2] 11, p. 199):

> . . . you are anxious that the institutions of the East and espe-
> cially of Egypt should be established in your province, which is at
> present without monasteries, although you are yourself perfect in
> all virtues and knowledge and so filled with all spiritual riches
> that not only your talk but even your life alone is amply sufficient
> for an example to those who are seeking perfection—yet you ask
> me . . . to contribute something from the scanty supply of my
> thoughts toward the satisfaction of your desire; and you charge
> me to declare . . . the customs of the monasteries which we have
> seen observed throughout Egypt and Palestine, as they were there
> delivered to us by the Fathers.

Let me begin by noting the leading principles that govern Cassian's
project.[9] The *Institutes* is designed to describe the outer structure of the
monastic life. The dress of the monks, their hours of prayer, the rules
governing the monk's entrance to the monastery, and remedies for the
Evagrian list of eight temptations are the topics treated. Cassian refuses
to "weave a tale of God's miracles and signs" and states his purpose is to
describe "the way to improve our character, and the attainment of the
perfect life, in accordance with that which we have received from our
elders."[10] Moreover, he recognizes the necessity of adapting Egyptian
monasticism to the conditions of Gaul (*Inst.* pref.; *NPNF*[2] 11, p. 200):

> . . . where I find anything in the rule of the Egyptians which
> either because of the severity of the climate, or owing to some
> difficulty or diversity of habits, is impossible in these countries, or
> hard and difficult, I shall to some extent balance it by the cus-
> toms of the monasteries which are found throughout Pontus and
> Mesopotamia.

It is obvious that Cassian's aim is a practical one and that he has a
commonsense approach to his enterprise. The *Conferences* presuppose
the outward structure established in the *Institutes*. Cassian's preface to
the *Conferences* puts it this way (*Con.* pref.; *NPNF*[2] 11, p. 293):

Let us therefore pass from what is visible to the eye and the external mode of life of the monks, of which we treated in the former books, to the life of the inner man, which is hidden from view.

Let us then follow the order Cassian establishes, beginning with the outward structure of the monastic life and moving on to its inner aspect.

The most important outward structure of the monastery is, of course, the round of canonical prayer. The nocturnal offices of vespers and nocturns Cassian borrowed from Egyptian monasticism. But his addition of the day offices of terce, sext, and nones is taken from the customs of Palestine and Mesopotamia and represents a moderation of "the perfection and immutable rigour of the discipline of the Egyptians" (*Inst.* 3.1; *NPNF*[2] 11, p. 212). The point is that the weaker brethren of Gaul are incapable of the perpetual prayer of the Egyptians and require a more fixed and fuller structure. The hours of prayer, together with directions about the psalms and prayers to be said as well as the manner of reciting them, are regarded as "movements of the outer man." Cassian promises that in the *Conferences* he will build on this foundation and treat the prayer of the inner man and so "build up the complete edifice of his prayers" (*Inst.* 2.9; *NPNF*[2] 11, p. 208). One confusion springs from Cassian's description of a new dawn office in *Institutes* 3.4–6 and his citation of Psalm 119:164 as the basis for seven times of prayer. The traditional solution of the problem is to give the following schedule: nocturns (i.e., matins), dawn office (i.e., lauds), prime, terce, sext, nones, and vespers.[11] Whether this is correct or not, the important point to make is that Cassian supplies his monks with a full outward structure of prayer.

To this structure and to the other requirements of the monastery the monk was obliged to yield absolute obedience. Cassian tells stories of the Egyptian monks to make the point (*Inst.* 4.24ff.). Abba John was ordered by his superior to plant a dead stick and water it twice a day. For an entire year he walked two miles twice daily with no result whatsoever. He passed the test. Abba Patermucius, we remember, was admitted to a monastery with his small son. Since this was contrary to custom, everything was done to purge him of his natural affection for the child. As a final test he was commanded to hurl the boy into the river to drown. Though the boy was saved, his father's obedience had been tested and found true. The requirements made of the "renunciants" upon their entrance to the monastery reflect this spirit of total obedience. They are not allowed to bring any possessions with them, and their very clothes are stripped from them to be replaced by the dress of the monastery. The clothes are kept so that if expulsion is necessary, the failed renunciant may leave the monastery as he came to it. All human ties are broken. Even letters from outside the monastery are a danger, and the monk who is able to burn them unread is commended.

Books 5–12 of the *Institutes* complete Cassian's description of the outer man by describing the eight temptations and the means for combatting them. Various ascetical disciplines supply outward bulwarks against greed, lust, avarice, melancholy, anger, accidie, vainglory, and pride. For example, fasting is an outward defense against greed. Moreover, it extinguishes "the fiery furnace of our body" and can deaden "the heats of fleshy lusts" (*Inst.* 5.14; NPNF[2] 11, p. 238). Placing cold leaden plates over the genitals during sleep helps ward off the nocturnal ghostly foe and leads to perfect chastity (*Inst.* 6.7). The midday demon of accidie or spiritual boredom may be fought by keeping busy and engaging in manual labor. Cassian is well aware of the ambiguities of the ascetical life. It is, from one point of view, only a propaedeutic to the life of the inner man, and it has no value unless it leads towards the goal of moral and spiritual perfection. Indeed (*Inst.* 5.9; NPNF[2] 11, p. 236),

> . . . each one should impose such a sparing diet on himself as the battle of his bodily struggle may require. The canonical observance of fasts is indeed valuable and by all means to be kept. But unless this is followed by a temperate partaking of food, one will not be able to arrive at the goal of perfection. For the abstinence of prolonged fasts—where repletion of body follows—produces weariness for a time rather than purity and chastity.

Asceticism must be treated as a means towards a greater end and must be used cautiously. From another point of view, ascetical practices are possible only when "the mind is fixed on the contemplation of divine things, and is the rather entranced with the love of virtue and the delight of things celestial" (*Inst.* 5.14; NPNF[2] 11, pp. 238f.). The interrelationship of outer and inner is presupposed throughout the *Institutes*.

It is in the *Conferences*, however, that Cassian gives us instruction about the progress of the inner man. Each Conference deals with a specific subject, and so we cannot speak of an argument that is advanced in any real order. Nevertheless, the point of view found in all the Conferences is reasonably coherent, and an attempt may be made to describe Cassian's view so long as one understands the description to be an interpretive one. The place to begin is with his view of the human mind, that is, the inner man. "The mind cannot possibly remain in one and the same state" (*Con.* 6.14; NPNF[2] 11, p. 360), because it must perpetually move towards good or evil. The movement of the mind can be regarded as an ascent towards God or a descent "to carnal and earthly things" (*Con.* 7.4; *NPNF*[2] 11, p. 363). One cannot avoid comparing Gregory of Nyssa's understanding of human nature, even in its redeemed state, as a perpetual becoming. It is unclear how far Cassian follows Nyssa's ideas, but it is certain he is concerned to develop the notion of the mobility of the soul in the context of a pragmatic concern for the spiritual life here and now. The mobility of the mind or heart, he says, is like that of a mill wheel (*Con.* 1.18; *NPNF*[2] 11, p. 303)

> . . . which the headlong rush of water whirls round, with revolving impetus, and which can never stop its work so long as it is driven round by the action of the water: but it is in the power of the man who directs it, to decide whether he will have wheat or barley or darnel ground by it.

Similarly, thoughts come into the mind from God, from the devil, and from ourselves; and we must decide which of these thoughts to accept. The emphasis is upon a right intent. However much outward structures facilitate the intent, it is really the mind's decision as to where it should direct its attention that counts. The idea is, of course, a commonplace and is an important aspect of the spiritual theology Cassian inherited from Evagrius and his predecessors. Moreover, it raises the issue of Pelagianism, which Cassian discusses in Conference 13 and which must be reserved for later treatment.

If the decisions of the inner man are of fundamental importance, one implication is that thoughts originating from the devil must be rejected. At this level, the spiritual life is a warfare against principalities and powers. Conference 8 discusses the matter at length. The devil and his angels have fallen from their original perfection and wage incessant warfare against us and even against one another. Every individual is accompanied by both a good and an evil angel. Cassian's view has its roots explicitly in the ancient Jewish-Christian theology of *The Shepherd of Hermas*.[12] But while we can still see this perspective, as well as the battle with the opposing powers that characterizes the *Life of Antony* and *The Sayings of the Fathers*, the ideas have been placed in a somewhat more sophisticated context that is reminiscent of Origen's treatment of the same themes in *De principiis* 3. The devil can bring thoughts to the mind, but like the owner of the mill, the Christian has the power to admit or reject them. Perpetual prayer enables the believer to reject the devil's proposals, and no prayer is more effective than "O God, make speed to save me: O Lord, make haste to help me" (Ps. 70.2, *Con.* 10.10). This perpetual prayer assists Christians in their struggle with Satan.

More important to Cassian than the metaphors of battle and struggle are those that revolve around the ascent of the soul to God. His description of this pilgrimage derives ultimately from Plato, particularly the *Symposium* and the *Phaedrus*. But there are more obvious links with the Christian Platonist tradition that go back to Origen via Evagrius and the Cappadocians. In Conference 3.6 Cassian speaks of three renunciations (*NPNF*² 11, p. 321):

> The first is that by which as far as the body is concerned we make light of all the wealth and goods of this world; the second, that by which we reject the fashions and vices and former affections of soul and flesh; the third, that by which we detach our soul from all present and visible things, and contemplate only things to come, and set our heart on what is invisible.

Towards the end of the chapter he equates the three renunciations with the three books of Solomon (*NPNF*² 11, p. 322):

> . . . Proverbs answers to the first renunciation, as in it the desires for carnal things and earthly sins are repressed; to the second Ecclesiastes corresponds, as there everything which is done under the sun is declared to be vanity; to the third the Song of Songs, in which the soul soaring above all things visible, is actually joined to the Word of God by the contemplation of heavenly things.

We seem to be in the presence of an Evagrian modification of an Origenist idea. For Origen and for the Cappadocians the three stages or aspects of the Christian life also correspond to the divisions of Greek philosophy. Ethics is followed by physics, and physics by speculation. Thus, the moral life should prepare one for the intellectual life, and the intellectual life for the contemplation of God. Cassian tends to allow the second of these stages to disappear. Either it is assimilated to the moral stage as a rejection of the vanity of one's former life, or it is merged with the contemplative life where little difference can be made between intellectual and spiritual. One suspects that behind the change lies a deeper suspicion of pagan culture and philosophy than we find in Origen and the Cappadocians.[13]

The old Origenist pattern of the three stages is reflected at several points in the *Conferences*. For example, the Pauline letters are used to describe three sorts of souls—carnal, natural, and spiritual (*Con.* 4.19). The transition from carnal to natural is described as the renunciation of vice and the acquisition of virtue. The natural stage is intellectual and is meant to yield to the spiritual one. Yet even here Cassian qualifies the Origenist pattern by regarding the natural stage as "lukewarm" and one to be passed over as quickly as possible. Another schema may be associated with the Origenist pattern (*Con.* 11.6ff.). There are three motives for spiritual progress—fear of punishment, hope of reward, and love. These three correspond to faith, hope, and love. (*NPNF²* 11, p. 417):

> For faith is what makes us shun the stains of sin from fear of future judgment and punishment; hope is what withdraws our mind from present things, and despises all bodily pleasures from its expectation of heavenly rewards; love is what inflames us with keenness of heart for the love of Christ and the fruit of spiritual goodness.

The three stages again appear, and again the second stage tends to lose its identity. It remains only as a turning from vice and towards the loving contemplation of God, thus retaining a connection with both the moral and the contemplative aspects of the Christian life, but losing its own identity.

That Cassian wishes to transform the traditional pattern in an Evagrian direction is made clear by the discussion of Conference 14. Spiritual knowledge is divided into practical and theoretical, precisely Evagrius' categories. One can have the first without the second, but the theoretical or contemplative cannot be gained without the practical. The practical consists in the renunciation of vice and the acquisition of virtue, and so is to be understood as the ethical stage of the Christian life. The theoretical knowledge turns out to be largely an understanding of Scripture. The historical sense is distinguished from the spiritual, and the spiritual is subdivided into tropological, allegorical, and anagogical. For example (*Con.* 14.8; *NPNF²* 11, p. 438):

> And so these four previously mentioned figures coalesce, if we desire, in one subject, so that one and the same Jerusalem can be taken in four senses; historically, as the city of the Jews; allegorically as the Church of Christ; anagogically as the heavenly city of God . . . ; tropologically, as the soul of man.

It is important to notice that Scripture plays a central role in the contemplative life. It is there that the Christian finds the deepest secrets of God revealed and there that he begins the contemplation of ultimate truth and the love of ultimate good. Thus a central emphasis of Origen finds expression in Cassian's spirituality.

Not only does Cassian follow Evagrius in reducing the Christian life to ethical and contemplative stages, he also reproduces Evagrius' emphasis on the successive character of these stages. The moral life is, of course, necessary. To put it in Cassian's words, while "the end of our way of life is indeed the kingdom of God" "the immediate aim or goal is purity of heart without which no one can gain that end" (*Con.* 1.4; *NPNF*^{2} 11, p. 296). Nonetheless, the story of Mary and Martha means that the Lord makes the chief good consist in meditation, i.e., in divine contemplation" (*Con.* 1.8; *NPNF*^{2} 11, p. 298). Cassian does not altogether lose a sense of the mutual involvement of the moral and the contemplative life, but he follows Evagrius in thinking of the latter as a higher form of spirituality. What is lost is the dialectical character of contemplation and action as found in the writings of Origen and of the Cappadocians. For them virtue enables contemplation, while contemplation expresses itself in virtue. For Evagrius and Cassian, at least in principle, contemplation is a higher form of life. Cassian does recognize the difficulty and even impossibility of this ideal (Con. 1.13; *NPNF*^{2} 11, p. 300):

> To cling to God continually, and as you say inseparably to hold fast to meditation of Him, is impossible for a man while still in this weak flesh of ours. But we ought to be aware on what we should have the purpose of our mind fixed, and to what goal we should ever recall the gaze of our soul; and when the mind can secure this it may rejoice; and grieve and sigh when it is withdrawn from this, and as often as it discovers itself to have fallen away from gazing on Him, it should admit that it has lapsed from the highest good. . . .

The ideal of contemplation is maintained, but Cassian more often than not treats it as an impossible one.[14]

The ambiguity of regarding the contemplative life as an ideal but not a practicable one is reflected in the analysis of different forms of monasticism given in Conferences 18–19. The coenobites, who live in communities, are thought to originate from the Jerusalem church described in the opening chapters of Acts. The anchorites or solitary monks sprang from the coenobites. The Sarabaites represent a perversion of monasticism, as do certain false anchorites, since neither group is subject to the discipline of a rule. In comparing the two authentic forms of monasticism, Cassian says (*Con.* 19.9; *NPNF*^{2} 11, p. 493):

> And so it is hard to find one who is perfect in both lives, because the anchorite cannot thoroughly acquire . . . a disregard for stripping

oneself of material things, nor the coenobite purity in contemplation. . . .

The ideal of perfect contemplation is found in the anchorite. But since the solitary life does not free a person from seeking the bare necessities of earthly life, it is rarely that the ideal is achieved. In any case, no one can expect to be a true anchorite without long training in the coenobitic monastery. The peculiarity of Cassian's view is that the ideal he holds up is not one that he advocates strongly in practice.

In another respect and for other reasons Cassian is obliged to qualify Evagrian monasticism. Not only is the absolute character of the contemplative ideal qualified, the emphasis on free will and the ability of the monks to turn toward God has to be reconciled to some degree with the issues of the Pelagian controversy. A dispute arose in southern Gaul over the writings of Augustine, and the monks of Marseilles ranged themselves against certain opinions of the bishop of Hippo.[15] But Augustine had his supporters in Gaul, notably Prosper of Aquitaine. And that meant that Cassian had to steer between an extreme Augustinianism and an outright Pelagianism. His adaptation of the Eastern tradition to the issues thus raised began with the assertion of the necessity of both grace and freedom (*Con.* 13.11; *NPNF*[2] 11, p. 428):

> These two then, viz. the grace of God and free will, seem opposed to each other, but really are in harmony, and we gather from the system of goodness that we ought to have both alike, lest if we withdraw one of them from man, we may seem to have broken the rule of the Church's faith: for when God sees us inclined to will what is good, He meets, guides, and strengthens us. . . . And again, if He finds that we are unwilling or have grown cold, He stirs our hearts with salutary exhortations, by which a good will is either renewed or formed in us.

At first this looks like nothing but a restatement of the problem. But it actually teaches that experience shows there are two ways in which we find God's grace working in us. Either God meets us as we make the first small move towards him, or, if our hearts are like flint, his grace strikes the spark of a response from us. Although Adam gained for humanity the knowledge of evil, he did not lose the knowledge of good. Hence, we retain to some degree a God-given power of turning towards good. Yet ultimately, "the God of all must be held to work in all, so as to incite, protect, and strengthen, but not to take away the freedom of the will which He Himself has once given" (*Con.* 13.18; *NPNF*[2] 11, p. 434).

Cassian concludes by appealing to the mystery of God's activity, and so makes it clear that his solution is a description of experience and not a satisfactory theoretical resolution of the problem.

Cassian's program for monasticism, then, is an ambiguous one. From one point of view, he is true to Evagrius. The monk embraces a special form of the Christian life and aims towards the superior goal of contemplation. This requires the fullest exercise of his God-given capacities and leads to the anchorite life. On the other hand, Cassian's common sense forces him to realize how few can attain this ideal; his pragmatism leads him to emphasize the coenobitic monastery and the outward structures which are requisite for any growth of the inner man; and the controversy over Augustine leads him to an emphasis upon grace that is characteristically Western, even though it is not Augustinian. If this assessment is correct, then it supplies a way of characterizing the Janus-like position of Cassian in the history of monasticism. The first set of emphases ally him with the earlier period and with the East; the second, with the Western monasticism as it developed in the early Middle Ages. His influence upon Benedict and his rule for beginners could not be doubted even if Benedict had not in the rule recommended that Cassian be read. But in Benedict Cassian's common sense and pragmatism come to fuller expression.[16] And the stage was set for giving the monasteries a role in the West that would have astonished Namatianus. What looked to him in 416 like a denial of the world on the part of the monks became the major institution for rebuilding Europe after the barbarian invasions. It is paradoxical that Cassian's work, which aimed at providing a structure for monks to attain the Kingdom of God, contributed to the rebuilding of earthly kingdoms. We shall be able to see at least the prelude to this reconstruction by turning in the next chapter to Christian attitudes towards the collapse of imperial authority in the West beginning in the fifth century.

8

The Collapse of the West

The Christian Roman Empire was short-lived in the West. Even if we extend its time as far as possible by beginning with Constantine's victory through the cross at the Milvian Bridge in 312 and by ending with the undoing of Justinian's reconquest of Italy by the Lombards at the end of the sixth century, Roman rule in the name of Christ lasted less than three hundred years. Needless to say, the reasons for the collapse of the West are highly complicated.[1] Social and economic problems can be pointed out ranging from inflation and excessive taxation to famine and plague. The absence of any generally accepted emperor in the West after the death of Valentinian III in 455 is a factor that helps explain why the West was more vulnerable than the East, for although the social and economic problems were by no means confined to the West, the Eastern Empire managed to survive until the fall of Constantinople in 1453. Nevertheless, while these factors and others must be included, there is little doubt that the barbarian invasions represent the most obvious explanation for the beginning of the Dark Ages in western Europe. However much the internal weakness of the Empire explains the destructive impact of the barbarian raids and settlements, without the invasions Roman rule might well have stumbled on in the West as in the East. The West bore the brunt of the incursions, since the barbarians were repeatedly deflected from Constantinople and driven towards lands easier to plunder. Ammianus Marcellinus (ca. 325–ca. 395), a Greek from Antioch who served in the emperor Julian's army, is probably correct in his history in singling out the Huns as the immediate cause of barbarian unrest. Moving westwards from the Asian Steppes, the Huns drove the other barbarian tribes before them into the Roman Empire.

Ammianus supplies a lengthy account of the Huns at the beginning of Book 31 of his history. A few of his comments will convey the general idea (31.2.1–3; LCL 3. pp. 381ff.):

> The people of the Huns . . . exceed every degree of savagery. . . . They all have compact, strong limbs and thick necks, and are so monstrously ugly and misshapen, that one might take them for two-legged beasts or for the stumps, rough-hewn into images, that are used in putting sides to bridges. But although they have the form of men, however ugly, they are so hardy in their mode of life that they have no need of fire nor of savory food, but eat the roots of wild plants and the half-raw flesh of any kind of animal whatever, which they put between their thighs and the backs of their horses, and thus warm it a little.

Ammianus goes on to describe their nomadic life and the terrible warfare they wage from their horses. It would be easy enough to deduce the usual romantic picture. Vast hordes of barbarians swept over the Empire, laying waste the land and enslaving the Roman population. The truth, however, is far more complicated and less dramatic. J. B. Bury estimates that "The total number of one of the large East German nations probably seldom exceeded 100,000, and its army of fighting men can rarely have been more than from 20,000 to 30,000."[2]

To understand the barbarian invasions we must remember some obvious facts about them. Another passage from Ammanius Marcellinus will make one point vividly. In describing the aftermath of the Battle of Adrianople (378), where the Goths defeated the Roman army and slew the emperor Valens, he tell the story of how the victorious Gothic army was repulsed from the walls of Constantinople. A troop of Saracens, mercenaries in the Roman army, sallied from the city to attack the Goths (31.16.5–6; LCL 3, pp. 501ff.):

> The contest was long and obstinate, and both sides separated on equal terms. But the oriental troop [the Saracens] had the advantage from a strange event, never witnessed before. For one of their number, a man with long hair and naked except for a loin-cloth, uttering hoarse and dismal cries, with drawn dagger, rushed into the thick of the Gothic army, and after killing a man applied his

lips to his throat and sucked the blood that poured out. The barbarians, terrified by this strange and monstrous sight, after that did not show their usual self-confidence. . . .

The Roman soldier proves to be more barbarous than the barbarians. The point, of course, is that by the fourth century the Roman army was largely made up of mercenary barbarian troops. This meant that a given battle must have looked more like warfare among barbarian tribes than a struggle between civilization and barbarism. Moreover, most of the important Roman officers were themselves barbarians; and once civil chaos and civil war became the norm, it would be hard to see which army was really the Roman one. Alaric the Visigoth, for example, who sacked Rome in 410, had probably been Master of Soldiers in Illyricum, an imperial post he may well have considered still his own. And much later, when Clovis was crowned King of the Franks, he was dressed as a Roman consul.

If from one point of view many barbarians thought of themselves as Romans or at least as closely tied to the Empire, from another perspective the Empire itself gave official recognition not only to barbarians as Roman soldiers but also to barbarian "nations" settled on Roman soil. When Theodosius the Great was co-opted as emperor by Gratian after Valens' defeat and death at Adrianople, he began the task of pacifying the Danube frontier. He made use of Federate nations, that is of barbarian tribes who committed themselves to supplying troops in return for imperial protection. But, as well, he allowed Federate Visigoths to settle within the Empire in Thrace. He did so on the basis of the ancient Roman system of *hospitalitas* by which soldiers had been quartered on the civilian population. The principle was applied to the land itself, the Goths gaining a one-third share of the territory they were given to occupy. Bury makes quite clear the important effect of this policy:[3]

> Thus the process of the dismemberment of the Empire was eased; the transition to an entirely new order of things was masked; a system of Federate States within the Empire prepared the way for the system of independent states which was to replace the Empire. The change was not accomplished without much violence and continuous warfare, but it was not cataclysmic.

Thus, from 378 and the Battle of Adrianople until 493 when the West found itself divided up into barbarian kingdoms, we find a gradual transition. There is no one point at which we can say the Western Empire ends. The barbarians were not without the possibility of claiming to be themselves Romans.

A more nuanced understanding of the character of the barbarians and of the "invasions" needs to be deepened by an examination of the diverse views of Romans towards them. Of course, the horror and hatred of barbarians suggested by Ammianus Marcellinus' account of the Huns was a common attitude, but it was by no means the only one. Even in the first-century Empire there was considerable respect for and fascination with the Germans, as Tacitus shows us. And in the fourth century the emperor Julian so admired his German troops that he adopted many of their customs and felt far more comfortable with them than with, say, the civilian population of Antioch. We must remember, as well, that the barbarians who established themselves within the Empire were Christians. The Goths, the Burgundians, and the Vandals owed their conversion to the fourth-century mission of Ulfilas to the Goths, and the fact that the mission was sent when the Empire was Arian meant that the barbarians were Arian heretics. Indeed, had it not been for Clovis' conversion to orthodox Christianity and the Franks' rise to hegemony in Western Europe, there would have been at least the possibility that Europe might have ended up Arian. Even though they were heretics, the barbarians were at least Christians; and this fact was understood by the old Roman population, which was often able to live in harmony with their Arian neighbors. Moreover, the barbarians were not only Christian but also had a civil government of law and a political structure that often drew admiration from Romans.

This last aspect of the matter deserves to be underlined. There were significant numbers of Romans who fled the Empire to take refuge with the barbarians. A specific example will best make the point. In 448 the historian Priscus accompanied his friend Maximin on his embassy to Attila the Hun. For some years the emperor Theodosius II had paid tribute to the Huns, and it is reasonably certain that Attila regarded himself as the master of the Roman Empire. His own empire extended from what is now southern Russia to Austria and far northwards. Priscus, therefore, realized that he was approaching a powerful and fearful monarch. The imperial embassy arrived at Naissus, halfway between modern Belgrade and Sofia and from there journeyed to Attila's headquarters beyond the Danube. Priscus' account is detailed, and he describes not only the barbarians but also representatives from the Western Empire present at Attila's court. At one point as he was waiting to arrange a meeting with Attila,[4]

> . . . a man, whom from his Scythian dress I took for a barbarian, came up and addressed me in Greek. . . . I was surprised at a Scythian speaking Greek. For the subjects of the Huns, swept

together from various lands, speak, besides their own barbarous tongues, either Hunnic or Gothic, or—as many have commercial dealings with the western Romans—Latin; but none of them easily speak Greek, except captives from the Thracian or Illyrian sea-coast; and these last are easily known to any stranger by their torn garments and the squalor of their heads.

The stranger whom Priscus meets, however, is well dressed as a Hun. He turns out to be Greek born, a Roman citizen who had settled in Viminacium near Belgrade and who had been captured when the Huns sacked the city. Buying his freedom, he married a barbarian and settled among the Huns.

According to Priscus, the transplanted Roman "considered his new life among the Scythians [Huns] better than his old life among the Romans." Priscus has him explain why as follows:

> After war the Scythians live in inactivity, enjoying what they have got, and not at all, or very little, harassed. The Romans, on the other hand, are in the first place very liable to perish in war, as they have to rest their hopes of safety on others, and are not allowed, on account of their *tyrants*, to use arms. And those who use them are injured by the cowardice of their generals, who cannot support the conduct of war. But the condition of the subjects in time of peace is far more grievous than the evils of war, for the exaction of the taxes is very severe, and unprincipled men inflict injuries on others, because the laws are practically not valid against all classes. A transgressor who belongs to the wealthy classes is not punished for his injustice, while a poor man, who does not understand business, undergoes the legal penalty. . . . The climax of the misery is to have to pay in order to obtain justice. For no one will give a court to the injured man unless he pays a sum of money to the judge and the judge's clerks.

Though the convert to the Huns admits, when Priscus presses him, that the theory of the Roman state is fair, he tearfully insists that the governing classes have so corrupted the state that life cannot be endured under it. This case was probably not isolated. Everything we know suggests that life was intolerable for many in the late Roman Empire. The autocratic and totalitarian rule that characterized the Empire from the late third century on so regulated the economy and the social structure that many were crushed beneath impossible economic obligations. A farmer, bound to the soil on which he was born, might struggle to raise a crop to see it devoured by taxes or by marauding armies. A decurion in one of the cities might find himself obliged to pay taxes he could not afford. It is no wonder that many found life under the barbarians at least no worse than life in the Empire.

A Synopsis of the Collapse of the West

Before turning to Christian attitudes towards the barbarian invasions, let me offer the briefest of sketches of the events that took place from the late fourth to the late sixth century. We should, of course, keep in mind the general points that have already been made. Roughly speaking, the history of the period can be divided into three parts. From 378 to 493 there was a gradual transition to the division of the West among barbarian kingdoms. From 493 until the 530s the barbarian kingdoms held sway under the leadership of Theodoric's Ostrogothic kingdom with its capital in Ravenna. In the 530s Justinian began the reconquest of the West for Byzantium, and his success in Italy was undone by the Lombard invasions of the late sixth century. By 600 the stage is set for the early middle ages, with the Franks as the most important power in western Europe. Part of the difficulty in telling the story is the result of our fragmentary evidence, but another part is to be explained by the fact that with the breakdown of unity in the Empire, different and somewhat unrelated events were taking place at the same time in different places. We have already seen the rough outline of the beginning of the story. Driven by the Huns, the Goths were forced across the Danube into Roman territory, where they eventually failed to obey Roman commanders. War broke out, and the emperor Valens was defeated and killed near Adrianople in 378. The surviving emperor, Gratian, co-opted Theodosius the Great, who pacified the Balkans by 382 at the price of allowing German Federates "hospitality" in Thrace. Two major rebellions broke out in the West, forcing Theodosius to wage constant war until his death in 395.

The next stage of the story can be told by giving a brief account of the life of one of the most interesting of ancient figures, Galla Placidia. She was Theodosius the Great's daughter and was probably born in 388; she died in 450, five years before her son, Valentinian III, who was the last undisputed Western emperor. When her father died in Milan in 395, for the first time Western and Eastern emperors were established, since Theodosius left two sons to inherit his throne. In the East Arcadius, who was barely eighteen years old, ruled under the guidance if not the control of Rufinus, the Praetorian Prefect of the East. In the West, Honorius, who was only ten years old, held the name of emperor, while real power was wielded by Stilicho, a Vandal who had married into the imperial family and who was Master of Both Services. Galla Placidia joined Honorius, and the Western court was soon moved from Milan to the safety of Ravenna.

Fifteen years later we find Galla Placidia in Rome during the sack of the city by Alaric's Visigoths. Alaric as early as 401 had posed a threat to Italy, but for reasons that are not altogether clear Stilicho allowed him to retreat in safety. After Stilicho's execution in 408 Alaric invaded Italy again, and in 410 he captured and sacked Rome. The event was immediately seen in mythic proportions. Jerome, amazed, asked if Rome fell, what was safe. And Augustine's *City of God* began as a response to pagans who blamed the Empire's allegiance to Christ for the sack of Rome. In any case, Alaric took Galla Placidia captive in 410, and for six years she wandered with the Visigothic army. Alaric died in the south of Italy shortly after the sack of Rome and was succeeded by Ataulf, who in 412 led the Visigoths across the Alps. In 413 they captured Narbonne, Toulouse, and Bordeaux, and the next year Ataulf married Galla Placidia. There is reason to believe that the marriage was not only a willing one on both sides, but was designed to be part of a plan to set up an Italo-Gothic empire in the West, a dream that was not in fact realized until Theodoric's Ostrogothic kingdom in 493. Ataulf's hopes vanished with his death in Spain in 415, and the following year Galla Placidia was released from her captivity with the Visigoths and married to Constantius, the chief Roman general in the West who, as Constantius III, reigned as coemperor of the West for seven months. Upon his death in 421 court intrigue opposed Galla Placidia to Honorius, and she was obliged to flee her half-brother's court for that of her nephew, Theodosius II, in Constantinople. She had scarcely arrived when news came of Honorius' death (423) and of the usurpation of John, who was an important civil servant. In the end Theodosius II gave his support to Galla Placidia's infant son, Valentinian III, for whom she served as regent. Thus, in 425 she returned to Ravenna and to the West, which she ruled directly or indirectly until her death in 450.

When Galla Placidia began her regency, the situation in the West was threatening. Federate barbarian kingdoms had been established in Spain and Gaul, and the foundations thereby laid for the Vandal, Visigothic, Burgundian, and Salian Frankish kingdoms. Two generals dominated the events of the next few years. Aëtius, who had been a supporter of John and whom Galla Placidia mistrusted, led the Romans to victory in Gaul. Bonifacius in Africa, however, lost ground to Gaiseric, the Vandal king.

In 430 Augustine died during the siege of Hippo, and two years later only Carthage and Cirta remained in Roman hands. The situation was complicated by war between Aëtius and Bonifacius, who won the war but died immediately afterwards, paving the way for Aëtius' restoration and sole supremacy. In 450 Attila the Hun invaded Gaul and Italy; but this threat, though extremely severe, was short-lived. Attila died in 453, and the Huns were once and for all defeatd by their German vassals the next year. At this point it looked as though the situation was about to be stabilized in the West with major losses confined to Africa, Spain, and parts of Gaul. But Valentinian III assassinated Aëtius in 454 and was himself assassinated in 455, surviving his mother, Galla Placidia, by only five years.

Who was to succeed to imperial authority in the West? The answer in the event proved to be in the hands of the barbarians, and for this reason the doom of the West was sealed. The Vandals in Africa were invited into the succession question when Valentinian III's widow appealed to Gaiseric, the Vandal king, to help her out of a forced marriage with an imperial pretender named Maximus. Gaiseric took the opportunity to sack Rome and to multiply marriages between his royal house and the children of Valentinian III. In Gaul the Visigoths were active in the proclamation of Avitus and, then, Majorian as emperors. Finally, Leo I, the Eastern emperor, sought to maintain Roman control over the West, first by supporting Majorian, and then, in 467, by nominating Anthemius. These names are scarcely worth remembering, since true power in the West lay in the hands of the generals who succeeded Stilicho, Constantius, and Aëtius. Ricimer from 457 to 472 and Odoacer from 476 to 493 came as close to controlling the situation as anyone could. Before his death in 491 the Eastern emperor (Zeno) was obliged to recognize Odoacer as the Patrician who administered the West for him. Thus, the de jure solution was to regard Zeno as emperor of East and West. De facto, however, the West had become divided up into barbarian kingdoms with here and there pockets of Roman resistance. At Soissons until 486, for example, Roman rule was maintained by Aegidius and his son Syagrius; but they were completely cut off from any central Roman authority. Something like this may lie behind the Arthurian legends in Britain. The absence of any alliance between a strong military figure and a legitimate emperor spelled doom for the Empire in the West.

Two final chapters to the story may be quickly told. In 493 Theodoric the Ostrogoth betrayed Odoacer, slew him, and assumed control in Ravenna. Until his death in 526 he ruled impartially over Roman and Goth alike and established a prosperous kingdom allied by marriage and treaty with the other barbarian kingdoms of Europe. The Roman civil

service remained in force, and Theodoric fully tolerated the orthodox
Christianity of the Roman population. Only towards the end of his reign
did the Italo-Gothic harmony break down. A number of Romans were
accused of conspiring with the Eastern emperor against Theodoric. Boe-
thius was so accused, doubtless unjustly, and was executed about 524.
What this conspiracy and its suppression demonstrated was the instabil-
ity of the Italo-Gothic alliance. The Goths themselves were divided into
pro- and anti-Roman factions, and this gave Justinian the opportunity to
reconquer the West for what can now be called Byzantium. The Eastern
forces under Belisarius easily recaptured Africa, but Italy was another
matter. War lasted from 535 until 554, and regaining control of Italy had
its price. The Byzantines appeared the foreigners, and the country was
left in a weakened condition. By 568 the Lombards began invading Italy.
By 600 the map of Europe looked something like this: in Britain, the
Celts and Anglo-Saxons; in France and Germany, the Frankish kingdoms;
in Spain and southwest France, the Visigothic kingdom; in Italy, the
Lombard kingdom and duchies, the papal states, and the vestiges of
Byzantine rule (the Exarchate of Ravenna); in Africa and Sicily, the
Byzantine Empire. It is the rise of the Franks more than anything else
that sets the stage for the Middle Ages, for the Franks had become
orthodox Christians. Their domination of the other barbarians was, as
well, a domination of Arianism by orthodoxy.

What might a Christian have thought and done in the face of so
radical a transformation of Western society as the one I have briefly
described? We have seen something of Christian attitudes towards perennial aspects of human life—the family, hospitality, the state. But now
we need to ask what role Christianity played in the way people dealt
with the misfortunes and changes of the fifth and sixth centuries. It
seems certain to me that broad and easy conclusions are impossible.
Nevertheless, we do possess the writings of a number of people who
were obliged to react as Christians to the collapse of the West, some of
whom were even concerned to explain what had happened. Obviously,
I can do little more than skim the surface, but let me begin by discussing three writers who took part in the story I have just told. Paulinus of
Pella was in Bordeaux when Ataulf the Visigoth took the city in 413.
Sidonius Apollinaris delivered a panegyric for Avitus when he was proclaimed emperor in 456, the year after Valentinian III died, and was
bishop of Clermont-Ferrand when the Auvergne was ceded to the Visigoths by Rome in 475. Cassiodorus was one of Theodoric's leading
officials; during the wars of reconquest under Justinian in the 530s he
retreated to his family estate in southeastern Italy, where he founded
two monasteries.

PAULINUS OF PELLA

In his eighty-third year Paulinus of Pella wrote an autobiographical poem called the *Eucharisticus* that has been preserved for us in the works of Paulinus of Nola. There is general agreement that the poem was written by a grandson of Ausonius, who was Paulinus of Nola's mentor and friend. The spiritual distance between Ausonius and his friend finds concrete historical expression in the distance between his own generation and that of his grandson. Ausonius (ca. 310–394) was a prominent rhetorician of Bordeaux who became the young emperor Gratian's tutor about 364. Gratian showered him with honors, culminating in a consulship in 379. After Gratian's murder in 383, Ausonius retired to Bordeaux, where he died in 394, the year before the death of Theodosius the Great. Consequently, his life was spent in the Indian summer of the Western Empire. Prosperous and cultivated, he belonged to the old Gallic aristocracy and wore his nominal commitment to Christianity very lightly. Indeed, his poems and letters suggest that he regarded being a Christian as only incidental to being a Roman. The two were equated in his mind as in the prevailing attitude of his time, but his fundamental commitment was to *Romanitas* and particularly to classical literature. He would no more have understood his grandson than he did his friend Paulinus of Nola.[5]

A number of letters between Ausonius and Paulinus of Nola have been preserved and must be read against the background of Paulinus' gradual conversion to a full commitment to Christianity that took him to St. Felix's shrine in Nola, where he founded a monastery and dedicated himself to the spiritual life and to the exercise of Christian hospitality. When Paulinus, who was a wealthy landowner, retired to the Spanish estates he had gained through marriage, Ausonius wrote repeatedly, complaining in one letter (27) that Paulinus had responded to everything but the one thing Ausonius asked, the promise to return and visit him. In another letter (29) he rebukes Paulinus for failing to write, saying that "even rocks make answer" by sending back an echo. We might suppose that Ausonius is simply the older man and the mentor to whom Paulinus means more than he to Paulinus. But there is more to the rift between the two than this. Paulinus responds finally (30) by declaring his abiding friendship and loyalty to Ausonius. He protests that he and his household continue to honor and love Ausonius, since "we are as agreed together as our hearts are linked together in worship of Christ." He concludes the letter with a moving poem that begins (LCL 2, p. 123):

> Through all the length of time given to mortals and ordained, so long as I shall be confined in this halting frame, though I be held

a world apart, thee neither parted by a world nor severed from
my sight I will keep implanted in my inmost being.

One can imagine that all Ausonius hears is "though I be held a world
apart," and the spiritual friendship of which Paulinus spoke must have
seemed cold in contrast to their earlier friendship in books and their
actual presence to one another. But the real division was Christ, as
Paulinus finally makes explicit (31; LCL 2, p. 125): "Why dost thou bid
the deposed Muses return to my affection, my father? Hearts consecrate
to Christ . . . are closed to Apollo."

The distance that separated Ausonius from his friendship spiritually
separated him from his grandson of the same name historically. Paulinus of Pella had grown up in Ausonius' generation, but his life extended
to a time when he had "outlived my fatherland" (*Euch.* 310; LCL 2, p.
329). He was born in 376, probably to Hesperius, one of Ausonius' sons,
and to Hesperius' Macedonian wife in Pella near Thessalonica. His father
was the vicar of Macedonia, and nine months after Paulinus' birth was
promoted to the proconsulship of Africa. After a year and a half in
Carthage the family returned to Bordeaux, where Paulinus grew up. His
education was the usual upper-class one of his time; he read Plato and
Homer, but had difficulty with Vergil because he was more accustomed
to Greek than to Latin. When he was fifteen an illness resulted in medi-
cal advice that he get "continual gaiety and amusement" (l. 126; LCL 2,
p. 317). He began to accompany his father on the hunt, and his youthful
desires began to shift from learning to "a fine horse bedecked with
special trappings, a tall groom, a swift hound, a shapely hawk, a tin-
selled ball, fresh brought from Rome, to serve me in my games of
pitching, to wear the height of fashion" (ll. 143ff.; LCL 2, p. 317). He
arrived at the usual stage of "youthful wantonness," which he satisfied
with "servile amours in my own home" (ll. 157ff.; LCL 2, p. 319).
Finally, at eighteen he married a propertied woman, whose father was
dead, and threw himself into the task of running her estates.

On the whole Paulinus takes a positive view of his early years. He is
grateful to Christ for his comfortable childhood and youth and exclaims:
"Of this life would that the enjoyment granted by Christ's rich bounty
had continued longer for us, the former times of peace enduring like-
wise" (ll. 226ff.; LCL 2, p. 323). At the same time, in his narrative there
is an undercurrent of dissatisfaction. He seems to recognize that he was
never able to make full and profitable use of the advantages he had been
given by birth and upbringing. Was it that the times prevented him from
making his contribution and mark in the world as his father and grand-

father had? Or was it that his spoiled youth robbed him of ambition? The answer was probably no clearer to Paulinus than it is to us. What is certain is that in 406 he suffered a double burden. His father died, and peace was broken when marauding tribes of barbarians crossed the frozen Rhine into the Empire and left behind them carnage and devastation. Life was never the same for Paulinus afterwards. His brother contested his father's will, which had made generous provisions for Hesperius' widow. Paulinus' house was pillaged by the barbarians because he lacked a Gothic guest to provide him with protection (l. 285). These misfortunes and those that followed quite naturally led him to think of his early years as a golden time.

The remainder of Paulinus' story revolves around the loss of his property. Forced from Bordeaux by the Visigoths in 413, he and his family fled to their property in nearby Bazas, where they soon found themselves again besieged. Paulinus' negotiations with Ataulf, however, resulted in the lifting of the siege. Prevented by his wife's wishes from fleeing to his estates in Macedonia and by his recognition of family responsibilities from seeking refuge in a monastery, Paulinus remained in Gaul "in perpetual exile" (l. 491). His sons failed to recover his property in Bordeaux, and they and his wife died. He moved to Marseilles, where he tried to eke out a living, and eventually returned to Bordeaux, where he appears to be living in genteel poverty at the time of writing his poem. There are hints that there is more to the story than Paulinus tells. A little before 410 he was given high office by Attalus, a puppet emperor of the Visigoths; and he appears to have been known to Ataulf at the siege of Bazas. For some reason he hesitates for long to return to Bordeaux. At one point he declares that his aim was "peace with the Goths" (l. 304; LCL 2, p. 329). It takes a good deal of reading between the lines, but it seems possible to me to argue that Paulinus played more of a public role in his mature years than he lets us know and that his virtual silence is to be explained by the failure of his pro-Gothic policy, because it made him seem a traitor to his fellow Romans.

Whatever the truth about the details of Paulinus' life after the barbarian invasions began, there can be little doubt that from a wordly point of view he was a failure. He lost not only his property but also any possibility of having a voice and a role in the events of his time. To what degree this was his own fault—whether by a natural tendency to withdraw or by putting his foot wrong in the politics of his day—we shall never know. What matters, however, is his attitude toward his own fate. We might expect anger or at least disappointment, but instead the name of his poem is "Thanksgiving." Paulinus makes his point in the preface to the *Eucharistus* (LCL 2, p. 305):

But—I am not ashamed to avow it—I, who in my lengthy pilgrimage have long languished in the misery of care-fraught idle-
ness, have been led on, as I surely believe, by divine mercy to seek
such consolations as befitted alike a good conscience in old age
and a devout purpose; I mean that I, who indeed felt that I owed
my whole life to God, should show that my whole life's doings
have also been subject to his direction.

I cannot help being reminded of Benjamin Jowett's final words: "I bless
God for my life." Paulinus does not think of success or failure, fortune of
misfortune. Instead, he regards his life as God's gift and gives thanks.
This attitude is clearly the fruit of experience, and what Paulinus has
learned is that (LCL 2, p. 307)

> . . .while reasonably chastening me with continual misfortunes,
> he [God] has clearly taught me that I ought neither to love too
> earnestly present prosperity which I knew I might lose, nor to be
> greatly dismayed by adversities wherein I had found that his
> mercies could succour me."

Later in the poem itself he sees "with perception improving with old
age" that his loss of earthly goods took place that "I might learn to seek
rather those which will endure for ever" (ll. 438ff.; LCL 2, p. 339). His
Christian faith did not empower Paulinus to take an active and constructive part in the events of his time, nor did it lead him to withdraw from
society to the security of a monastery. But it did enable him to endure,
and in that enduring there is testimony to the victory of Christ.

SIDONIUS APOLLINARIS

Another writer for whom the crisis of the West supplied a geological
fault running through his life and cutting it in two was Sidonius Apollinaris. Born in Lyons about 430 of a noble and wealthy Gallic family, he
died in Clermont sometime after 479 as bishop of the Auvergne in the
Visigothic kingdom. He began his career in emulation of his father and
grandfather, both of whom had been praetorian prefects of Gaul, and he
ended it serving the Church under barbarian rule. As we shall see, the
contrast is more apparent than real; but it was Sidonius himself who
made it that way. Let me give a brief sketch of his life before turning to
his letters as evidence for his attitude toward the barbarian triumph and
toward Christianity. Little is known of his early years, but his poems and
letters demonstrate that he had received an excellent education by the

conventions of the aristocratic Gallic society of the time. He was thoroughly versed in the classics, and his letters constantly echo with his love of and commitment to Latin literature. He married well. His wife was Papianilla, the daughter of the Avitus who was proclaimed emperor in 455 upon Valentinian III's death. Sidonius accompanied his father-in-law to Rome, where he delivered an official panegyric and received the honor of a bronze statue in the Forum of Trajan. Sidonius survived the fall of Avitus, and in 458 delivered a panegyric for Majorian, Avitus' successor, in Lyons. He delivered a third panegyric in 468 for the new emperor Anthemius in Rome and was rewarded by being named urban prefect of Rome, a post of great honor. It looks as though Sidonius was obliged to do some sharp tacking to keep the wind in his political sails, but in 468 he looked well on the way toward a promising and important public career.

It is at this point in his life that Sidonius' fate suddenly changed. By 472 he was enthroned at Clermont as bishop of the Auvergne. We simply do not know what happened. Had he come to realize the futility of a political career when one did not know who was to be emperor from one year to the next? Did he see the Church as the only hope for his culture in Gaul? Or was it simply that the local people decided they needed him as their bishop? This last possibility is a reasonable one, since it was common for powerful men to be chosen bishop regardless of their religious convictions and knowledge. The point is that the bishop was a patron for Christians, and to find one who had prestige and authority was regarded a stroke of luck. Ambrose, of course, is an earlier and more familiar example of these forces at work. In any case, from the moment he became bishop Sidonius worked hard to prevent what inevitably happened in 475, the cession of Auvergne to Euric, the Visigothic king. He assisted his brother-in-law, Ecdicius, who led the resistance to the barbarians, engaged in diplomacy, attempted to boost the morale of the Auvergnians, and introduced the "Rogations," prayers which Bishop Mamertus had introduced in Vienne.[6] When Clermont fell to the Visigoths, Sidonius was, obviously, suspect. He was imprisoned by the Goths, but eventually was allowed to return to Clermont, where he resumed his episcopal duties.

Sidonius' letters enable us to fill in some details in the sketch of his life just given, but more importantly they give us a good idea of his attitudes and, in particular, of the role played by Christianity in them. What comes across most clearly is his double commitment to Rome and to his native land. In his panegyric on Avitus, for example, Jupiter gives a speech in which he explains the disasters suffered by Rome. Fate, which governs even the king of the gods, decrees that what "has reached its highest bourne must needs be afflicted" (ll. 124ff.). The explanation, however, is but the prelude to an assurance (ll. 137ff.; LCL 1, p. 129):

> And now [says Jupiter], that it may be plain to thee how thou mayst rise again, worn out as thou art, hearken and I will declare it in few words. I have a land which carries its head high as sprung from Latin blood, a land famed for its men, a land to which Nature, the blessed creator of all things, vouchsafed no peer in days gone by.

The land, of course, is Gaul, specifically the Auvergne, and the man is Avitus. Through him Gaul will prove its loyalty by turning defeat to victory for Rome. What Sidonius really had in mind, however, is the civilized life of the Gallic aristocracy on their country estates. His description of a friend's country estate reveals where his heart lies (Ep. 8.iv; LCL 2, p. 413):

> Close to the city [Narbonne], the river [Aude], and the sea, it [your property] feeds your guests with feasts and you with guests; moreover, its lay-out charms the eye of the beholder. In the first place the house rises high, with walls skillfully arranged so as to produce an undoubted architectural symmetry. Again, it sends forth a gleam far and wide from the chapel, the colonnades and the baths, which are all conspicuous. In addition, its fields and springs, vineyards and olive-groves, its entrance court, its park, its hill present a most lovely view. Then, besides a well-stocked larder and abundant furniture, it is liberally filled with stores of books, amid which you expend as much energy on the pen as you give to the ploughshare, so that it is hard to decide whether the owner's land or his mind has been the better cultivated.

The passing allusion to the chapel is the only detail that enables us to remember that Sidonius is speaking of a Christian country house. Moreover, the Arcadian setting functions primarily in his view to house a library.

Sidonius believes himself committed to a Roman culture that no outward circumstance can destroy. He praises his friend Arbogastes for having "drunk deep from the spring of Roman eloquence" and for speaking "the true Latin of the Tiber." Though dwelling on intimate terms with barbarians, Arbogastes is "innocent of barbarisms." Sidonius concludes that "with you and your eloquence surviving, even though Roman law has ceased at our border, the Roman speech does not falter" (Ep.

4.xvii; LCL 2, pp. 127f.). In another letter he goes further (Ep. 8.ii; LCL 2. pp. 403f.):

> . . . for they [your pupils] have been so moulded and trained by your teaching that, though now in the very midst of an unconquerable and alien race, they will preserve the signs of their ancient birthright; for now that the old degrees of official rank are swept away . . . the only token of nobility will henceforth be a knowledge of letters.

Sidonius worries about the impact of German on his culture. The seven-foot barbarians pose the danger that six-foot poetry may be destroyed (Poem 12). And though Syagrius (great-grandson of Afranius Syagrius of Lyons) is to be commended for his excellent command of German, he must beware of losing his Latin (Ep. 5.v). Sidonius, of course, aimed at expressing his commitment to Roman culture by publishing his poems and letters. Though modest even by the standards of his own time and contrived and artificial to modern taste, his works at least show us his deepest enthusiasms.

The obvious question to ask is what does Christianity have to do with Sidonius' basic loyalties. The first point to make is that, like the chapel on the country estate, the Church is simply part of the landscape, an ingredient in the sort of *Romanitas* Sidonius defended with his life and letters. An example offers itself in Sidonius' description of the annual festival of St. Justus in Lyons. After the procession before daylight and the celebration of the Vigils, the large crowd temporarily disperses to rest before the Mass of the feast. Sidonius and his friends go to the tomb of Afranius Syagrius of Lyons, where they repose themselves in the shade or "on the green turf, which was also fragrant with flowers." Pleasant conversation follows; and many of those present fall to sport, some to ball games, others to dice. Sidonius is challenged to write a verse in honor of the towel that has just dried the face of one of the more energetic ballplayers. He completes his verses, and immediately they are told that the bishop is proceeding to the church. And so, they all arise and return to Mass (Ep. 5.xvii; LCL 2, pp. 227ff.). The remarkable aspect of Sidonius' description is that the church seems as natural a part of the day's festivities as the bath or a banquet would be in a country house party. The same can be said of Sidonius' poetic efforts. If he can write an epigram for a towel, he can also write poetry for his grandfather's grave (Ep. 3.xii) and for the rebuilt church of St. Martin at Tours (Ep. 4.xviii).

From one point of view, then, Sidonius understands the Church as a

prop of Roman culture, threatened as it was by the barbarians whom he
shuns "even if they are good" (Ep. 7.xiv; LCL 2, p. 381). Before the
cession of Auvergne he mobilizes the Church against the Visigoths. His
fear is that Euric will oppose the orthodox faith, and he is alarmed at the
many vacant bishoprics in Gaul (Ep. 7.vi). His imprisonment after the
fall of Clermont does nothing to improve his attitude towards the barbarians. What strikes him most about the jail is his inability to sleep,
"for a din would immediately arise from the two old Gothic women near
the skylight of my bedroom, the most quarrelsome, drunken, vomiting
creatures the world will ever see" (Ep. 8.iii; LCL 2, p. 407). At the same
time and perhaps in some contradiction, he sometimes displays a grudg-
ing admiration for the barbarians. He describes Prince Sigismer's wedding as "a pageant of Mars no less than of Venus" (Ep. 4.xx; LCL 2, p.
139). Perhaps it was this part of his complicated reaction to the barbarians that enabled him to live out his days at his episcopal post in a
homeland captive to the Visigoths. For Sidonius Roman culture would
continue so long as the Church remained its patron.

On the other hand, it would be far too simple to suppose that Sidonius
sees the Church as nothing but a cipher for Roman culture.[7] What he
says makes it abundantly clear that he takes his responsibilities as bishop
with utmost seriousness. He speaks of the burden of the calling that has
been thrust upon him (Ep. 5.iii) and of his own unworthiness to exercise
such a dignity (Ep. 6.i, 7.xiv). And he insists that bishops rank higher
than civil officials (Ep. 7.xii). He sees the role of the bishop as a patron
for his people, caring for their physical and social needs as well as for
their spiritual ones (Ep. 6.xii). One of his letters contains an address he
gave to decide an episcopal election in Bourges, where the root issue
seems to have been whether the best patron for the Church would be a
holy man or someone from the old aristocracy who would know how to
protect the Church in concrete ways.[8] Sidonius attempts to avoid what he
sees as a false dichotomy between a monk and a civil servant, but it is
clear enough where his true sympathies lie: The man he most admires is
holy, but also an aristocrat (Ep. 7.ix). Sidonius' ideal is best found in his
description of one Vettius (Ep. 4.ix). Vettius runs an efficient estate with
good servants, and he is highly hospitable. He is good with horses, dogs,
and hawks, but he is also devoted to prayer and the reading of Scripture.
In sum, Sidonius feels "bound to admire a priest-like man more than a
man in the priesthood" (LCL 2, p. 99). The point of view does seem a
trifle odd, but surely it indicates that in Sidonius' mind the Church is
more than an institutional way of preserving Roman culture; it must be
taken seriously in its own right. Indeed, the point is that what we should
see as an uneasy amalgam of *Romanitas* and Christianity is for Sidonius

a single whole. And it is his commitment to the Church that enables him to take an active part in helping his people to adapt to a new life under barbarian rule.

CASSIODORUS

Cassiodorus is remembered because he founded a double monastery on his family estate at Scyllacium in southeastern Italy and because his monks prepared and preserved manuscripts that enabled Christian and pagan classics of late antiquity to be passed down to later generations. Thus, his story is bound up with that of the monasteries of the Dark Ages that preserved civilization by withdrawing from the chaos of the world. And yet most of his life was spent not in retirement but at the centers of power in the Ostrogothic kingdom of Theodoric with its capital at Ravenna. Like Paulinus of Pella and Sidonius, he found his life broken in two by outward circumstance. In his case, however, it was not barbarian invasions that brought his old life to an end, but the impact of Justinian's reconquest of the West in the 530s. The Goths were increasingly pressed towards an anti-Roman position, which meant there was no longer any place to stand for people like Cassiodorus, who though Romans, had been committed to Theodoric's policy of Italian and Gothic cooperation. The irony of his life, then, is that the circumstances that forced him to withdraw from the world had nothing to do with barbarian victories, but on the contrary with barbarian defeat. Like Sidonius, he and his family had adapted to life under barbarian rule, save that since Theodoric preserved the Roman civil service, it was there rather than in the Church that Cassiodorus served.

Cassiodorus followed in the footsteps of his father, who had been the chief financial officer of the Western Empire under Odoacer, and who was employed by Theodoric the Ostrogoth after 493 as governor of Sicily, administrator of his home province, and praetorian prefect. It was in 503, the year his father became praetorian prefect, that Cassiodorus, in his early twenties, began his own public career. He became an assessor in his father's court, and soon afterwards he came to public attention because of his panegyric on Theodoric and was rewarded by being made a quaestor, a rare honor for so young a man. Later he followed his father as praetorian prefect and was named consul for the year 514. He received the title Patrician and like his father became governor of his native province. He pursued letters as well as public office, publishing about 520 his *Chronicon* and *Gothic History*, books which glorified the Goths and made them a part of Roman history. It was probably because of this work that Theodoric appointed him master of the offices ("chief of the civil service") in 523, a post he held until 527, the year after Theodoric's death. He remained active during the troubled years that followed and was praetorian prefect from 533 until 537. In 536 Justinian's general, Belisarius, captured Naples and soon afterwards laid siege to Rome. By 540 the Byzantines had captured Ravenna and Cassiodorus had been obliged to retire from public life. In the late 540s Cassiodorus went to Constantinople. By then Totila had become king of the Ostrogoths and had committed himself to a strong anti-Roman policy, successfully reconquering Italy. Cassiodorus was forced to side with Byzantium, but when he returned to Italy in the early 550s it was not as a public servant for Justinian.[9] Instead, he returned to his family estate and founded one monastery for hermits on Mount Castellum and another for coenobites named Vivarium after the fish ponds Cassiodorus had constructed on his estate.

Cassiodorus' project is quite self-conscious, and he explains it in the preface to his *Introduction to Divine and Human Readings*, which was in a sense the charter for his monasteries. His original aim was to persuade Pope Agapetus to cooperate with him in founding a school for Christian letters in Rome on the model of the school that had once existed in Alexandria or on that of the Jewish school in Nisibis of which Cassiodorus has heard. But "the struggles that seethed and raged excessively in the Italian realm" stood in the way. His treatise is designed to set forth a curriculum for the school he would have founded; and, while he envisages a wider audience than his own monasteries, it is clear from chapter 32 ("An Admonition for the Abbot and the Community of Monks") that he thinks of them as putting his ideas into practice so far as possible. In the first instance, "divine letters," of course, means Scripture. But though Cassiodorus recognizes that divine inspiration can sometimes open the meaning of Scripture miraculously, he is convinced that "we, however, ought not to long for such things frequently, but we ought rather to abide by the common practice of teaching" (Pref.). What he means is that the works of the Fathers ought to be consulted in order to make the true meaning of Scripture plain. Moreover, secular learning is not to be despised. It is true that "many illiterate persons attain true understanding," and there are bound to be monks unable to cope with philosophical and scholarly writings. Nevertheless, those capable of entering upon the study of humane letters ought to be bold in doing so, since these studies, if rightly used, will assist the attainment of true wisdom in interpreting Scripture (DL 28).

The course of study Cassiodorus recommends is to be part of a community engaged in contemplation and action. Indeed, the study is itself the contemplative life (DL 32; Jones, p. 137):

You have therefore been given a city of your own, O pious citizens, and if with the help of the Lord you spend your time concordantly and spiritually, you already enjoy a prefiguration of the heavenly home. . . . The authentic documents of the Sacred Scriptures together with their interpreters attend you, and they are truly the flowery fields, the sweet fruits of the heavenly paradise, with which faithful souls are imbued to their salvation and by which your tongues are instructed in a diction not destined to die but to bear fruit.

To study the Scriptures is to participate in the age to come, and in this way the monks have withdrawn from this age. On the other hand, Cassiodorus insists that the monastery has an obligation to be active in caring for the stranger and for the neighboring people. Baths have been built conducive to the healing of the sick, and the monastery exists in part to be sought by others (*DL* 29).

The more interesting aspect of the active life of the monastery, however, consists in its relation to those nearby. The peasants must be instructed "in good morals," and they may not be burdened "with the weight of increased taxes" (*DL* 32; Jones, p. 136). The comment is interesting because it presupposes a dependence of the local people on the monastery. Already we begin to see the double function of monasteries in the early Middle Ages. On the one hand, they were refuges from the storm and sanctuaries that enabled people to escape and be delivered from the doomed world outside. On the other hand, they were little pockets of order in a disordered age, and as such, the seeds of a renewed order in Europe. Cassiodorus seems to have recognized both these aspects of monasticism. While he certainly sees his enterprise as one of finding deliverance from a world fallen apart, he also sees it as a way of preserving what little order could be salvaged from the ruin of the time.

CHRISTIAN ATTITUDES TOWARD THE FALL OF THE WEST

Toward the end of chapter six I suggested that in the writings of Namatianus, Salvian, and Augustine we could find the themes of deliverance and of ordering playing themselves out somewhat as they had done in the earlier period where deliverance from the world was eventually transformed into the Christian reordering of the world in the fourth century. To conclude this chapter, let me reflect for a moment on that claim, substituting Orosius, who was a Christian, for the pagan Namatianus. The first point I should like to make is that the attitudes displayed by Paulinus of Pella, Sidonius, and Cassiodorus supply us with a

spectrum that bears striking resemblance to the points of view of Orosius, Salvian, and Augustine. There must have been those, like Sidonius,
who found in Christ the power to adapt themselves to changed circumstances and yet remain faithful to their own heritage. Others, like Cassiodorus, must have found Christ calling them out of this world altogether. Still others, like Paulinus of Pella, must have found in Christ the
power to endure without fully participating in or fully withdrawing from
the changed world around them. These different attitudes must have
been, of course, the product of differing circumstances. But, I believe, at
another level they represent a spectrum of attitudes found among Christians in every period of history, attitudes that represent differing human
responses to similar sets of similar of circumstances.

Orosius, who was born about 385 in Spain, became associated with
Augustine in Hippo some five or six years after the sack of Rome by
Alaric. He joined Augustine in seeking to refute the pagan claim that it
was the Christianization of the Empire that explained its present ill
fortune. In his dedication of the *History against the Pagans*, written in
418, Orosius tells us that Augustine had given him the task of investigat-
ing the past to see what sort of disasters could be found with a view to
answering the question whether the sack of Rome was anomolous or
simply one more tragedy in a long list. Orosius has discovered "that the
days of the past were not only as oppressive as those of the present but
that they were the more terribly wretched the further they were removed
from the consolation of true religion" (Dedication; Raymond, p. 31).
Orosius' thesis is an anti-apocalyptical one. The sack of Rome cannot be
understood as the prelude to a final doom of some kind. Instead, it is no
worse and even less a disaster than many events to be found in the past.
Indeed, Christianity, far from causing the disaster, actually blunted its
effect.[10] The thesis is a simple one, and it is designed not only to deny an
apocalyptic view of the present but also to maintain the prevailing Christian view that the Roman Empire was sacred and part of God's providential guidance of the whole world toward the truth of Christ. The practical conclusion to be drawn from Orosius' assessment is the optimistic
one that Christian Rome is destined to survive and triumph. Obviously,
Sidonius was obliged to abandon this conviction at a literal level; but it
seems to me that his is a stance toward events that fits Orosius' interpretation. Not only does he implicitly dismiss the idea that all is over, he
also believes that Christian Rome will survive in the Church. Though he
is not a reactionary deluding himself that the clock can be turned back,
he is a conservative who believes that his views and his commitment to a
Christian Rome can be maintained by being adapted to changed circumstances. He has hope that Christianity can continue to order society.

Salvian's view is at the opposite end of the spectrum from Orosius'. Little is known of Salvian's life save what can be deduced from his writings and from the brief biographical note given by Gennadius in his *Catalogue of Illustrious Men.* He seems to have been born to a family in the upper echelons of the imperial civil service in Gaul, so his background is not to be understood as significantly different from that of Sidonius. He and his wife became ascetics and lived for a time in the monasteries at Lérins. According to Gennadius he was a priest of Marseilles. His treatise *On the Government of God* must have been written between 439 and 450. His thesis is a very simple one. God rules the world with justice, and the barbarian conquests, together with the sufferings of Christians, are trials "he suffers us to endure . . . because we deserve to endure them" (4.12; Sanford, p. 119). The treatise is an indictment of the Roman Christian Empire as a social and economic system totally rotten and unjust. Implicit in the argument is the apocalyptic view that a well-deserved doom has begun to take effect and that the only sane option in the face of it is to follow the monks in their total renunciation of society (8.4–5; Sanford, pp. 228ff.). Cassiodorus' stance may not have been quite so apocalyptic and his withdrawal from society seems more passive than active, but I think it can be argued that he belongs toward the end of the spectrum represented by Salvian. To be a Christian obliges one to withdraw, and the monastery presents itself as an alternative to a hopeless society.

Augustine's attitude is harder to define. His reflections in *The City of God* take us beyond the two extreme alternatives we have just seen. He refuses to admit that present disasters can be interpreted apocalyptically, but he also denies that they can be minimized and made anything less than tragic. And his ruminations lead him to deny the accepted theory of his day that the Christian Empire was sacred, employed providentially by God. Instead, the Empire for Augustine is merely secular, neither good nor evil in and of itself, but instead the tragic setting in which the two mingled cities find their destiny being worked out. The paradox of the Christian life is that the evils we suffer in our earthly pilgrimage must be taken with absolute seriousness, but so must the destiny that awaits us in the City of God. There are no victories or defeats in the present that really matter. All that counts is the final victory for the saints in the age to come. The practical implication of Augustine's view is that what matters is to endure. The Christian can be neither fully involved in his society nor fully withdrawn from it. Instead, he must keep his sight on the pilgrim's path. Paulinius of Pella, I think, best fits the stance taken by Augustine, though I should admit that certain aspects of Sidonius' and Cassiodorus' attitudes may ally even them with

Augustine's insistence on the paradox of alien citizenship. I need scarcely confess that this last attitude makes most sense to me, but perhaps I should admit why: I am persuaded by Faulkner's view that we cannot alter the tragic character of human life, but that we can endure and so prevail.

One last comment is in order. What I have tried to suggest is that different Christians were empowered in different ways to react to the collapse of the West. And, in a sense, Augustine's pilgrim ideal would be in principle applicable both to those who sought to endure by adapting and to those who sought to endure by withdrawing. But we are talking here of individual responses. If we stand back from the historical development, an additional conclusion can be drawn. As I have pointed out, the monasteries in the early Middle Ages served the double function of refuges and of foundations for the reordering of society. There is something to be said for the view that the Church began by providing deliverance from the disasters that attended the collapse of Roman rule in the West, but ended by becoming the basis for a new order of society. A pattern that can be discerned in the first centuries of the Church's existence, leading to the new order of the Christian Empire, seems to repeat itself when we examine the end of late antiquity and the birth of the new order of the Middle Ages. Is this a way of looking at our own times? And are we living in the midst of the death of an old culture in which Christ brings us not so much an ordering of our society as a deliverance from it?

Epilogue

Despite the fact that my major concern in what I have been arguing has been to emphasize the diversity of Christianity in idea and in practice, it is impossible for me to resist the temptation to draw the threads together so far as that is possible. Looked at in detail the theological themes we have encountered are rich and diverse, drawing upon Scripture and the Platonizing lingua franca of the late antique world. They are indeed broken lights that point towards a total vision of truth available only in the age to come. And in the same way the mending of lives by these visionary lights takes place in many different ways. For some redemption means deliverance from past and present circumstances; for others, a reordering of present experience. Again, redemption sometimes focuses upon the hope beyond this world order; sometimes, on the ways in which that hope informs the present. There are, however, some least common denominators that run through the evidence we have examined. The theological themes comprise a vision of the Christian destiny that, in part, functions as a vision of life rooted in Christ and in the community that bears allegiance to him. And the application of these themes to the mending of human lives immediately involves the tensions between the Church and the world and between this world and the next that I have just noted.

The theological themes, of course, all meet in Christ. He is not only the victor, but his fate supplies us with a paradigm of the victory the Christian will share with him. In this sense, early Christianity is a religion of salvation more than it is a way of life. For this reason it is Christ's triumph over Satan, over death and sin, that really matters. That story is more important than his teachings and even than his example of righteous obedience. As well, since the story of Christ's victory is really the story of God's victory, it is immediately placed in the framework of the greater story embracing the whole of human history from Creation to the end of the world and what lies in the eternal future prepared by God. Thus, for the Fathers the "Incarnation" is not the nativity or even an account of Christ's person, but instead is the "Economy," the activity of God in Christ from his conception in Mary's womb to his Resurrection and exaltation. And *the* Economy, far from being an isolated event, is simply what brings to focus God's other economies in Creation, in the calling of Israel, in the sending of the prophets, and even in the gift of philosophy to the Greeks. Redemption not only overcomes the effects of Adam's fall, it also brings to completion God's creative work. Indeed, Redemption as the completion of Creation is simply a way of talking about one aspect of a total process initiated at what we normally call Creation and consummated in the age to come.

The technical aspects of patristic theology need to be seen in the context of the points I have just made. To put it as clearly as possible, if the Christian message focuses upon the story of God's victory in Christ, it becomes important to ask who the Victor is. As Irenaeus says, it was necessary that the victory be human; and yet only God could win it, and only the union of God and humanity could make it effective. The development of the doctrine of the Trinity serves to enable the Church to define the Victor as God without compromising Christian commitment to the heritage of Jewish monotheism; the christological debates revolved around how to maintain that the divine Victor was also the human Victor and the human being given victory. Christ is the Mediator. Both divine and human, he is the saved Saviour and the sanctified Sanctifier. Thus, the Christian can see in him not only the power of God to save, but the ways in which that power works: It conquers death, whereby the Resurrection of Christ becomes the principle for the general resurrection in which all shall partake, and it conquers the sin and blindness that separate human beings from God. And so redemption carries with it the idea of God's triumph over sin and his self-disclosure as perfect Truth, Goodness, and Beauty. The physical, moral, and spiritual dimensions of Redemption are all rooted in the classical accounts of Christ as divine and human, as the Victor who also supplies the paradigm of what victory means.

The theological themes encountered in Part Two, while retaining their focus on Christ, spring largely from understanding him as the paradigm of victory. The vision of Christian destiny and of the Christian life is a vision of salvation. In the first instance, this vision involves some account of the relation between grace and human freedom. What God has done in Christ, he also does and will do in us. At the same time his work involves our response, and we must choose to receive and use the gift he gives us. It is impossible not to confront this issue from the perspective of the Pelagian controversy. Where the early Fathers had simply seen grace and freedom as two coincident activities at different levels and so as two sides of the same coin, Pelagius and Augustine became embroiled in the question which comes first. Complicated questions arise. Did Christ bring Redemption for all? Is God's grace irresistible? Who will be saved? I have largely avoided these issues on the grounds that to speak of the Christian life, even in an Augustinian context, presupposes our ability to respond to God's grace and to exercise some freedom in choosing the good. But the issue has been implicit in much of what has been said. Generally speaking, all the different ways in which we have seen Christians trying to live their lives have been understood as human responses to the saving work of Christ.

More explicit in what we have seen is one of the leading themes in patristic thought, Irenaeus' idea that "the vision of God is the life of humanity." What he means by this is that the empowered mind is made capable of governing the body to such a degree that it renders the body incorruptible. What Irenaeus and the others are talking about, of course, is the resurrection of the body. The Fathers employ Stoic themes to explain what this means. The control of the body by the mind is more than just the life of virtue; it culminates in incorruption and impassibility, giving humanity a likeness to God so far as possible. We saw these themes most fully in discussing virginity in its relation to Christian attitudes toward the family. Chastity becomes a sign that the mind's governance of the body is indeed leading us toward the incorruption that is our resurrection destiny. This set of ideas, then, is primarily oriented toward the age to come, when physical redemption will take place; however, it also involves the moral dimension of salvation, which is present to us now. Finally, moving beyond the physical and moral aspects of salvation, the conviction that only when the mind is empowered by its vision of God can it begin to perform its destined task takes us in the direction of a spiritual understanding of salvation that is not always integrated with the Irenaean schema. A contemplative ideal stands in tension with the hope of moral and physical incorruption.

The vision of God, treated in its own right, is developed in Platonizing terms that revolve around interpretations of Plato's teachings above love. The ascent toward perfect beauty of which Plato speaks in the *Sympo-*

sium and the *Phaedrus* enables the Christian to take wings and fly toward God, in whom his soul will find rest. The ascent is often thought to consist of three sequential stages, moral, intellectual, and spiritual. And, as we have seen, what are three stages from the point of view of the Christian's destiny are three simultaneous aspects of his life. Moreover, with Nyssa the movement toward God has no term but is a continual progress, a movement to infinity. This contemplative ideal became central to monasticism in the West as well as in the East; wherever we have encountered monasticism we have also encountered this way of thinking of the Christian victory. Taken together, "incorruption" and "contemplation" label an extremely rich and complicated understanding of the Christian victory in its moral, intellectual, spiritual, and physical dimensions. And that victory makes us what we were intended to be in God's creative purpose.

Putting it this way means that the themes I have been discussing all drive toward a corporate understanding of human nature, since the Creator intended humanity to be social. So it is that Christ's victory necessarily involves the establishment of a community, and at every step of the way in the discussions in Part Two we have seen this communal ideal at work in differing ways. Even in virtue of Adam the human race is social, and the Fathers can expound the idea by employing the stock Stoic notion of "appropriation": To preserve myself I must preserve my family, my neighbors, my city, and ultimately all humanity. Christ as the new Adam establishes a humanity in which racial, economic, and social differences are abolished. The new family of the Church is established. Nyssa's development of the corporate theme is particularly important because it shows how the Christian community is understood in the light of the soteriological themes already mentioned and because it betrays the impact of solutions to the technical trinitarian and christological disputes. Humanity, as the image of God, must mirror God and by doing so find the power to govern the body and to harmonize and divinize the entire created order; contemplation leads to incorruption not only for the individual but also for the whole of creation. Moreover, the functions of the image are corporate because human nature, as the image of the Trinity, must be defined as a single, ineffable nature. Properly speaking, according to Nyssa, human individuals correspond to the persons of the Trinity and no more abolish the unity of human nature than Father, Son, and Spirit take away the unity of the Godhead. Just as the three divine persons are individuated as relations of a single nature, so human persons are in principle defined as relations of one nature. We have also encountered Augustine's rather different way of characterizing the corporate character of the Christian life, including his doctrine of the ordering of loves. All these themes inform the patristic understanding of the Church as Christ's family, expressing its unity in hospitality and in alien citizenship.

Applying these themes to the Christian life, as we have seen, proves to be a complicated task. Two tensions emerge, and they have been the preoccupation of chapters six to eight. First, there is the ambiguous relationship between the Christian life and Christian destiny. How is the age to come at work in the present? How are heaven and earth related to one another? I suggested we can distinguish participation from anticipation. On the one hand, sometimes the emphasis is upon ways in which human life can actually participate here and now in Christian destiny. The most obvious example is the widespread fourth- and fifth-century conviction that the Roman Empire was a sacralized order; participation may not have been complete, but it was possible and real. On the other hand, sometimes the present is cut off from the future: Hope can anticipate our destiny, but we cannot confuse our pilgrimage with its goal or our convalescence with perfect healing. This, of course, is Augustine's view, and it involves him in denying the usual view of the Empire and in insisting that Rome is secular. The root issue is the degree to which Redemption *from* this age can be Redemption *in* this age.

The second tension is more strictly this-worldly and involves the relationship of the Church to the world and of Christ to culture. There is, up to a point, a correlation with the first tension. Those who believed that the Christian life could participate in the age to come could also believe that this participation was meant to leaven the whole of society. Similarly, to say we can only anticipate the age to come could lead to the kind of withdrawal from the world that characterized some forms of early monasticism and that seems to represent Salvian's ideal. On the other hand, the correlation is deceptive. The tension between a this-worldly and an otherworldly Christianity is not quite the same as the tension between a catholic view that Christianity is meant for all and a holiness view that treats the Church in opposition to the world. In sum, it looks as though the Church is healthiest when the tensions are preserved—so that the Christian lives both in this world and in the light of the next and seeks to preserve both the holiness and the catholicity of the Church. Moreover, the course of history seems to act in such a way as to prevent the dominance of one or another of the poles of tension.

To list the theological themes and the tensions with which I have been preoccupied in one sense summarizes the argument. Yet I believe a more fundamental lesson is taught by what we have observed. The attempt to integrate theology and life is more important than apparent success in the enterprise. This is, I think, partly because there can be no one way of putting theology into life. We cannot identify our theological convictions with truth, since as Hooker said, "The things that are most certain are least certainly perceived." Since theology is a business of broken lights, we cannot have exact knowledge of the ideal we want to actualize. Moreover, lives can be mended in any number of ways, and therefore a number of valid ways exist for translating the vision into virtue. The trouble is that the very terms with which we are dealing lie outside any infallible grasp we might have upon them. Nevertheless, the reason the attempt to bring theology to life is more important than success in the enterprise is not just a sour grapes reaction. We can take seriously Augustine's insistence that we are pilgrims; what matters for us is the journey. We can neither know the destination with exactitude nor avoid the detours along the way, but we can constantly raise the question of how the destiny affects our next steps. We need to grow in our apprehension of the broken lights of God's truth and to learn how those lights can show us the next steps in a mending that can never be completed in this life.

Notes

INTRODUCTION

NOTES

1. What I am assuming is that there is no contradiction between the beliefs of the leaders and intelligentsia of the Church and those of the common people. Both were fully involved in the life of the Church; and however much their understanding of that life differed, they were both interpreting the same phenomenon. I am happy to find Peter Brown rejecting any "two-tiered" model for assessing the early Church and arguing that we cannot oppose popular to official piety. See his persuasive discussion in *The Cult of the Saints*, pp. 12–22.

2. The development is, of course, more complex than this; and the particular ancestors of the Apostles' and the Nicene Creeds are to be found not in rules of faith, but in the baptismal interrogations. See J. N. D. Kelly, *Early Christian Creeds*, especially pp. 94–99. Nonetheless, in broad terms the content of rules of faith does not differ significantly from that of the interrogative baptismal creeds.

3. See R. P. C. Hanson, *Tradition in the Early Church*, p. 256: "Perhaps it is an overstatement to say that tradition *is* interpretation of the Bible; it would be better to say . . . that tradition is created and formed by interpretation. The two overlap and interact."

4. Cf. Alexander Schmemann, *For the Life of the World* (Crestwood, N.Y.: St. Vladimir's Press, 1973), p. 38: "In and through the Eucharist the whole creation becomes what it always was to be and yet failed to be." Schmemann elaborates the patristic perspective from a modern Orthodox point of view.

5. For the citations see Theodore of Mopsuestia, *Commentary on Nahum* (Migne, *Patrologia Graeca* 66.401–4) and *Commentary on Jonah* (Migne, *Patrologia Graeca* 66.320B). See my discussion in *The Captain of Our Salvation* (Tübingen. J. C. B. Mohr, 1973), especially chapters 1 and 5. See also volume 1 of *The Cambridge History of the Bible*.

6. I am indebted to a lecture given by Morton Smith at Yale some years ago in which he argued that Iamblichus' *On the Mysteries* is to be regarded as a *summa theologica* of magic. So far as I can discover, Smith's lecture was never published.

7. See Michael Gough, *The Origins of Christian Art*, plates 10, 14, 15; pp. 19, 21–22.

8. It is often supposed that the "Law" replaces the "Gospel" in the Church after New Testament times. Maurice Wiles in *The Christian Fathers* (New York: Oxford University Press, 1982) deals judiciously with the question on pp. 163–65. See p. 165; "Baptism embodied God's free gift of salvation which could not be earned by any keeping of the moral law. But once received that gift had to be preserved. And the requirement for its preservation was the keeping of God's law. . . . It is here that the note of legalism creeps into early Christian teaching." It is not so much the absence of a doctrine of grace that characterizes the Fathers' teaching before Augustine as the absence of the issues of the Pelagian controversy.

9. See Carl Andresen, *Logos und Nomos*, especially pp. 393–400.

SECONDARY SOURCES

Of the many books treating the history of the later Roman Empire I have found J. B. Bury, *History of the Later Roman Empire* to give the most helpful chronological narrative of the fifth and sixth centuries. A. H. M. Jones, *The Later Roman Empire* covers more ground and supplies excellent and detailed discussions of aspects of late Roman society. On the Christian side Hans Lietzmann, *A History of the Early Church* remains a standard account of the Church in the apostolic and patristic period, though W. H. C. Frend, *The Rise of Christianity* (Philadelphia: Fortress Press, 1984) may well replace Lietzmann as the standard work in English. Frend's bibliographies are extensive and up-to-date. Henry Chadwick, *The Early Church* (Harmondsworth: Penguin Books, 1967) and Robert M. Grant, *Augustus to Constantine* (London: Collins, 1971) deserve mention as useful introductions to the period; and *The Cambridge Ancient History* (Cambridge: Cambridge University Press, 1923–39) remains important for both general and Church history. Ramsay MacMullen, *Christianizing the Roman Empire* is a provocative study of the role of wonder-working in the "triumph" of the Church.

The history of Christian doctrine in the patristic period is treated thematically by Jaroslav Pelikan, *The Emergence of the Catholic Tradition*. For the beginner the more chronological approach of J. N. D. Kelly, *Early Christian Doctrines* is probably to be recommended; and Justo L. Gonzalez, *A History of Christian Thought*, volume 1 (Nashville: Abingdon, 1970) supplies a textbook approach to the period. Louis Bouyer, *The Spirituality of the New Testament and the Fathers* gives a survey of theology from the point of view of the spiritual life. Aloys Grillmeier, *Christ in Christian Tradition: From the Apostolic Age to Chalcedon (451)* (Eng. tr. J. S. Bowden; New York: Sheed & Ward, 1965, enlarged & rev. 1975) is a standard treatment of Christology. Johannes Quasten, *Patrology* is the reference work most widely used; and Frances Young, *From Nicaea to Chalcedon* is not only useful as an introduction to the conciliar period, but also has extensive bibliographical information and judicious assessments of the present state of patristic scholarship.

A number of particular studies deserve mention. *The Cambridge History of the Bible*, volume 1, describes the origin and development of the Biblical canon; and part 5 includes articles on Origen, Theodore of Mopsuestia, Jerome, and Augustine as Biblical exegetes. R. P. C. Hanson, *Tradition in the Early Church* examines the relation of Scripture and tradition, while J. N. D. Kelly, *Early Christian Creeds* is the standard work on the development that leads to the Nicene and the Apostles' Creeds. Three books that are important for the study of the early liturgy are: Dom Gregory Dix, *The Shape of the Liturgy* (London: Adam & Charles Black, 1945); Joachim Jeremias, *Infant Baptism in the First Four Centuries* (London: SCM Press, 1960); and Josef A. Jungmann, *The Early Liturgy* (Notre Dame, Ind.: University of Notre Dame Press, 1959).

With respect to individual writers the reader may consult Quasten and Young for full bibliographical information. The books that have been particularly influential on my ideas in the Introduction are: Carl Andresen, *Logos und Nomos*; L. W. Barnard, *Justin Martyr: His Life and Thought* (Cambridge: Cambridge University Press, 1967); Charles Bigg, *The Christian Platonists of Alexandria* (2nd ed. London: Oxford University Press, 1913); Jean Daniélou, *Origen* (London: Sheed & Ward, 1955); and Hugo Rahner, *Greek Myths and Christian Mystery* (New York: Harper & Row, 1963). Rahner makes considerable use of Clement of Alexandria's writings in the course of his argument.

CHAPTER ONE

NOTES

1. See Michael Gough, *The Origins of Christian Art*, pp. 34–39; plate 30.

2. See Matthew 12:38–42 and 16:4 (cf. Luke 11:29–32). Matthew understands "the sign of Jonah" in reference to Christ's death and resurrection, as well as to repentance. Luke has only the second interpretation.

3. Cf. Samuel Laeuchli's discussion of the "arcane" character of early Christianity as implying "a new religious-psychological search for security and return . . . the craving of ancient man for a safe, exclusive society. . . ." *Mithraism in Ostia* (Evanston: Northwestern University Press, 1967), p. 99.

4. Cf. Ramsay MacMullen, *Christianizing the Roman Empire*. MacMullen underlines the role of miracles and exorcisms in the process he seeks to describe. For example, he says (pp. 108f.): "In taking our measure of Christian wonders, on which Christians so continually insist, what needs emphasis is not that they were reported and believed. . . . We need not struggle, either . . . with the question Did they really occur? . . . Nor do we need to stress the fact that the most talked-about Christian miracles were routinized, in the hands of special officers of the congregation. . . . No, the unique force of Christian wonder-working that does indeed need emphasis lies in the fact that *it destroyed belief as well as creating it*—that is, if you credited it, you had then to credit the view that went with it, denying the character of god to all other divine powers whatsoever." This judgment seems a sound recognition of the fact that it was not the wonders alone that produced conversion. We shall find in the patristic theologians a tendency to omit or even to downplay the miraculous. Their concern is less with the "wonder-working" than with "the view that went with it." Origen, for example, does not deny Celsus' view that Jesus was a wonder-worker, but insists that Jesus used "his tricks to call the spectators to moral reformation" (*CC* 1.68; Chadwick, p. 63). See Eugene V. Gallagher, *Divine Man or Magician?: Celsus and Origen on Jesus*, SBL Dissertation Series 64 (Chico, CA: Scholars Press, 1982).

5. Cited by Eusebius *HE* 5.20.5–6; LCL 1, p. 497.

6. Cited by Eusebius *HE* 5.1.4–63; LCL 1, pp. 407–37.

7. One problem with Irenaeus' theology is assessing how far he is original and how far he simply duplicates previous traditions that are often contradictory of one another. F. Loofs, *Theophilus von Antiochien Adversus Marcionem und die anderen theologischen Quellen bei Irenaeus* (Texte und Untersuchungen zur Geschichte der altchristlichen Literatur, vol. 46, pt. 2; Leipzig, 1930), grants Irenaeus no originality and explains problems in his thought by his failure to integrate his sources. Loofs' view seems exaggerated, and we can safely assume that Irenaeus is in some measure a constructive theologian. The major point to make, however, is that to Irenaeus the task is not so much being an original thinker as articulating what he regards as the common theology of the Church.

8. Albert Houssiau, *La Christologie de saint Irénée*, argues for the coherence of Irenaeus' account of Christ and concludes that "la christologie d'Irénée sera largement sanctionée, durant les siècles qui suivront, par l'orthodoxie catholique" (p. 256). I should agree that the main lines of Irenaeus' thought lend themselves to an "orthodox" understanding, but am more doubtful than Houssiau that all problems have been solved.

9. Irenaeus' *Against Heresies* is preserved for us in an ancient Latin translation of the Greek. The three English phrases all translate the Latin "recapitulans."

10. A rabbinic comment on Leviticus 26:39 ("and also because of the iniquities of their fathers they shall pine away like them") supplies a way of explaining Romans 5:12 (*Sifra* 112a; ed. I. H. Weiss: Vienna, 1862). The verse is contrasted with Deuteronomy 24:16, where "the fathers shall not be put to death for the children nor shall the children be put to death for the fathers; every man shall be put to death for his own sin." Thus, the comment begins by recognizing the contradiction in Scripture between passages teaching corporate guilt and passages insisting upon individual responsibility. The resolution of the problem is: "At the time when they embrace the deeds of their fathers generation after generation after generation, they will be judged on their own responsibility." In other words, we may distinguish the explanation for the sons' sins and their moral responsibility for following the bad example of their fathers.

11. This seems to me the best way of handling a complicated problem. Irenaeus can say or imply that Adam was created in the image and likeness of God (*AH* 3.18.1, 3.22.1–2)—or at least in the likeness of God (*AH* 4.pref.4, 5.6.1). But he can also say that the full image and likeness have been given only in the Incarnate Lord (*AH* 4.38.4, 5.16.2). We cannot avoid saying that Irenaeus contradicts himself in interpreting Genesis 1:26f. At the same time, it is clear that he wants to resolve the problem by insisting that what was intended for Adam was actualized only in Christ. For a discussion of the important secondary literature on the question see John Lawson, *The Biblical Theology of Saint Irenaeus*, pp. 8–19, 13–14, 155–56, 200–203, 204–6. For Lawson's own view see pp. 209–11.

12. Cf. *Dem.* 5; *AH* 1.22.1, 3.8.3; Theophilus of Antioch, *Ad Autolycum* 1.7.

13. Cf. Gustav Wingren, *Man and the Incarnation*, p. xiv, summarizing the argument of part three: "Thus, in the Church the original Creation breaks through afresh and extends towards the resurrection, when the Devil and death will be destroyed and annihilated. Not until the Consummation will Creation be fully realised, for not until then will God's primal decision concerning man, *Let us make man in our own image* (Gen. 1.26), be accomplished, and this fulfilment of God's purpose is wholly dependent on the fact of Christ's becoming

man, His conflict, and His victory." It is in this context that Wingren believes we must discuss "recapitulation."

14. For a full discussion of early Christian views of the millennium see Jean Daniélou, *Théologie du Judéo-christianisme*, pp. 342–66.

15. Hippolytus in *The Apostolic Tradition* (early third century) gives us our best evidence for the Christian passover. Of course, we cannot be sure that what was customary at Rome was also customary in Gaul and Asia Minor twenty or thrity years earlier. And we know that there was a dispute over the date of Easter (the Quartodeciman controversy) in which Irenaeus was himself involved. And there is also the temptation to read Hippolytus in the light of what we know about the paschal feast from much later evidence. Nevertheless, the problems can be exaggerated. There seems no reason to doubt that the general features of the feast remained stable throughout the early period.

SECONDARY SOURCES

One of the best introductions to Irenaeus' thought is to be found in chapter three of Richard A. Norris, *God and World in Early Christian Theology* (New York: Seabury Press, 1965). Norris describes the broad structure of Irenaeus' thought, but manages to combine a lucid overview with penetrating analysis of problems of detail. André Benoit, *Saint Irénée: Introduction à l'Étude de sa Théologie* (Paris: Presses Universitaires de France, 1960) is a more technical but a sound discussion of literary and historical problems that must be faced in studying Irenaeus. John Lawson, *The Biblical Theology of Saint Irenaeus* and Gustav Wingren, *Man and the Incarnation* expound the broad structure of Irenaeus' theology with particular emphasis on its Biblical character. Albert Houssiau, *La Christologie de saint Irénée* and Juan Ochagavía, *Visible Patris Filius: A Study of Irenaeus' Teaching on Revelation and Tradition*, Orientalia Christiana Analecta 171 (Rome: Pont. Inst. Orient. Stud., 1964) deal with particular problems in Irenaeus' thought. Two books, one old and one new, are good introductions to the study of Gnosticism: Hans Jonas, *The Gnostic Religion: The Message of the Alien God and the Beginnings of Christianity* (2nd ed. rev.; Boston: Beacon Press, 1963) and Kurt Rudolph, *Gnosis: The Nature and History of Gnosticism* (San Francisco: Harper & Row; 1983).

CHAPTER TWO

NOTES

1. See Michael Gough, *The Origins of Christian Art*, pp. 154–55; plates 149–50.

2. See *Life of Saint Macrina* 15ff.; Grégoire de Nysse, *Vie de Sainte Macrine*, French tr. & ed. Pierre Maraval, Sources chrétiennes 178 (Paris: Les éditions du cerf, 1971), pp. 190ff.

3. The roots of the image theology may be found as early as Justin Martyr (ca. 155 c.e.), who speaks of "the seed of reason [the Logos] implanted in every race of men . . ." (*2 Apol.* 8; *ANF* 1, p. 191). The eclectic philosophical background of Justin's doctrine includes the Platonizing idea that individual human souls participate in the World Soul. That participation enables them to know the good and so to do the good. And Justin identifies the World Soul with the pre-existent Christ (*1 Apol.* 60). In Origen we find the pattern set in a broader

context. The eternal Word of God is the image of the Father (cf. 2 Cor. 4:4, Col. 1:15); rational beings are created *according to* the image of God (cf. Gen. 1:26), that is, modelled after the Word. This Origenist theology is also found in Athanasius' *De incarnatione*. The problem, of course, is that it implies the sort of distinction between the Father and the Word that played into the hands of the Arians, for whom the distinction was one of nature. Consequently, the later Athanasius abandons the Origenist theme; and with the Cappadocians we find the theme redefined so that humanity is the image of the Trinity.

4. Posidonius lived from ca. 135 to ca. 50 B.C.E. He went to Rome in 87 B.C.E. to represent Rhodes, and Cicero studied under him in 78 B.C.E. His ideas are reflected in Cicero's *Somnium Scipionis and De natura deorum*. For a discussion of Posidonius and his influence on Nyssa, see D. L. Balás, *Metousia Theou*, pp. 36–40, especially footnotes, 95, 96, 110, 118. The possible parallels may be explored by comparing Nyssa's *On the Making of Man* with Cicero, *De natura deorum* 2.73–end. Cicero is retailing the "Stoic" arguments, but the opinions of Posidonius are certainly a part of his account.

5. The point can be made more easily with respect to Basil the Great. See especially Ep. 361, where he is unwilling to understand the one *ousia* of the Godhead as a "common genus transcending" the Three or as a "material substratum pre-existing them" or any "partition of the original." His language implies a rejection of the usual philosophical models. For Ep. 361 see G. L. Prestige, *St. Basil the Great and Apollinaris of Laodicea* (London: S.P.C.K., 1956). The Cappadocians virtually equate *ousia* and nature, and they argue that the three *hypostaseis* are not to be understood at the level of the nature of God. This position reflects the refusal to handle the problem of the one and the three by using the available philosophical models. Cf. also Nyssa's own attitude towards "the insipid salt of the pagan wisdom" in the passage I cite below, p. 56.

6. This way of putting it depends to some degree on understanding what Nyssa means by using terms found in the theology of Maximus the Confessor (*diaphora* 'difference'; *diairesis* 'division'). Cf. Lars Thunberg, *Microcosm and Mediator: The Theological Anthropology of Maximus the Confessor* (Lund: C. W. K. Gleerup, 1965), pp. 54ff.

7. Chapter 16 of *On the Making of Man* is notoriously difficult to explain. Part of the problem can be understood as Nyssa's retention of certain Origenist themes, while rejecting Origen's notion of a pre-cosmic creation. For one attempt to resolve the difficulties see E. Corsini, "Plérôme humain et plérôme cosmique chez Grégoire de Nysse," in *Écriture et culture philosophique dans la pensée de Grégoire de Nysse*, ed. Marguerite Harl (Leiden: E. J. Brill, 1971), pp. 111–26.

8. It may be that this is going too far as an interpretation of the passage in question. Note 24, p. 294, in LCC 3 interprets "logical limits" to mean "all humanity." Nonetheless, we need only place this view in relation to Nyssa's understanding of the role of humanity to arrive at the interpretation I am suggesting.

9. Discussions of Apollinaris' Christology may be found in the secondary sources listed after the footnotes for the Introduction. The reader may also consult R. A. Norris, *Manhood and Christ: A Study in the Christology of Theodore of Mopsuestia* (London: Oxford University Press, 1963), part 2.

10. For the Arians the human experiences of Christ in the Incarnation prove that the Word is mutable and, consequently, less than God, i.e., a creature. Francis A. Sullivan in *The Christology of Theodore of Mopseustia* (Rome: Analecta Gregoriana 82, 1956), p. 162, puts the argument "in the form of a syllogism:

Maj. The Word is the subject even of the human operations and sufferings of Christ.

Min. But whatever is predicated of the Word, must be predicated of him *kata physin.*

Ergo: The nature of the Word is limited and affected by the human operations and sufferings of Christ."

The Antiochene Christology attacks the major premise by positing two subjects in the Incarnate Lord; the Alexandrian, the minor premise by positing two modes of predication, natural and economic.

11. I am suggesting a difficulty in the passage. The "beast" on which the Good Samaritan rides must signify the humanity of Christ and not just a human body appropriated by the Word of God. Nyssa can use the expressions "body" and "flesh" to refer to a full human nature, the part standing for the whole. Only if we interpret him this way does what he says here accord with his usual Christology.

12. The point is made explicitly in *De perfectione:* ". . . so that he might make you again the image of God he himself became the image of the invisible God through his love for humanity. . . ." (Jaeger 8.1, pp. 194–95)

13. See, for example, Nyssa's discussion of the hardening of Pharaoh's heart in *LM* 73ff., CWS, pp. 70–74. Cf. my discussion in "The Analogy of Grace in Theodore of Mopsuestia's Christology," *Journal of Theological Studies* 34 (1983), pp. 82–92.

14. See the introduction to *LM* in CWS, pp. 5–9. The parallels with Philo are given in the notes.

15. Here I should disagree with Jaeger's tendency to treat Nyssa as something of a Pelagian before Pelagius. See Werner Jaeger, *Two Rediscovered Works,* pp. 85–114, especially p. 89; "From the point of view of orthodox faith, which rejected Pelagius' doctrine as heresy, Gregory's attempt at reconciling grace and nature is not much better. It would have to be classified as Semipelagianism. But such a classification would be anachronistic. . . ." My point is that such a judgement is not only anachronistic but fails to respect the context in which Nyssa locates the theme of divine assistance.

16. For an excellent treatment of the subject see John M. Rist, *Eros and Psyche.*

17. For an interesting discussion of a similar idea, namely the movement out of time towards eternity, see Hannah Arendt, *Thinking,* pp. 202–13.

SECONDARY SOURCES

I have found the best general introductions to Nyssa's thought to be Hans von Balthasar, *Présence et Pensée: Essai sur la philosophie religieuse de Grégoire de Nysse* (Paris: G. Beauchesne, 1942) and Jean Daniélou, *Platonisme et Théologie Mystique: Doctrine Spirituelle de Saint Grégoire de Nysse* (Paris: Aubier, 1944). Daniélou's essays in *L'Être et le Temps chez Grégoire de Nysse* (Leiden: E. J. Brill, 1970) provide helpful discussions of particular themes. Nyssa's image theology is treated by Jérome Gaïth, *La Conception de la Liberté chez Grégoire de Nysse* (Paris: Librairie Philosophique J. Vrin, 1953) and by Roger Leys, *L'image de Dieu chez saint Grégoire de Nysse* (Brussels: Desclée de Brouwer, 1951). David L. Balás, *Metousia Theou* is an extremely suggestive treatment of Nyssa's account of the hierarchical structure of the universe. Ronald E. Heine, *Perfection in the Virtuous Life: A Study in the Relationship Between Edification and Polemical Theology in Gregory of Nyssa's De Vita Moysis,* Patristic Monograph Series 2 (Cambridge, Mass.: Philadelphia Patristic Foundation, 1975) and Walther Völker, *Gregor von*

Nyssa als Mystiker (Wiesbaden: Franz Steiner Verlag GMBH, 1955) examine Nyssa as a mystic. Werner Jaeger, *Two Rediscovered Works*, Part 1.5, pp. 70ff., focuses upon Nyssa's doctrine of grace and his relationship to themes that come to be thought of as Pelagian. Even though he does not discuss Nyssa, John M. Rist in *Eros and Psyche* describes in detail the sort of Platonizing doctrine of love that informs Nyssa's thought.

CHAPTER THREE

NOTES

1. Émile Bréhier, *The Philosophy of Plotinus*, Eng. tr. J. Thomas (Chicago: University of Chicago Press, 1958), pp. 13–19.

2. We need to remember, however, that there is nothing unusual about this opinion. Pelagius' elitist brand of Christianity envisaged, if anything, a smaller number of "saved" than Augustine did. Cf. Peter Brown, *Augustine of Hippo*, p. 372: "There is a cold streak in the mentality of the whole Pelagian movement. . . . It is Pelagius, not Augustine, who harps on the terrors of the Last Judgment. . . ."

3. The beginning of the prayer suggests that Augustine already begins to see complications in the dialectic of contemplation and action. We should expect him to pray either that his life be purified in order to see God or that he may see God in order to purify his life. Instead, he says: "O God, Creator of the universe, give me first that I may pray aright, then that I may conduct myself worthy of being heard by thee, and finally that I may be set free by thee." (*Sol.* I.i.2; LCC 6, p. 23) Contemplation is meant to lead to action, but both are transcended by being "set free."

4. In *Of True Religion* Augustine seems to be moving away from Christian Platonism towards his mature view. Christian Platonism would understand "faith" to be an innate capacity and the starting point of knowledge. (See S. R. C. Lilla, *Clement of Alexandria*, pp. 118ff.) Augustine comes to mistrust this view and redefines faith as the Catholic faith, an external confession rather than an innate capacity. Cf. *Of True Religion* x.20; LCC 6, p. 235: "I have come to the conclusion that this is the method I must use. Hold fast whatever truth you have been able to grasp, and attribute it to the Catholic Church."

5. It may be possible to distinguish the point of view of Book III from that of the earlier books, since Augustine wrote the treatise over a long period of time. In the long run, however, Augustine seems poised between an earlier Christian Platonist view that would argue we are able to choose good as well as evil and his mature view that we are not only incapable of choosing the good, but also incapable of responding to God's grace before election.

6. On the other hand, the predestinarian schema of his mature thought may also be found in the *Confessions*. See the summary in *Conf.* 13.34 and cf. *Conf.* 13.14, 17, 20.

7. Cf. the Stoic texts assembled by C. J. DeVogel, *Greek Philosophy*, vol. 3, pp. 80–82; and see the entire section pp. 78–85.

8. Note that they thus constitute themselves a perverse mirror image of the Trinity and of the triune structure of being, knowledge, and love.

9. Augustine is the first to think through what we do when we will and to move beyond the usual Christian Platonist view that willing is choosing between

good and evil. Hannah Arendt calls him "the first philosopher of the will." See her excellent and provocative discussion in *Willing*, pp. 84–110.

10. In the phrase from Romans 5:12 translated by the RSV "because all men sinned" Augustine's Latin reads *in quo* for "because." The Latin words are meant to express a Greek idiom for "because" (*eph' hōi*), and *quo* should be construed as neuter. Augustine, following Ambrosiaster, treats the *quo* as masculine and understands "in whom, *sc.* Adam, all men sinned." See Eugene TeSelle, *Augustine the Theologian*, p. 158.

11. Cf. Hannah Arendt, *Willing*, p. 104.

12. Augustine certainly does not deny that even pagans can do good deeds. The point is that he shifts attention to the motives of human actions and argues that motives are always tainted with love of self. From this perspective even the good we do is not really good; and since the will is enslaved because of original sin, it is an evil tree that always brings forth evil fruit.

13. There is, however, one place where Augustine casually refers to what appears to be his solution to the problem (*CG* 18.47; PC, p. 829): ". . . those among other nations who lived by God's standards and were pleasing to God, as belonging to the spiritual Jerusalem. But it must not be believed that this was granted to anyone unless he had received a divine revelation of 'the one mediator between God and men, the man Christ Jesus' (1 Tim. 2:5) whose future coming in a material body was foreannounced to the saints of antiquity. . . ." Calvin builds upon Augustine's apparent recognition of the elect before Christ. See *Institutes* 4.1.7, LCC 21; *Calvin: Institutes of the Christian Religion*, ed. J. T. McNeill (Philadelphia: Westminster Press, 1960), p. 1021: "Sometimes by the term church it [Holy Scripture] means that which is actually in God's presence. . . . Then, indeed, the church includes not only the saints presently living on earth, but all the elect from the beginning of the world." See note 14 on p. 1022 of LCC 21, where references are given to the theme in Augustine, Wycliffe, Hus, Luther, Zwingli, and others and to articles 6 and 8 of the Augsburg Confession.

14. See the clear statement in *DT* 13.12.16 (*NPNF¹* 3, p. 175): "By the justice of God in some sense, the human race was delivered into the power of the devil; the sin of the first man passing over originally into all of both sexes in their birth through conjugal union, and the debt of our first parents binding their whole posterity." The whole of the discussion that follows is relevant.

15. For a good discussion and analysis of his argument see John Burnaby's introduction and notes to the *DT* in LCC 8, *Augustine: Later Works* (Philadelphia: Westminster Press, 1955).

16. For the best discussion see John Burnaby, *Amor Dei*.

SECONDARY SOURCES

The secondary literature on Augustine is vast. C. Andresen, *Bibliographia Augustiniana* (Darmstadt: Wissenschaftliche Buchgesellschaft, 1962) includes bibliographical information arranged topically to 1961. Peter Brown, *Augustine of Hippo* allows Augustine to tell his story in his own words and is essential for an understanding of Augustine's intellectual and religious pilgrimage, as well as important for a general understanding of late antiquity. Eugene TeSelle, *Augustine the Theologian* traces Augustine's pilgrimage by examining what he read at different periods of his life and showing how he was influenced by his reading. John Burnaby, *Amor Dei* avoids the predestinarian structure of Augustine's thought, but gives a comprehensive account of his theology and spirituality under the rubric of love. Etienne Gilson, *The Christian Philosophy of St. Augustine* (New York: Random House, 1960) is a more or less systematic treatment of the Augustine that becomes central to medieval theology. R. A. Markus, *Saeculum* argues convincingly that Augustine breaks with the prevailing view of his time by refusing to see the Empire as sacral.

Chapter Four

NOTES

1. See Federico Fellini, *Fellini's Satyricon*, ed. Dario Zanelli, tr. E. Walter and J. Matthews (New York: Ballantine Books, 1970), p. 8, where Fellini calls the film a "fantasy" and "a species of nebula."

2. The information given in what follows is taken from Balsdon and Carcopino; see the secondary sources for this chapter.

3. For a discussion of the Christian population in the Empire see R. M. Grant, *Early Christianity and Society*, chapter 1.

4. See H. I. Marrou, *A History of Education in Antiquity*, pp. 355ff. The quotations that follow are taken from pp. 362–63.

5. See David L. Balch, *Let Wives be Submissive: The Domestic Code in 1 Peter*, SBL Monograph Series 26 (Chico, CA: Scholars Press, 1981). For the household as the basic unit in earliest Christianity, see Wayne A. Meeks, *The First Urban Christians*, pp. 29–30, 75–77.

6. W. D. Davies in *The Setting of the Sermon on the Mount* (Cambridge: Cambridge University Press, 1964), pp. 393–95, interprets the passage in relation to Matthew's interpretation of the new Law.

7. See Raymond E. Brown, *The Gospel according to John XIII–XXI*, The Anchor Bible 29A (New York: Doubleday, 1970), pp. 918–31.

8. See 1 Corinthians 11:2–16. Cf. C. K. Barrett, *The First Epistle to the Corinthians*, Black's New Testament Commentaries (London: Adam & Charles Black, 1968) ad loc., especially p. 255: ". . . her veil represents the new authority given to the woman under the new dispensation to do things which formerly had not been permitted her."

9. See Jean LaPorte, *The Role of Women*, p. 77, including his footnotes. See also Elizabeth A. Clark, *Jerome, Chrysostom, and Friends*, part 4, which includes a translation of John Chrysostom's *Treatises on the Subintroductae*.

10. See Johannes Quasten, *Patrology*, vol. 1, pp. 171–73. The translation cited is on p. 172.

11. See also A. D. Nock's judgment in *Conversion* (1933; London: Oxford University Press, 1961), p. 14: "It is wholly unhistorical to compare Christianity and Mithraism as Renan did, and to suggest that if Christianity had died Mithraism might have conquered the world. It might and would have won plenty of adherents, but it could not have founded a holy Mithraic church throughout the world."

12. See J. P. Broudéhoux, *Mariage et famille chez Clément d'Alexandrie* (Paris: Beauchesne et ses fils, 1970), pp. 196f.: "L'Alexandrin professe incontestablement une estime très haute pour le mariage: il n'a pour cet état que des paroles d'éloge. Il affirme la sainteté du mariage, et il faut bien reconnaître que cette attitude n'a pas de parallèle dans l'Église de cette periode." On the other hand, Broudéhoux argues that Clement also preaches the ideal of virginity, treating it

". . . comme un mieux par rapport à un bien. . . . Il reste que Clément n'est pas parvenu à réaliser cette difficile synthèse . . ." (p. 198). See also his bibliography.

13. See Hippolytus *Ref.* 9.7; *ANF* 5, p. 131. Hippolytus is following what was permitted by Roman law. See Ludwig Friedländer, *Roman Life*, vol. 1, p. 238. Cf. also Peter Brown's discussion of Augustine's concubine in *Augustine of Hippo*, pp. 61ff.

14. The quotation that follows is taken from Lewis and Reinhold, *Sourcebook II*, p. 606. In the West clerical celibacy began to be legislated as early as the late fourth century.

15. Fear of homosexuality seems to have become a factor in refusing boys admission to the monasteries. But this does not seem to have been an issue in the early generation of the desert fathers, nor does it appear to be involved in the story of Patermucius. See Derwas J. Chitty, *The Desert a City*, pp. 66f.

16. See Elizabeth Clark, *Jerome, Chrysostom, and Friends*, where the "friends" are women. See also Jean Chrysostome, *Lettres à Olympias*, French tr. & ed. Anne-Marie Malingrey, Sources chrétiennes 13 (Paris: Éditions de cerf, 1947); J. N. D. Kelly, *Jerome*, especially chapters 10 and 23.

17. See Peter Brown, "Aspects of the Christianization of the Roman Aristocracy," "Pelagius and His Supporters: Aims and Environment," and "The Patrons of Pelagius: The Roman Aristocracy between East and West," in *Religion and Society*, pp. 161–226, especially pp. 187ff. See also Brown's discussion of Pelagian perfectionism and its appeal in the early fifth century in *Augustine of Hippo*, pp. 346–51.

18. See A. Moulard, *Saint Jean Chrysostome, le défenseur du mariage et l'apôtre de la virginité* (Paris, 1923); C. Baur, *John Chrysostom*, vol. 1, pp. 373–86.

19. See the discussion in Eric Osborn, *Ethical Patterns in Early Christian Thought* (Cambridge: Cambridge University Press, 1976), pp. 214–20, especially p. 216: "From the New Testament on, there is a strong positive emphasis on the moral life. . . . At the same time there is a negative emphasis which insists that mere morality is a dangerous corruption."

20. Methodius was both a Christian Platonist and an opponent of Origen. See H. A. Musurillo's judgment in his introduction to *The Symposium*, ACW 27, p. 17: "Methodius writes rather like the 'self-taught' Platonist, and it is my view that his aim was much more subtle [than purely an infatuation with form and language] and it is perhaps connected with the paradox that he, one of the first to write against the Neoplatonist Porphyry and the allegorist Origen, should make extensive use of both Platonism and allegory. In both cases perhaps it was a question of invading the adversary's armory for weapons to turn against him."

21. Cf. Grégoire de Nysse, *Traité de la Virginité*, French tr. & ed. Michel Aubineau, Sources chrétiennes 119 (Paris: Éditions du cerf, 1966), p. 212 (intro.): "Enfin sur *la doctrine même de la virginité* . . . retenons ces pages où Grégoire de Nysse montre que la virginité chrétienne, vouée à Dieu et pratiquée pour Dieu, est d'abord *affaire d'âme*, plus encore qu'intégrité du corps." Chrysostom's point of view seems more matter of fact and involves treating virginity as both physical and spiritual, defining it as a higher stage than marriage. See Jean Chrysostome, *La Virginité*, French tr. & ed. Bernard Grillet, Sources chrétiennes 125 (Paris: Éditions du cerf, 1966), p. 64 (intro.): "Jean considère ces deux états sous le rapport de la perfection que doit atteindre l'âme du chrétien pour parvenir au ciel; dans ce cas la virginité est un état privilégié . . . alors que le mariage est un 'vêtement servile,' à l'usage des médiocres. . . ."

22. The doctrine is a common one among the Stoics, though it has roots in Theophrastus and even Aristotle. See the texts and notes on secondary literature in C.J. DeVogel, *Greek Philosophy*, vol. 3, pp. 127ff.

SECONDARY SOURCES

A number of books have been helpful to me in trying to imagine life and manners in the Roman Empire and have informed my thinking in this and the following chapters. J. P. V. D. Balsdon, *Life and Leisure*, Jérôme Carcopino, *Daily Life*, Samuel Dill, *Roman Society from Nero to Marcus Aurelius* (2nd ed; New York: MacMillan & Co., 1905), and Ludwig Friedländer, *Roman Life and Manners* treat in detail the social, political, and economic structures of late antique society. Glanville Downey, *A History of Antioch in Syria from Seleucus to the Arab Conquest* (Princeton: Princeton University Press, 1961) and *Antioch in the Age of Theodosius the Great* (Norman: University of Oklahoma Press, 1962) and J. H. W. G. Liebeschuetz, *Antioch: City and Imperial Administration in the Later Roman Empire* (Oxford: At the Clarendon Press, 1972) examine what can be known of urban life in one of the largest cities in the East. H. I. Marrou, *A History of Education in Antiquity* gives a detailed account of what education was like under the Empire. Ramsay MacMullen, *Enemies of the Roman Order, Soldier and Civilian in the Later Roman Empire* (Cambridge, Mass.: Harvard University Press, 1967), and *Roman Social Relations, 50 B.C. to A.D. 284* (New Haven: Yale University Press, 1974) discuss various aspects of Roman society.

Turning to Christianity in the Roman Empire, Robert L. Wilken, *The Christians as the Romans Saw Them* gives a general but accurate and imaginative account of how Christians appeared to Romans at different periods. R. A. Markus, *Christianity in the Roman World* (London: Thames & Hudson, 1974) is to some degree concerned with the same issue. Richard Krautheimer, *Three Christian Capitals: Topography and Politics* (Berkeley: University of California Press, 1983) examines the archaeological evidence in Rome, Constantinople, and Milan for what it tells us of the place of Christianity in Roman society in the fourth century. Cecil John Cadoux, *The Early Church and the World* (Edinburgh: T. & T. Clark, 1925) is an older book and, consequently, not fully informed by studies of Christianity as a social phenomenon. The best general introduction to the issues with which I am concerned in chapters four to six is Robert M. Grant, *Early Christianity and Society*. His essays are on the Christian population, Christian devotion to monarchy, taxation and exemption, work and occupations, private property, the organization of alms, and endowments. Wayne A. Meeks, *The First Urban Christians*, though limited to the first century, is also important.

In addition to the books mentioned in the footnotes to this chapter and to the treatments of the family found in Balsdon and Friedländer, several works have helped me to try to understand Christian attitudes toward the family, marriage, and virginity. Elizabeth Clark, *Jerome, Chrysostom, and Friends* gives brief but perceptive treatments of issues that largely revolve around the place of women in the early Church; and her translations of important primary works allow the reader access to these materials. Jean LaPorte, *The Role of Women in Early Christianity*, Philip Rousseau, *Ascetics, Authority, and the Church*, and Korbinian Ritzer, *Formen, Riten, und Religiöses Brauchtum der Eheschliessung in den Christlichen Kirchen des ersten Jahrtausends* (Münster: Aschendorffsche Verlagsbuchhandlung, 1962) are also helpful.

CHAPTER FIVE

NOTES

1. Cf. Robert F. Evans, *One and Holy*, which explores the dilemma in terms of ecclesiology. Should the Church be a club of saints or a school for sinners?

2. See Luke T. Johnson, *The Literary Function of Possessions in Luke-Acts*.

3. Cf. K. F. Nickle, *The Collection: A Study in Paul's Strategy*, Studies in Biblical Theology 48 (Naperville, Ill.: Allenson, 1966).

4. See George Foot Moore, *Judaism in the First Centuries of the Christian Era: The Age of the Tannaim* (Cambridge, Mass.: Harvard University Press, 1927), vol. 2, pp. 166–73. That almsgiving brings a reward is reflected in Luke 6:37–38, 14:13–14, and Acts 10:4.

5. See the note on 104:2 in *The Apostolic Fathers, volume 6, Hermas*, Eng. tr., ed., and comm. G. F. Snyder (London: Thomas Nelson & Sons, 1968), p. 153.

6. See A. H. M. Jones, *The Later Roman Empire*, vol. 2, chapter 22, and R. M. Grant, *Early Christianity and Society*, chapter 5.

7. Jerome tells the story in *Contra Ioannem Hierosol.* 8. Praetextatus is the one who made the remark. See P. V. Davies, Eng. tr., ed., and intro., *Macrobius, The Saturnalia* (New York: Columbia University Press, 1969), p. 6 and (for a description of Praetextatus) pp. 4–5. Praetextatus was in the circle of Symmachus, the pagan urban prefect of Rome who addressed the famous *relatio* to Theodosius the Great in 384 for the restoration of the Altar of Victory to the Senate House and who recommended Augustine for the chair of rhetoric in Milan.

8. For a full discussion see Stanislas Giet, *Les idées et l'action sociales de saint Basile* (Paris: Libraire Lecoffre, 1941).

9. The whole of *On Pilgrimages* is worth consulting. Nyssa's hostility towards pilgrimages and their emphasis on sacred places associated with Jesus' life seems to be a conservative reaction to a development in Church life that is an innovation, at least as something with wide appeal. While the cult of the martyrs and the care of relics is clearly older than the fourth century, there does seem to be a growing emphasis upon relics and pilgrimages from the later fourth century on.

SECONDARY SOURCES

Peter Brown, *The Cult of the Saints* and Henry Chadwick, *The Role of the Bishop in Ancient Society* (Berkeley: University of California Press, 1979) are important studies that enable us to understand some of the ways in which the Church found an ecumenical unity. In addition to R. M. Grant, *Early Christianity and Society* several books deal with property and wealth in late antiquity and in the early Church: A. R. Hands, *Charities and Social Aid in Greece and Rome* (London: Thames & Hudson, 1968); Luke T. Johnson, *The Literary Function of Possessions in Luke-Acts*; L. William Countryman, *The Rich Christian in the Church of the Early Empire: Contradictions and Accommodations* (New York: Edwin Mellen Press, 1980). Robert F. Evans, *One and Holy* is an excellent discussion of Latin patristic doctrines of the Church.

CHAPTER SIX

NOTES

1. See, for example, John 17:11–19, Rom. 13:1–8, 1 Cor. 5:9–13, Gal. 4:26, Phil. 3:20, Hebr. 12:22–24, 1 Peter 2:11–17.

2. Eusebius, *HE* 5.5.1–7. Cf. also the legend that the emperor Philip was a Christian (*HE* 6.34). These legends are not confined to Christian sources. According to the *Historia Augusta* Alexander Severus included in the sanctuary of his Lares statues not only of the deified emperors but also of Apollonius of Tyana, Christ, Abraham, and Orpheus (*Life of Alexander Severus* 29).

3. See *Apol.* 8–9, *Ad nationes* 15–16.

4. See *Apol.* 40, *To Scapula* 4.

5. *To Scapula* 2 (*ANF* 3, p. 106); cf. *Apol.* 37; *ANF* 3, p. 45: ". . . almost all the inhabitants of your various cities being followers of Christ."

6. See *Apol.* 40, *Ad nationes* 9.

7. See *On Idolatry* and *De spectaculis*, passim.

8. *On Idolatry* 7–11, 17; cf. Hippolytus, *The Apostolic Tradition* 16.

9. See *On Idolatry* 24, *De spectaculis* 30.

10. See *On the Soul*, 2, 20; *The Soul's Testimony* 5–6; *Apol*, 17, 46–49.

11. Justin employs his Logos theology to show that because "reason" (the soul or mind) is akin to "Reason" (the Logos or Truth), the philosophers had access to the Truth. Thus, philosophical truth is in continuity with Christian truth. At the same time, the Logos incarnate for the first time reveals the whole truth and in such a way that all may receive it. Consequently, Christian truth is also discontinuous with philosophical truth, which is partial and available only to an elite.

12. See *On the Soul* 1; *Apol.* 14, 22, 39; *The Prescription against Heretics* 7.

13. *Ad martyras* 2.

14. Eusebius, *Martyrs of Palestine* 11.7–19, cited by Ramsay MacMullen, *Enemies of the Roman Order*, p. 91.

15. For a full discussion see S. R. C. Lilla, *Clement of Alexandria*, pp. 9–59.

16. *Ex.* 7, 5–6 (*ANF* 2, pp. 193, 190ff.); *Strom.* 1 (*ANF* 2, pp. 299ff.).

17. *Strom.* 1.2, 7; 6.8.

18. See Norman H. Baynes, *Constantine the Great and the Christian Church*. Baynes does not adopt the conclusion I have suggested, but he does conclude that Constantine was not "merely a philosophical monotheist whose faith was derived from the religious syncretism of his day—a faith into which Christianity had been absorbed. . . . The emperor has definitely identified himself with Christianity, with the Christian Church and the Christian creed. Further, here is a sovereign with the conviction of a personal mission entrusted to him by the Christian God. . . ." (p. 29).

19. Peter Brown, *The Making of Late Antiquity* (Cambridge, Mass.: Harvard University Press, 1978), p. 7.

20. Cf. Arthur Darby Nock, "The Emperor's Divine *Comes*," in *Essays on Religion and the Ancient World*, ed. Zeph Stewart (Oxford: Clarendon Press, 1972), vol. 2, pp. 653–75.

21. Cf. Timothy D. Barnes, *Constantine and Eusebius*, p. 254.

22. *Div. inst.* 6.8, citing Cicero's *Republic* 3.22,16; *ANF* 7, p. 171.

23. Hom. 16 on 2 Cor. (*NPNF*[1] 12, p. 359). Cf. Hom. 12 on Mt. (*NPNF*[1] 10, p. 78); Hom. 23 on Eph. (*NPNF*[1] 13, p. 166); Hom. 15 on 2 Cor. (*NPNF*[1] 12, p. 353); Hom. 56 on John (*NPNF*[1] 14, p. 203); Hom. 79 on John (*NPNF*[1] 14, p. 293).

24. Hom. 34 on 1 Cor. (*NPNF*[1] 12, p. 204). Cf. Hom. 19 on John (*NPNF*[1] 14, p. 67): "In this it is that we differ from beasts, for this we have built cities, and markets, and houses, that we may be united with one another, not in the place of our dwelling only, but by the bond of love."

25. Gregory Nazianzen, *Panegyric on Saint Basil* 63 (*NPNF*[2] 7, p. 416). Cf. Basil, Ep. 94; Theodoret, *Ecclesiastical History* 4.18; Sozomen, *Ecclesiastical History* 6.34.

26. Hom. 47 on Mt. (*NPNF*[1] 10, p. 295); Hom. 77 on Mt. (*NPNF*[1] 10, pp. 468f.).

27. Hom. 5 on 1 Cor. (*NPNF*[1] 12, p. 28); Hom 14 on 1 Cor. (*NPNF*[1] 12, p. 80); Hom. 30 on 1 Cor. (*NPNF*[1] 12, pp. 178f.).

28. Hom. 21 on Eph. (*NPNF*[1] 13, p. 155); *On the Priesthood* 6.2–8 (*NPNF*[1] 9, pp. 75ff.).

29. Cf. Charles N. Cochrane, *Christianity and Classical Culture*, chapter 5, "The New Republic: Constantine and the Triumph of the Cross," pp. 177–212, especially pp. 179f.: "In this way, it ["Render to Caesar," Mt. 22:21] pointed to an utterly novel idea—the project of a Christian commonwealth. Through this idea, the tendency of centuries was to be reversed, and *Romanitas* was to secure a fresh lease of life under the aegis of the Church."

30. A. H. M. Jones, *The Later Roman Empire*, vol. 2, p. 979.

31. See R. A. Markus, *Saeculum*.

32. St. Bernard of Cluny; Hymn 597 in 1940 Episcopal Hymnal.

SECONDARY SOURCES

There is a considerable literature regarding the relationship of Church and state in late antiquity. Robert L. Wilken, *The Christians as the Romans Saw Them* and Charles N. Cochrane, *Christianity and Classical Culture* cover the entire period. Before Constantine the reader may consult A. N. Sherwin-White, *Roman Society and Roman Law in the New Testament* (London: Oxford University Press, 1963) and W. H. C. Frend, *Martyrdom and Persecution in the Early Church: A Study of a Conflict from the Maccabees to Donatus* (Oxford: Basil Blackwell & Mott, 1965). And in this period Timothy D. Barnes, *Tertullian: A Historical and Literary Study* (London: Oxford University Press, 1971), S. R. C. Lilla, *Clement of Alexandria*, and E. F. Osborn, *The Philosophy of Clement of Alexandria* (Cambridge: Cambridge University Press, 1957) are important studies that involve the relationship of Christianity to pagan culture. For Constantine let me mention Timothy D. Barnes, *Constantine and Eusebius*, Norman H. Baynes, *Constantine the Great and the Christian Church*, and Ramsay MacMullen, *Constantine* (London: Weidenfeld & Nicolson, 1970). Robert M. Grant, *Eusebius as Church Historian* (London: Oxford University Press, 1980) should not be neglected. The essays collected and edited by Arnaldo Momigliano, *The Conflict between Paganism and Christianity in the Fourth Century* (London: Oxford University Press, 1963), treat a number of important dimensions of the Constantinian revolution. For Chrysostom, C. Baur, *John Chrysostom* should be consulted; and for Augustine, R. A. Markus, *Saeculum*.

CHAPTER SEVEN

NOTES

1. See L. Bouyer, *The Spirituality of the New Testament and the Fathers*, pp. 317 and 523f. With Evagrius Ponticus and the Pseudo-Dionysius we find the

contemplative life treated as a higher form of the Christian life, and it seems reasonable to correlate this development with the emergence of the monastic life as a special and higher kind of Christian life. See Bouyer, p. 393.

2. See Arthur Voöbus, *History of Asceticism in the Syrian Orient*, vol. 2, pp. 157ff. He argues that Syrian monasticism cannot be explained "as a transplanting of the monachal ideas from Egypt" or "by means of the biblical examples or the primitive idea of a mission to fight the demons." ". . . in spite of their fragmentary condition, the features of the primitive monasticism which we have encountered leave no doubt that they are in reality a fusion with elements derived from a source which claims a very different inception." He identifies this source with Manichaeism. Indian features were introduced into Mesopotamia "by the medium of the Manichees" (p. 169).

3. See Gerald Lewis Bray, *Holiness and the Will of God: Perspectives on the Theology of Tertullian* (Atlanta: John Knox Press, 1979).

4. The "liturgies" imposed upon the curial classes in the cities are discussed in A. H. M. Jones, *The Later Roman Empire*, vol. 1, pp. 734–57, and the flight of peasants from their land in ibid., vol. 2, pp. 808–12, 817–23, 1043–44; see also the primary materials collected by Lewis and Reinhold in *Sourcebook II*, pp. 478ff.

5. Cf. Pierre Humbertclaude, *La doctrine ascétique de saint Basil de Césarée* (Paris: Gabriel Beauchesne et ses fils, 1932), p. 322: "Parallèlement à cette marche individuelle vers la sainteté, l'âme s'y sent encore élevée avec tout le système social dans lequel elle gravite. Dieu a fait l'homme sociable, il a voulu que le chrétien se sanctifie dans l'Eglise, *société* de tous les fidèles. . . ." See also Bouyer, pp. 338f.

6. The preface to *The Longer Rules* makes it clear that Basil is primarily interested in "the life of piety" and only secondarily in monasticism as the context in which that life should be pursued. "Since, by the grace of God, we who have set before ourselves one and the same end, namely, the life of piety, are met together in one place in the name of our Lord Jesus Christ; and you indeed are plainly desirous to learn somewhat of the things that concern salvation; I for my part must proclaim the righteous acts of God . . ." (Clarke, p. 145).

7. See Owen Chadwick, *John Cassian*, pp. 32–36.

8. For discussions of the controversy see C. Baur, *John Chrysostom*, vol. 2, chapters 18–22; J. N. D. Kelly, *Jerome*, chapters, 18, 21, 22.

9. The text tradition of Cassian's works poses a number of difficult problems, but for consideration of them let me simply refer to Owen Chadwick's magisterial discussion of the issue in *John Cassian*, pp. 37–50.

10. Cassian's mistrust of miracles is difficult to assess. We cannot always suppose that it has colored his versions of stories that are to be found in other sources. For example, he tells (*Inst.* 4.24) of Abba John of Lycopolis' obedience in watering a dry stick twice a day for a year without adding the miracle of the stick's flowering that we find in the *Sayings of the Fathers* and in *The Dialogues* of Sulpicius Severus. But his version seems to be the original one (see Chadwick, p. 21, where full references to the sources may be found). On the other hand, we can at least raise the question whether his mistrust of miracles is allied to the Evagrian and Origenist mistrust of the simple. See Chadwick's brief assessment of the Tall Brothers controversy as a sign of "the stresses of which Evagrius was the centre; learning versus simplicity, Egyptian versus foreigner" (p. 26).

11. See Chadwick, pp. 67ff.

12. See J. Daniélou, *Théologie du judéo-christianisme*, chapters 5 and 14.

13. One argument for this conclusion may be found in the evidence of the *Apothegmata*, where Evagrius is cited with approval. One story is significant: "Abba Evagrius once said to Abba Arsenius: 'How is it that we educated and learned men have no virtue, and Egyptian peasants have a great deal?' Abba Arsenius answered: 'We have nothing because we go chasing worldly knowledge. These Egyptian peasants have acquired virtues by hard work' " (LCC 12, p. 106; see also pp. 37, 42, 44, 50, 78, 109, 132, 141, 160, 176). On the other hand, Chadwick concludes: "It is not likely that Evagrius asked this question or that Arsenius gave this answer" (*John Cassian*, p. 26).

14. It is difficult to explain why Cassian has such an ambiguous attitude towards the Evagrian ideal. Perhaps he reacted to the controversies in which he must have been involved. P. Rousseau in *Ascetics, Authority, and the Church*, p. 235, describes Cassian as "a diplomatic man." Perhaps he also shared with others a feeling that what Chitty (in *The Desert a City*, p. 60) call "the freshness of the first generation" of monks had faded. Chitty also points out that Cassian fails ever to mention Evagrius (p. 52 and p. 60).

15. See J. Pelikan, *The Emergence of the Catholic Tradition*, pp. 318–31; J. N. D. Kelly, *Early Christian Doctrines*, pp. 369–72.

16. See the brief discussion in LCC 12, pp. 25–30.

SECONDARY SOURCES

Derwas J. Chitty, *The Desert a City* supplies the best introduction to Egyptian and Palestinian monasticism. Arthus Voöbus, *History of Asceticism in the Syrian Orient* examines asceticism somewhat more broadly and argues that Syrian asceticism does not primarily derive from Egyptian sources. W. K. L. Clarke, *St. Basil the Great: A Study in Monasticism* (Cambridge: Cambridge University Press, 1913) and E. F. Morison, *St. Basil and His Rule* (London: Oxford University Press, 1912) are the best introductions to Cappadocian monasticism. Owen Chadwick, *John Cassian* and Philip Rousseau, *Ascetics, Authority, and the Church* are basic to an understanding of the late fourth and the fifth centuries in the West.

CHAPTER EIGHT

NOTES

1. See Peter Brown, "The Later Roman Empire," in *Religion and Society*, pp. 46–73; Mortimer Chambers, ed., pp. 46–73; *The Fall of Rome: Can it be Explained?* European Problem Studies (2nd ed.; New York: Holt, Rinehart, & Winston, 1970).

2. Bury, *The Later Roman Empire*, vol. 1, p. 309.

3. Ibid., p. 206.

4. Priscus' account is translated by Bury, pp. 279–88. The citations here are from p. 283 and p. 284.

5. See the discussion in Helen Waddell, *The Wandering Scholars* (1927; Garden City, N.Y.: Doubleday Anchor Books, 1955), pp. 1–13.

6. See the brief discussion in J. M. Wallace-Hadrill, *The Frankish Church* (Oxford: At the Clarendon Press, 1983), pp. 10–12.

7. This view seems to be taken by Wallace-Hadrill, pp. 3–4.

8. Synesius of Cyrene (ca. 370–ca. 413) was another aristocrat who became a

bishop. (There were many Ambroses.) His letters reflect the problems he faced in giving up a life of leisure and philosophy to be the patron of his people. See especially letters 11, 13, and 57 (Eng. tr. & ed. A. Fitzgerald, *The Letters of Synesius of Cyrene* [London: Oxford University Press, 1926], pp. 96f., 97f., 127ff.).

9. Momigliano discusses Cassiodorus' attitude towards Justinian's reconquest of Italy in relation to his new edition of *The Gothic History*. See Arnaldo Momigliano, "Cassiodorus and Italian Culture of His Time," in *Studies in Historiography* (New York: Harper Torchbooks, 1966), p. 195: "His last chapters evidently expressed the hopes of the Italian aristocratic exiles who wanted to go back to Italy with a part to play in the reorganization of the country. They did not contemplate the utter destruction of the Goths—and of so much else—that Narses was soon to perpetrate. They may well have thought that the most advantageous situation for themselves would be one in which enough Goths were left to counterbalance Byzantine influence." In the event Byzantine policy of total war against the Goths left Cassiodorus no place to stand.

10. Augustine does, of course, employ this argument in *The City of God*. See, for example, *CG* 1.1 (PC, p. 6): "The benefits are unmistakable: those enemies [of the City of God] would not today be able to utter a word against the City if, when fleeing from the sword of their enemy, they had not found in the City's holy places, the safety on which they now congratulate themselves. The barbarians spared them for Christ's sake; and now these Romans assail Christ's name. . . . In this way many escaped who now complain of this Christian era, and hold Christ responsible for the disasters which their city endured. But they do not make Christ responsible for the benefits they received out of respect for Christ, to which they owed their lives."

SECONDARY SOURCES

English translations of primary sources that deserve to be underlined are L. W. Jones, *Cassiodorus Senator, An Introduction to Divine and Human Readings*; Harold Isbell, *The Last Poets of Imperial Rome*; I. W. Raymond, *Seven Books of History Against the Pagans: The Apology of Paulus Orosius* (New York: Columbia University Press 1936). Samuel Dill, *Roman Society in the Last Century of the Western Empire* (New York: MacMillan Co., 1906) remains an important work. The impact of the barbarian invasions is described in J. B. Bury, *The Invasion of Europe by the Barbarians* (New York: W. W. Norton & Co., 1967) and Stewart Irvin Oost, *Galla Placidia Augusta* (Chicago: University of Chicago Press, 1968). *The Transformation of the Roman World: Gibbon's Problem after Two Centuries*, ed. Lynn White, Jr. (Berkeley: University of California Press, 1966) is a collection of essays dealing with different aspects of the end of late antiquity.

Selected Bibliography

Ackroyd, P. R., and C. F. Evans, eds. *The Cambridge History of the Bible*. Vol. 1, *From the Beginnings to Jerome*. Cambridge: Cambridge University Press, 1970.

Andresen, Carl. *Logos und Nomos: Die Polemik des Kelsos wider das Christentum*. Berlin: Walter de Gruyter, 1955.

Arendt, Hannah. *The Life of the Mind*. Vol. 1, *Thinking*; vol. 2, *Willing*. New York: Harcourt Brace Jovanovich, 1977, 1978.

Balás, David L. *Metousia Theou: Man's Participation in God's Perfections according to Saint Gregory of Nyssa*. Studia Anselmiana 55. Rome: Libreria Herder, 1966.

Balsdon, J. P. V. D. *Life and Leisure in Ancient Rome*. London: The Bodley Head, 1969.

Barnes, Timothy D. *Constantine and Eusebius*. Cambridge, Mass.: Harvard University Press, 1981.

Baur, Chrysostomus. *John Chrysostom and His Time*. 2 vols. Westminster, Md.: Newman Press, 1960–61.

Baynes, Norman H. *Constantine the Great and the Christian Church* London: Oxford University Press, 1929, 1972.

Bouyer, Louis. *The Spirituality of the New Testament and the Fathers*. New York: Burns & Oates, 1963.

Brown, Peter. *Augustine of Hippo: A Biography*. Berkeley: University of California Press, 1969.

———. *Religion and Society in the Age of Saint Augustine*. New York: Harper & Row, 1972.

———. *The Cult of the Saints*. Chicago: University of Chicago Press, 1981.

Burnaby, John. *Amor Dei: A Study of the Religion of St. Augustine.* London: Hodder & Stoughton, 1938.

Bury, J. B. *History of the Later Roman Empire: From the Death of Theodosius I to the Death of Justinian.* 2 vols. London: Constable, 1958.

Carcopino, Jérôme. *Daily Life in Ancient Rome.* New Haven: Yale University Press, 1965.

Chadwick, Owen. *John Cassian.* Cambridge: Cambridge University Press, 1950.

Chitty, Derwas J. *The Desert a City: An Introduction to the Study of Egyptian and Palestinian Monasticism under the Christian Empire.* Oxford: Basil Blackwell, 1966.

Clark, Elizabeth A. *Jerome, Chrysostom, and Friends: Essays and Translations.* New York: Edwin Mellen Press, 1979.

Cochrane, Charles N. *Christianity and Classical Culture: A Study of Thought and Action from Augustus to Augustine.* London: Oxford University Press, 1940.

Daniélou, Jean. *Théologie du Judéo-christianisme.* Paris: Desclée, 1958.

DeVogel, C. J. *Greek Philosophy.* Vol. 3, *The Hellenistic-Roman Period.* Leiden: E. J. Brill, 1959.

Evans, Robert F. *One and Holy: The Church in Latin Patristic Thought.* London: S. P. C. K., 1972.

Friedländer, Ludwig. *Roman Life and Manners.* 4 vols. Eng. tr. 1907; rpt. London: Routledge & Kegan Paul, 1965.

Gough, Michael. *The Origins of Christian Art.* New York: Praeger, 1974.

Grant, Robert M. *Early Christianity and Society.* New York: Harper & Row, 1977.

Hanson, R. P. C. *Tradition in the Early Church.* London: SCM Press, 1962.

Houssiau, Albert. *La Christologie de saint Irénée.* Louvain: Publications universitaires de Louvain, 1955.

Jaeger, Werner. *Two Rediscovered Works of Ancient Christian Literature: Gregory of Nyssa and Macarius.* Leiden: E. J. Brill, 1965.

Johnson, Luke T. *The Literary Function of Possessions in Luke-Acts.* SBL Dissertation Series 39. Missoula, Mont.: Scholars Press, 1977.

Jones, A. H. M. *The Later Roman Empire, 284–602.* 2 vols. Norman: University of Oklahoma Press, 1964.

Kelly, J. N. D. *Early Christian Creeds.* London: Longmans, Green & Co., 1950.
———. *Early Christian Doctrines.* New York: Harper & Bros., 1958.
———. *Jerome: His Life, Writings, and Controversies.* New York: Harper & Row, 1975.

LaPorte, Jean. *The Role of Women in Early Christianity.* New York: Edwin Mellen Press, 1982.

Lawson, John. *The Biblical Theology of Saint Irenaeus.* London: Epworth Press, 1948.

Lewis, Naphtali, and Meyer Reinhold, eds. *Roman Civilization, Sourcebook II: The Empire.* New York: Harper & Row, 1966.

Lilla, S. R. C. *Clement of Alexandria: A Study in Christian Platonism and Gnosticism.* London: Oxford University Press, 1971.

MacMullen, Ramsay. *Enemies of the Roman Order: Treason, Unrest, and Alienation in the Empire.* Cambridge, Mass.: Harvard University Press, 1967.
———. *Christianizing the Roman Empire (A.D. 100–400).* New Haven: Yale University Press, 1984.

Markus, R. A. *Saeculum: History and Society in the Theology of St. Augustine.* Cambridge: Cambridge University Press, 1970.

Marrou, H. I. *A History of Education in Antiquity.* Eng. tr. 1956 by George Lamb. New York: A Mentor Book, 1964.

Meeks, Wayne A. *The First Urban Christians: The Social World of the Apostle Paul.* New Haven: Yale University Press, 1983.

Pelikan, Jaroslav. *The Emergence of the Catholic Tradition (100–600).* Chicago: University of Chicago Press, 1971.

Quasten, Johannes. *Patrology.* 3 vols. Westminster, Md.: Newman Press, 1950–60.

Rist, John M. *Eros and Psyche: Studies in Plato, Plotinus, and Origen.* Toronto: University of Toronto Press, 1964.

Rousseau, Philip. *Ascetics, Authority, and the Church in the Age of Jerome and Cassian.* London: Oxford University Press, 1978.

TeSelle, Eugene. *Augustine the Theologian.* London: Burns & Oates, 1970.

Voöbus, Arthur. *History of Asceticism in the Syrian Orient.* CSCO Subsidia 14 and 17. Louvain: CSCO, 1958, 1960.

Wilken, Robert L. *The Christians as the Romans Saw Them.* New Haven: Yale University Press, 1984.

Wingren, Gustav. *Man and the Incarnation: A Study in the Biblical Theology of Irenaeus.* Edinburgh: Oliver & Boyd, 1959.

Young, Frances. *From Nicaea to Chalcedon.* Philadelphia: Fortress Press, 1983.

Index